# Our Responsibility
# to One Another
## A VISION OF HUMAN PROGRESS
## FOR THE THIRD MILLENIUM

"Kurt Koerbel has reminded us of a particularly important call: the call to responsibility. Indeed, in Mr. Koerbel's experience as a counsellor and teacher, he has seen firsthand that people have free will to make choices and that these choices — made responsibly — can be a powerful force for change in their lives and in our world, today and tomorrow. Throughout his book, we are reminded that our responsibility to one another is at the apex of human existence and has a bearing on the very well-being of society and the natural environment upon which we depend. By being responsible now we are reminded that we can leave an important legacy for our children and the generations that will follow: a legacy characterized by hope for the future, the sustainability of life, and equality among peoples."

**— Maurice F. Strong**
**Executive Director for United Nations reform**
**President of the United Nations Earth Summit,**
**Rio de Janeiro, 1992**

"Recommending an ethics of responsibility and applying it to different age groups and various walks of life, Kurt Koerbel's book renders an important service in a civilization that honors personal rights yet has little to say about corresponding duties."

**— Gregory Baum**
**Professor of Ethics**
**McGill University, Montreal, Canada**

"This important book endeavours to make us more responsible, as we strive to fulfill our goals in life. In a world increasingly cut off from profound values, where money and profit have become ultimate aims, Kurt Koerbel's book is a beacon of hope showing the way to individual happiness and collective well-being."

**— Jacques Marois**
**Director of Student Services, École de Technologie supérieure**
**Université du Québec, Montréal**

**Cataloguing in publication data (Canada)**

Koerbel, Kurt H., April 15, 1928-

Our responsibility to one another : a vision of human progress for the third millenium

ISBN 1-55207-001-8

1.  Responsibility.     I. Title

BJ1451.K63 1997              170              C97-941055-X

Readers may consult our ever-evolving catalogue on the Internet at:
http:/www.rdppub.com

Kurt H. Koerbel

# Our Responsibility to One Another

## A VISION OF HUMAN PROGRESS
## FOR THE THIRD MILLENIUM

*Robert Davies Publishing*

MONTREAL-TORONTO-PARIS

Robert Davies Publishing
311-4999 St. Catherine St West
Westmount, Qc H3Z 1T3 Canada
514-481-2440 Fax 514-481-9973
e-mail: rdppub@vir.com


The publishers wish to thank the Canada Council for the Arts,
the Department of Canadian Heritage, and the Sodec(Québec)
for generous support for their publishing program.

*Dedication*

*This book is dedicated to*
*my wife Hilda*
*and my son Robert,*
*whose love, moral and personal integrity,*
*and constant encouragement inspired and motivated me greatly*
*and whose support made it possible to write this book.*

They shall beat their swords into plowshares and their spears into pruning hooks; nation shall not take up sword against nation; they shall never again know war.

—Isaiah 2:4

Thou shalt not kill.

—Exodus 20:13

It is important we pay attention to save the planet. If we develop good and considerable qualities within our own minds, our activities will naturally cease to threaten the continued survival of life on earth. We have the responsibility as well as the capability to protect the earth.

—The Dalai Lama

Philosophy should be an energy; it should find its aim and its effect in the amelioration of mankind.

—Victor Hugo

It is not only what we do, but also what we do not do, for which we are accountable.

—Moliere

Morality should be placed ahead of politics.

—Vaclav Havel

Where there is no vision, the people perish.

—Proverbs 29:18

The integration of unconscious contents is an individual act of realization, of understanding, and moral elevation. It is a most difficult task, demanding a high degree of ethical responsibility. Only relatively few individuals can be expected to be capable of such an accomplishment and they are not the political but themoral leaders of mankind. The maintenance and further development of civilization depend upon such individuals.

—Carl Gustav Jung

The price of greatness is responsibility

—Winston Churchill

There is nothing training cannot do. Nothing is above its reach. It can turn bad morals into good; it can detsroy bad principles and recreate good ones.

—Mark Twain

# Contents

# Foreword

After reading the work of Mr. Koerbel, my prevailing impression is of a privileged encounter with a philosopher and spiritual master, full of experience and wisdom.

The work is divided into 14 chapters of 134 units, and an average of two pages per unit. This means that the very structure of the text leads the reader to think deeply about every unit rather than rushing through the volume.

I think that Mr. Koerbel's work is a part of the long series of ethical codes stretching from the prophets of Israel, the Buddha, and Confucius down to the genuine ethical guides of our time. Focusing on responsibility, the book deals with the whole range and total aspects of contemporary life and discusses the major issues of our age. The value and interest to the reader come mainly from both the major central theme and the scope of thinking which attest to an undeniable richness of culture and experience. It will be of interest to readers of all ages and of great help in the world of education.

Long life to the work of Kurt Koerbel.

Jacques Langlais, Ph.D., C.H.C.
President, Canadian and French speaking section
The World Conference on Peace and Religion
Founder of the Intercultural Institute
Montreal, Quebec, Canada

# Preface

As a counseling psychologist specializing in vocational and career counseling, I have helped countless people during more than thirty years of professional practice to become successful in their studies, jobs, and careers. What helped me to a great extent was my strong belief in personal, social, and moral responsibility, and my ability to communicate it to my clients. As a result, I helped awaken and foster in them the sense of duty and responsibility that considerably strengthened their motivation to use their aptitudes and talents to prepare for and succeed in their careers.

I am more and more convinced that personal, social, and moral responsibility cannot only help to achieve success in employment and in people's careers; it is also the key to solving most of the many other problems that confront people individually and collectively. It is my belief and faith that personal, social, and moral responsibility is the foundation of the moral law of the universe that influences all our activities in almost every sphere of human endeavor, and that, similar to the law of gravity, to ignore and violate this law of responsibility has disastrous consequences.

Even though I am not a specialist in the strict sense of the word in other fields but my own, I nevertheless also have a great interest in and think a lot about psychological, spiritual, moral, philosophical scientific, health, social, educational, political, economic, legal, environmental, and cultural issues, as well as about current events.

This book deals with many of the spiritual, moral, philosophical, social, educational, psychological, health, political, economic, legal, and cultural issues and problems that confront people individually and collectively. Its purpose is to make people aware of these issues and problems, to stimulate and motivate them to think about them in order to understand them, and, above all, to develop their sense of personal, social and moral responsibility in order to be able to respond to the needs of individuals, society, and humankind and to find solutions that will make it possible to improve the world as well as their own lives.

To do all this, people have to become aware that they are responsible to God, to humankind, to other individuals, and to themselves. They must know what their duties and responsibilities are.

This book contains a great number of relatively short units, each one dealing with one responsibility. The large number of units is absolutely necessary, considering the great quantity of individual and collective duties and responsibilities. The responsibilities mentioned in this book are by no means exhaustive, and it will be up to other enlightened thinkers to add additional responsibilities in the future in order to make the list more complete. This book, however, is an important and essential step in the right direction.

Some of the units deal with ideas that are partially covered in other units. However, considering the complexity of some of these topics, it is important that they are mentioned and discussed again in a different unit in a related but different context, by adding additional information and insights.

Each unit of the book can be read alone and separately as it is in a certain way a self-contained entity and informs and educates on a specific responsibility. At the same time, however, it is also an element of the various chapters into which the book is divided as well as a constituent of the book as a whole.

The book is divided into various chapters dealing with categories of responsibilities. Each chapter is divided into units, each unit dealing with one specific responsibility. The order, disposition, and priority of the various chapters of the book are based on the great importance attached by the author to faith in God and to moral, philosophical, educational, health, scientific, social, and psychological responsibilities. By no means does this signify that political, economic, environmental, legal, and cultural responsibilities are not as vital as the other responsibilities mentioned above. To create a peaceful, socially and morally responsible world dedicated to the general wellbeing of all people on earth, all responsibilities mentioned in this book are indispensable.

# Introduction

Many social scientists, philosophers, environmentalists, and politicians, including the Canadian businessman and environmentalist Maurice Strong and the Czech president and playwright Vaclav Havel, believe that profound changes in values and beliefs are necessary and essential in order to enable humankind to solve the many problems that confront it today—the rapid deterioration of the environment, the global population explosion, the danger of a nuclear holocaust, the existence of widespread hunger, sicknesses, poverty, unemployment, child exploitation, illiteracy, as well as the need for economic development in the third world without destruction of the environment.

On top of this, we witness a moral breakdown and rejection of traditional values and moral principles. Roger Conner, executive director of Washington's liberal American Alliance for Rights and Responsibility said that the word responsibility has dropped from the policy dialogue in America. A society can't operate if everyone has rights and no one has responsibilities.

Many people throw out the baby together with the dirty bath water, discarding the good in traditional values together with the evil. We must not only rediscover the important moral values like altruism, responsibility, and integrity, but spiritual values like faith, and use them in everyday life as well as in politics, business, and public administration.

Countless people in various countries, especially the young, have become disenchanted and even outright cynical concerning politics and politicians, equating them with opportunism, selfish lust for power, corruption, and in some cases even despotism, oppression, and tyranny. This is sad, as there is a desperate need for politicians to solve the many problems of the world. This can only be done by a combination of vision, efficiency, and personal, social, and moral responsibility. Morality has to penetrate politics and make it honorable and highly decent and responsible. This would attract many gifted and competent people into this vitally important field.

This book was written in response to the problems described above and suggests bold, imaginative, idealistic, and at the same time practically realistic solutions, based on the application of the principles of personal, social, and moral responsibility, which can help us to cope with these difficulties. It is evident that people cannot live meaningful lives without responsible values and moral, ethical, guidelines. The author reintroduces responsibility into many areas of human activity and uses it to mean the performance of a duty, often without being ordered by a superior, which becomes self-initiated and self-motivated, and for which there must be accountability, should there be shirking and evasion of obligation. It also includes the additional meaning of responsiveness, the psychological quality of responding to other people's as well as to one's own needs and to satisfy them. The concept of responsibility is introduced into the psychological, political, social, spiritual, educational, cultural, ecological, scientific, business, technological, and health fields. All these human activities must be guided by social, moral, personal, and collective responsibility.

Psychologists, sociologists, and many others today believe that countless people don't know what their duties are. Many of these duties are described and dealt with in this book.

Another important issue discussed in this book is the fact that modern science and secular humanism have rejected God. This has contributed to a weakening of faith in general. Successful, responsible living needs faith in God and in people's capacity to deal effectively with the many problems confronting them. This book—inspired to a great extent by the faith and vision of the bible, predicting the eventual transformation of our planet into a peaceful, tolerant, harmonious world—emits the idea that man's relationship with God becomes one of partnership and cooperation. By bringing God into many daily activities and working together with him, people can develop the necessary confidence and resourcefulness to successfully solve many of the world's problems which at times appear insurmountable.

Economic development and technical progress that occurs in a manner that does not pollute the environment is indispensable to the achievement of moderate global prosperity and the elimination of sicknesses, illiteracy, poverty, and unemployment. Government must cooperate with the business community, with social organizations, and with private citizens to ensure that people's rights to positive freedom, social security, health, happiness, moderate prosperity, development of their potentials, and to peace are satisfied. It is also extremely important that the explosive growth of the world's population becomes controlled.

Many of the issues described above can only be realized by a world federal central authority. This implies the necessity of the eventual creation of the "United States of the World." Ideally and realistically this body should consist of a strong federal center cooperating with strong regional states.

It is my firm belief that individual and collective responsibility are the foundation of the moral law of the universe. On a personal level, living responsibly leads to genuine success, authentic maturity, physical and psychological health and wellbeing, and moderate prosperity. On a global level, social and moral responsibility leads to peace, international solidarity, and worldwide moderate prosperity.

The author also expresses his belief that a great variety of individual and group differences are necessary, comparable to a jigsaw puzzle, where every piece, by virtue of its difference, becomes an indispensable part of the total puzzle.

This book is based on the conviction that comprehensive reality includes an awareness of the way things are as well as the responsibility to form an idealistic vision as to how things could and should be. It is the author's faith that responsible education can help to develop socially, morally, and personally responsible people, able to deal effectively with the many problems confronting individuals, society, and humanity as a whole.

The book also deals with the responsibility to choose and live according to responsible values.

Excessive and irresponsible competition at all levels and in any field is detrimental to human wellbeing. Likewise, all forms of exploitation, domination, prejudice, greed, and exaggerated lust for power are morally and personally irresponsible. Cooperation, on the other hand, allows the combination of the specific talents of all and makes it possible through the choice of common goals to transform personal and group conflicts into peaceful coexistence. Other qualities denoting a high degree of social, moral and personal responsibility are altruism, commitment to a responsible cause, decency, and moral and personal integrity as well as compassion and generosity. All these responsible qualities contribute to the survival of humankind.

The point is stressed in this book that freedom is only valuable if it is responsible. This means respect for and compliance with the obligation to avoid engaging in destructive behavior that is harmful to others and to oneself, and the obligation to espouse only causes that are just and socially and morally responsible. The concept of positive, responsible freedom outlined above is of very great importance.

In my thirty years experience as as counseling psychologist and career counselor, I have motivated many people of all ages to gain insight and understanding of themselves, to develop their potentials and talents, to choose careers and find jobs in accordance with the unique constellation of their interests, aptitudes, talents, values, personality traits, expectations, as well as the needs of the labor market, and to help them make a responsible success of their careers and working lives. I am aware of both the merits and the limitations of psychology. I am nevertheless convinced that the introduction of responsibility as well as of responsiveness (which are based to some extent on psychology as well as on morality) into many areas of daily activities, as well as into various fields of the social and human sciences, is of crucial importance.

It is my belief that our ultimate responsibility is to God, humankind, and individuals, including oneself. A further conviction, based on evidence from social research, is that violent human behavior, including war, is socially and culturally conditioned and learned. People can be educated not to engage in war, to become peaceful, and to avoid any violent, destructive behavior.

Many of these noble and realistically responsible ideals and values can and must assume an increasingly prominent role in people's lives. This can be achieved through responsible education starting as early as possible in life. The guiding principles of the education toward social, moral, and personal responsibility should be that people must think globally and must assume global responsibility. They must also become empowered to achieve a responsible degree of success in their lives. Responsible education is ideally suited to help people realize these lofty, yet also realistic and practical, goals.

May this book, with the help of God, make a contribution to stimulate people to work toward the goal of building a better and more responsible world.

# CHAPTER ONE

# *Definition and Advantages of Responsibility*

## 1. Definition and Meaning of Responsibility

According to the dictionary the word responsibility has the following meanings: 1. the duty, obligation to perform a task demanded by an authority, whether parent or institutional leader; 2. being accountable to the authority which assigns the duty; 3. being able to meet an obligation by acting without superior authority or guidance; 4. the capacity to perceive the distinction of right and wrong.

In this book responsibility is used to signify the duty or obligation to be responsive to the needs of society, of other people, of humankind, of God, and to one's own needs — and to satisfy them. The responsibility to satisfy needs could be in answer to an order by a superior authority or self-motivated. Both forms of responsibility are important. Highly mature and socially and morally responsible people, however, would be more inclined to respond to and satisfy these needs without external constraints than people with a less developed sense of personal, social, and moral responsibility.

The needs dealt with in this book (and which should and must be satisfied) are life-preserving and life-enhancing, humanitarian, and promote general well being. These needs could be conscious or unconscious; many people might not be consciously aware of the great importance of some of these needs as well as the duty and obligation to satisfy them. Dealing with these needs in this book will make the reader aware of their existence and importance as well as of the responsibility to satisfy them. Failure to respond to and satisfy the life-enhancing and society-furthering individual and collective needs discussed in this book should and must

23

lead to accountability. People must be made accountable for shirking their responsibilities. The highest responsibility must be to God, to humankind, and to the individual person, including oneself. Knowing to whom we are ultimately responsible is of great psychological, spiritual, and moral value, because this will galvanize and motivate us to develop the necessary energy, efficiency, and courage to successfully meet most challenges and to find satisfactory solutions to the pressing problems troubling humankind.

## 2. The Manifold Advantages of Responsibility

Many people today feel insignificant — that they can't change the system or society, believing that they are a mere cog in a wheel, anonymous victims of an impersonal social structure. But we can overcome feelings of powerlessness and insignificance and become genuinely and responsibly empowered by acting responsibly and by assuming responsibility for others as well as for ourselves, by accepting the idea that we are God's partners and coworkers, that every person has a triple responsibility to God, humankind, and to the individual (including oneself), and by responding to other people's needs in a self-motivated manner, beyond the call of duty.

Immense amounts of potentially untapped human energy are buried in the depth of our personalities, similar to the tremendous amount of latent energy stored in an atom. These can be released when we are responsive to other people's needs as well as to our own, and when we satisfy these needs in a responsible manner. A good example is the extraordinary strength a mother possesses to save her child's life — even managing to lift a truck to rescue the child pinned beneath it.

Acting responsibly by responding to positive needs of others and oneself is also the cornerstone of responsible, genuine success. It allows us to solve many human problems, to improve people's lives, to better the human condition, and to find solutions to economic, ecological, social, political, and personal difficulties.

Responsibility through responsiveness to human needs leads to wholeness and integrity of personality. It also bridges the gap between altruism (helping others) and egoism (having an inordinate concern for one's own welfare). Through responsibility one responds at the same time to the needs of others as well as to one's own need to help others; this leads to a responsible development of potentials, to self-realization, and to personal fulfillment and contentment. Besides, altruistically responsible people are emotionally and socially mature and mentally, physically, and psychologically healthier than egotistical people. Behaving in a personal, social, and moral way is also highly meaningful. Responsible behavior also forges bonds of solidarity with God and humanity, overcomes feelings of isolation, and fosters the psychological, spiritual, and moral evolution of people.

# CHAPTER TWO

# *Spiritual Responsibilities*

### 3. The Responsibility to God and the Duty to Have Faith

THE DICTIONARY DEFINES FAITH AS: 1. CONFIDENCE IN OR DEPENDENCe on a person, statement, or thing as trustworthy; 2. belief without need of certain proof; 3. belief in God; 4. anything given adherence, for example a person's political faith. One can have faith in God, but also in people, in a cause, in humanity, and in oneself. Many atheists who deny the existence of God nevertheless have faith in people or in a cause. I believe, however, that people who lack faith in God lack an essential spiritual component, namely the capacity to find profound meaning in life, to become rooted and anchored—in spite of the shortness of human existence—in eternity, to see order and purpose in the universe and in the world, and to have hope and faith in humankind's ability to eventually create a peaceful, moderately prosperous, harmonious, and united world.

It is important to mention that one can have faith in God and believe in the inspired prophetic wisdom of many passages of the bible without necessarily being a part of organized religion or without attending religious services in a church, synagogue, or in any other place of worship. The important thing is to believe that God has a plan and purpose for the world, that humankind is the caretaker of God's world, and that revelation concerning God's purpose is a continual, progressive process.

Some of the most important responsibilities that people need to assume toward God are the duty to bring God into everyday life as well as into major human activities. It is important to believe that God created science and all the scientific laws and that God created all living creatures, and to integrate and synthesize the religious belief in creation with the scientific belief in evolution. Bringing God into politics means to introduce morality and integrity into political life, to strive for the creation of a world government, to abolish war and to promote peace, to create the social, economic, and political conditions that will eliminate poverty, unemployment, and overpopulation throughout the world. It also means to create the necessary national and international institutions as well as to make public administrations and bureaucracies more efficient and more responsible.

People should also see themselves as God's partners and coworkers in continuing the work of creation, transforming the world into a socially and morally more responsible place. People must learn to live in harmony with God, their fellow human beings, and with nature. Human beings owe it to God to develop solidarity with humankind and to manage wisely and responsibly, as well as protect, the environment. We should consider it our obligation to pray, to thank God for the blessings bestowed on us, and to ask God to enable us to live more responsible lives. It is our responsibility to realize that just as we need God, God also needs us, and we must respond to God's need and desire to improve the world. It is also our duty to develop the talents given each one of us as much as we can and use them wisely and responsibly.

It is also vital that one understand that human beings ultimately derive much of their dignity and self-respect from the awareness and knowledge of the passage in the bible stating that human beings were created in God's image. One is intellectually in tune with God when one understands the physical laws of the universe as well as the biological processes and laws regulating and controlling living organisms. Creative abilities are also God-like qualities, and one should be sure to use them wisely and responsibly.

Traditionally, God has been regarded as a father. This is due to a great extent to the fact that throughout most of history authority was exercised by men. It is normal that we think of God as a parent. Since God is a spirit, and as such asexual, he should ideally be considered as an authoritative, parental figure, consisting of a synthesis of paternal and maternal qualities.

It is also extremely important to be aware of the fact that genuine faith in and responsibility to God presupposes that one must not worship idols, not only the old idols (inanimate objects, animals, or human beings), but also the modern idols (race, class, state, nation, science, technology, ideology, wealth, and power). Responsibility to God means not to delude and deceive oneself by mistaking what is relative, finite, temporary, and changeable for the ultimate, eternal, spiritual reality.

Some people consider it their ultimate responsibility to love God, since they see the goodness and beauty of creation, while others are in awe of God's authority and power and fear him. I think that emotionally, one should love God as the creator of life, but at the same time one must understand the people who fear him, because of his supreme power and the many dangers, uncertainties, and mysteries of life.

It must also be understood that faith gives meaning and sustenance to life. It taps profound emotional reservoirs and energies, both at the conscious and unconscious levels. Faith is also based on intellectual explanations, but does not provide absolute, scientific proof. It is not necessary. Profound faith, whether in people, a cause, or a responsible ideology, uses a combination of qualities of the head with qualities of the heart.

Responsible, creative thinking, which makes use of both logical reasoning as well as of intuition and uses the intelligence of the head as well as that of the heart, helps us to understand in a creatively insightful manner what has to be done to improve the world in a socially and morally responsible manner. This helps us to be on the same wavelength with God's purpose or plan for the world and motivates us to respond to our insights as well as to God's plan and to carry them out.

Karl Marx and Sigmund Freud were part of an intellectual, philosophical wave that went against, to an extremely exaggerated degree, the traditional patriarchal, biblical God, to the point where they threw away the baby with the dirty bath water. They went so far as to deny the existence of God altogether. Marx saw in religion the opium of the people, a means of the dominant classes of society to divert and distract the attention of the exploited, oppressed majority of ordinary people from their poverty and misery by encouraging them to engage in hallucinatory fantasizing, thus preventing them from rising against the oppressors and freeing themselves from their dire predicament, and improving their condition. He saw only part of the truth. Similar to the situation in India, where the low status of the pariah was (and still is to some extent) believed to be caused by divine will, Marx believed that religion, by promising the poor a better life after death in heaven, justified and upheld the status quo and the establishment. Of course, it is socially irresponsible and immoral to keep any human group in ignorance, servitude, and in a submissive role. Every group and every person must be encouraged to strive to become fully emancipated. Yet Karl Marx, in spite of his social conscience to improve the condition of the dispossessed, did not understand the absolute human need for God and for spiritual values, which give meaning and purpose to life. The resurgence and reemergence of religion in Eastern Europe and all parts of the former Soviet Union in the late 1980s and 1990s and the important role it plays to motivate people and support them spiritually and morally in their quest for responsible freedom indicates the onesidedness and even superficiality of Marx's beliefs.

Similarly, Sigmund Freud also saw in religion only the negative, unhealthy, and neurotic. Rather than being unhealthy and neurotic, responsible religion and responsible faith in God allow human beings to transcend their transitory, ephemeral life by finding meaning, purpose, sustenance, and strength in the everlasting, eternal existence of God. Faith in God and understanding of his purpose for the world also motivates us to work in cooperation and partnership with him to improve the world.

Friedrich Nietzsche was another thinker who in his writings proclaimed the death of God. He too threw away the baby with the dirty bath water and did not understand that faith and belief in God, undergo transformation and evolutionary growth just as many other things in life. What was about to die toward the end of the nineteenth century and disappeared to a great extent in the twentieth, was a calcified, sclerotic, extremely rigid, and exaggerated patriarchal, authoritarian, and immature concept of God, to be replaced by a more mature vision, which portrays God as more benevolent, understanding, loving, and caring.

Biblical wisdom and responsible, genuine faith in God continue to guide, inspire, and motivate increasing numbers of people. The commandment of Moses, "Thou shalt not kill," assumes greater importance in our age. The refusal of many Americans to fight in Vietnam, in what they considered an unjust war, as well as the relatively bloodless overthrow of the communist rule in Eastern Europe and all parts of the former Soviet Union, when compared with the bloody social revolutions of the past, illustrates this point very well. Faith in God inspired the German Lutheran pastor and resistance fighter Dietrich Bonhoeffer to oppose the Nazi tyranny, an act for which he was executed by Hitler. Similarly, the Polish Catholic priest Maximilian Kolbe sacrificed his life to save a family in the extermination camp Auschwitz. Albert Schweitzer, the Protestant theologian, humanitarian, philosopher, and doctor, was inspired by faith in God to devote his life to cure the sick in Gabon and to write about the importance of developing reverence for all living creatures. Albert Einstein, the inventor of the physical relativity theory, believed in God, the creator of the universe and of all its scientific laws.

Finally, it is very important that people gradually change their conception concerning God's gender and accept the realistic idea that God has no gender. God created the world and every living creature and is a parent, rather than a father, since God has both masculine and feminine parental qualities. If God, who is a spiritual power, is seen as a father, then authority, power, creativity, and order would be associated exclusively with men and maleness. A parent loves, protects, nurtures, and disciplines his or her children and is both powerful as well as loving. God is one power, having all the masculine and feminine parental qualities. To view God as a parent, having both masculine and feminine qualities (which is starting to be accepted by some enlightened Christian and Jewish theologians and thinkers) will empower both men and women, and will help people to develop a greater sense of responsible personal and moral integrity. Men and women will find encouragement to be loving, fostering, protecting, and responsive to other people's needs. They will also become creative, authoritative, and powerful in a personally, socially, and morally very responsible manner.

## 4. Believing Only What Is True

Belief means acceptance with or without proof of something. To have responsible beliefs necessitates that we carefully check the foundation on which our beliefs rest, that we find factual, realistic proof to validate them, and reject them if they are unfounded. Furthermore, these beliefs must also be moral and humanitarian.

In the November 1986 issue of *Psychology Today*, Fuller Torrey mentions a book written by Robert Jay Lifton, entitled *The Nazi Doctors: Medical Killing and the Psychology of Genocide*. In this book the author analyzes the role played by Nazi doctors and psychiatrists in the extermination of the Jews. Some of the doctors said that as doctors their aim was to preserve life, but that in order to respect and save life they would remove a gangrenous appendix from a diseased body. For them, the Jews were the gangrenous appendix in the body of mankind. This false and criminally insane belief was responsible for the horrendous crimes committed by these Nazi physicians. It would have been their moral duty to reject these crazy, untrue, inhuman beliefs and not to participate in the criminal actions of the Nazis.

All this indicates the absolute necessity of scrutinizing one's own beliefs as well as those of others, and, while respecting freedom of thought, also making certain that these beliefs are in accordance with truth and scientific fact as well as being responsible and humanitarian.

## 5. Appreciating the Blessings of Life

Dr. David Goodman says that we draw to ourselves the good of everything we appreciate, but the evil of everything we belittle. He further says that to have something to do, someone to love, and something to hope for are the true essentials of a happy and meaningful life. Those who keep free of self-centeredness by seeing the good in people and things live full and satisfying lives.

The saying "count your blessings" contains a lot of wisdom. Some people learn to appreciate their blessings only as a result of major or minor tragedies. The death of a loved one makes them aware of the finiteness and preciousness of life and helps them to live each day more fully. Losing a job, for example, through being laid off from a job which one did not like too much, can motivate a person to readjust his or her career and lead to more fulfilling employment. Even a severe accident, resulting in partial paralysis, forcing a person to use a wheelchair for the rest of his or her life, has motivated some people to study and start new careers, leading to more fulfilled lives, which would not have been the case had they not experienced the accident. One can truly say that their tragedy turned out to be a blessing in disguise. A person can also take his or her health for granted, and can quite often only start to appreciate it as a result of sickness.

Life is full of marvelous blessings. Appreciating the beauty of the world created by God, as well as the many beautiful creations of man's creative genius is imperative as well as meaningful and satisfying. A sunset, mountains, rivers, oceans, a rainbow, flowers, an inspiring poem, a good novel, melodious music, aesthetic works of art, and architectural creations satisfy our need for beauty and contribute to our happiness. Scientific and technological inventions make our lives more comfortable. It is our duty to appreciate them as well and to pay homage to the creative, inventive genius of outstanding men and women who got their talents and inspiration from God. We must also appreciate such human qualities and values as intelligence, truth, love, friendship, integrity, human solidarity, wisdom, social justice, courage, and personal, social, and moral responsibility.

It is also our responsibility to appreciate all the people who have contributed throughout the ages to create culture and civilization, as well as to those who through their courage, decency, humanitarianism, and altruism have made our world socially and morally more responsible.

31

## 6. Coping Responsibly with Adversity

It is obvious that experiencing adversity is very painful. Yet it can also awaken in us the readiness to respond to the challenge, bringing unsuspected resources of courage and creative adaptation to the surface. In 1940, after the capitulation of France, which left Britain alone to face the military might of Nazi Germany, Winston Churchill, the newly appointed British prime minister, brought out in the British people the indomitable and unconquerable spirit, essential for Hitler's eventual defeat.

Alfred Adler, the Viennese founder of Individual Psychology, coined the term compensation and overcompensation for the psychological mechanisms used by many people to cope with difficulties. It lies at the very heart of human progress and helps many people remain optimistic, retain their practical and realistic idealism in spite of all the setbacks and defeats they experience, and prevents them from becoming cynical. It has great relevance for education, politics, economics, morals, psychology, and medicine. From a position of weakness and dependency a loved and well-brought-up child develops into a responsible and mature adult. Human beings have a tendency to be challenged by a negative situation, and attempt and often succeed in transforming it into a positive condition. The small state of Israel, overcoming tremendous military economic and geographical odds, surviving and prospering in spite of everything, is a good example. Japan, completely ruined during the Second World War, has become the world's second economic giant. Similarly remarkable is West Germany's post-Second World War recovery.

Another superb and highly pertinent illustration of overcompensation and responsible coping with adversity concerns the Canadians Terry Fox and Steve Fonyo. Each of these two young men lost a leg to cancer. They decided to run from the Atlantic Ocean to the Pacific coast of Canada to raise money for cancer research. The first ran until Thunder Bay and was forced to drop out due to the resurgence of cancer. The second covered the whole distance. There are many other examples of people who coped successfully with adversity, even under the most difficult circumstances. Some survivors of Nazi concentration camps as well as prisoners of war treated extremely harshly by their captors succeeded in preserving their will to live as well as their sanity by communicating their pain and anguish to fellow victims, by managing to exercise some degree of control over their lives, and by setting goals for the future. Surprisingly, quite a few survivors succeeded after their liberation from captivity in building successful lives for themselves, in spite of their immense suffering. Some even benefitted from their ordeal by becoming more determined, courageous, and compassionate.

There are also examples of severely handicapped people who completed their academic schooling and became successful professionals. All these sorely tried and tested people triumphed in spite of everything and are shining examples of personal, social, and moral responsibility. They are, in the   real sense of the word, genuine human heroes.

# CHAPTER THREE

# *Moral Responsibilities*

### 7. Understanding What Causes Wars and Preventing Them

WAR IS AN ARMED CONFLICT BETWEEN STATES OR NATIONS OR BETWEEN different parties in the same state. We have to distinguish aggression from war-making. There is no way that life could be sustained or reproduced without some degree of mild or moderate aggression. War, however, is a particular type of institutionalized destructive aggression, in which social pressure is used to force individuals to kill other people they may not even fear or hate. Hatred of the enemy to be destroyed through war is usually instilled by propaganda. War is an institution for satisfying socially defined needs.

Anthropological evidence indicates that not all primitive societies made war. Some were peaceful. Hunters were the least warlike. There are primitive societies today, such as the Hopi and pygmies, who do not wage war.

The intensity and bloodiness of wars has increased with the growth of civilization. If wars were caused by innate human destructive impulses, the number of wars and casualties would have decreased with the advance of civilization. This has not been the case. The truth is the exact opposite, indicating that people have no innate destructive warlike impulses and that waging war is due to learned behavior.

Twenty leading psychologists and social scientists from twelve nations gathered in 1986 in Seville, Spain and declared that it is incorrect to say that we have inherited a tendency to make war from our animal ancestors. Warfare is a peculiar human phenomenon and does not occur in other animals. It is scientifically incorrect to say that war is genetically pro-grammed.

Traditionally, war was an institution, respected and even sanctified by society and romanticized in literature. Peace might have had a better chance in the past if war had been described in its terrifying horror, in the form of the countless dead and crippled and the immense suffering it caused. There is nothing humane about war. It is atrocious, ferociously inhuman and criminal. Even a defensive war against an evil aggressor is a necessary lesser evil.

Throughout most of history and especially in patriarchal and authoritarian societies, what was valued and emphasized was the expression of struggle, aggression, domination, and conquest. Life was considered relatively cheap, of no great value. Leading military commanders like Napoleon Bonaparte, looked upon soldiers as cannon fodder, to be sacrificed at will to fight irresponsible and unnecessary wars.

It is important in this context to ask why soldiers throughout most of history, most of whom didn't want war, fought to the end and did not prevent and stop wars. The answer lies in the fact that the soldiers fought in order not to lose the war and bring disaster and disgrace to the nation. They were afraid to be shot if caught running away They had little other choice than to kill or be killed. They were also indoctrinated and programmed to submit blindly and totally to authority as a moral and religious obligation and to be ready to give their lives when so commanded.

It is essential to understand what causes wars to start. The main reasons are territorial disputes and aggressions, religious, ethnic, national and class struggles and conflicts, ideological differences, humiliation of a defeated state by the victors (Germany in 1918), underestimation of an enemy country and misperception (Napoleon and Hitler regarding their invasions of Russia), human rights violations (American Civil War). Other motives are struggle for world markets, economic rivalries and alliances between states, or forcing fellow members of an alliance to go to war if another member is at war. Additional motives for starting wars are conquering lands for cultivation or because they are rich in raw materials, energy resources, or drinking water.

There is good reason for optimism that humankind is slowly on the way to outlawing and ending mass killings and wars—this despite the fact that there were 22 wars in 1988—and that the creation of a lasting peace on earth might occur only sometime in the future. The revolutions that removed communism and restored democracy in Eastern Europe and the former Soviet Union were relatively bloodless when compared with previous revolutions. The spread of democracy in the world lessens the chance of the occurrence of wars, including civil wars. This is due to the fact that it is immoral and illegal in a democracy for the state or a private citizen to kill other human beings in order to achieve political objectives. Conflicts of interest continue to occur between individuals and groups, but elections, courts, and parliaments settle them by nonviolent means.

Another reason for hope lies in the fact that in many  western countries in the second part of the twentieth century, soldiers have become

35

more human and responsible. Not long ago, soldiers would have viewed the shedding of tears for a fallen comrade as a loss of manhood. This attitude has changed, and even commanding officers will accept their emotions and weep openly to mourn a fallen officer or soldier. After the Second World War the parliament in West Germany enacted a law making it a crime for a soldier or officer in the German army to obey a criminally irresponsible order given by a superior. This is another step in the right direction.

It is also important to understand the teaching of history: There is progress toward an increase in social and moral responsibility. Thousands of years ago many people were cannibals. In the eighteenth and a large part of the nineteenth centuries, millions of Americans believed that God had ordained white people to be free and blacks to be slaves. Yet slavery was abolished. Human beings became morally more responsible, developed a more responsible faith in God in accordance with the teachings of the bible, and abolished slavery.

History also teaches us that people often abandon their bad habits only after a disaster or when a catastrophe is close at hand. The word crisis in Chinese connotes opportunity as well as danger. The threat of the possibility of a nuclear holocaust, of the global destruction of the environment through pollution, or of overpopulation can and must shake people up to behave responsibly and create a lasting worldwide peace, global environmental protection, and take up measures to limit the number of people on earth, to allow everyone to live in moderate prosperity.

Still another reason for hope lies in the fact that a survey of opinion done in France has revealed that a majority of French people consider Louis Pasteur, the founder of modern bacteriology, a greater human being than Napoleon Bonaparte, the emperor and military commander.

Insofar as the practical aspects of the relationship between armament and war is concerned, there are those thinkers and politicians who see arms races as the basic cause of war, and who believe that stopping arms races and producing fewer weapons will lead to a reduction in political conflicts, resulting in a further reduction in weapons. On the other hand, other political and military analysts believe that disarmament efforts are bound to fail if not preceded by political accommodations. I believe that both viewpoints reflect part of the truth and must be synthesized. Countries should reduce their level of armament and should also strive to build bonds of respect, friendship, and solidarity.

It is imperative that all nuclear, chemical, and biological weapons be destroyed by all countries who have them, and that production of new weapons of this kind be universally prohibited. Every country should possess conventional weapons for defensive purposes only, and should help the United Nations or a future world government to maintain peace in every part of the world.

It is important that nations and people everywhere on our planet transcend, psychologically and philosophically, the false belief that in a conflict situation between groups of people, all the bad is on the side of the enemy and all the righteousness is on one's own side. This perversion of truth often transforms a conflict between nations, states, or other groups of people into violent and armed hostilities. It must also be realized that the reason why war appealed to people is that it allows the individual to transcend himself through personal sacrifice to the cause of the glory and destiny of the nation.

People must be educated to realize that iIt is morally irresponsible to sacrifice themselves for a cause that requires the destruction of innocent people. It is also sad that throughout history many religious leaders prayed to God for victory of their nation against the enemy without thinking that solidarity with mankind is more important than victory in war and that the enemy was also a part of humankind. From a moral and ethical viewpoint the only justification to fight in a war is defense against unwarranted aggression.

It must also be understood that war releases solidarity and even altruism among people fighting for their country, but that even these highly positive emotions must under no circumstances be misused, channeled and directed to unify a nation to fight an enemy except when the enemy is cruelly immoral and out to destroy civilization as in the case of Nazi Germany.

War must be waged and fought against the real enemies of humankind: hunger, poverty, unemployment, sickness, personal, social, and moral irresponsibility, dishonesty, lack of psychological and moral integrity, ignorance, illiteracy, prejudice, discrimination, social and legal injustice. War must be waged against any form of murder, unless it is for defending one's life or the lives of innocent victims of aggression. A worldwide solidarity and community of interest must develop to unite people all over the world to fight these real enemies of humankind.

Furthermore, to abolish war on a worldwide basis, people must individually and collectively create the psychological, spiritual, cultural, moral, philosophical, economic, social, and political conditions for making peace. The next chapter in this book is dedicated to the responsibility to create peace.

## 8. Creating a Responsible and Permanent World Peace

Creating conditions for making universal peace necessitates the out-lawing and elimination of war. It necessitates much more however. Traditions, values, and beliefs responsible for the glorification and institutionalization of war have to be changed and peace must become institutionalized. All the institutions and corporations benefitting from war and the production and sale of weapons would have to undergo a profound transformation to adjust to a peaceful world. This new peaceful world order must be based on armies who maintain peace and on the prohibition of the production and use of weapons, except for defensive purposes. The worldwide sale of weapons must also be severely curtailed. People need to gain insight and understand the reasons for their violent behavior, their prejudices, and scapegoating of innocents. The death penalty must be abolished in every country where it is still used. Conflicts between states and feuding groups will have to be referred to an International Court for binding arbitration. Democracy has to become the accepted form of government all over the world. Hunting for pleasure and sport must be abolished. Torture and every form of abuse of human rights and dignity have to stop. Educators and parents must teach children the virtue of peace. The creation of a world government having authority over the "United States of the World" must become a reality. Warlords and conquering military leaders of the past and present have to be devalued. The fact that the majority of people in France considered Louis Pasteur a greater human being than Napoleon Bonaparte is a hopeful sign and a great example of what people all over the world must value. People who advance the well being of the human race must be eternally remembered and glorified, whereas war-making leaders who murder and ruin the lives of countless people through unprovoked, conquering wars must be branded as evildoers, even though they might have achieved some positive gains for their people in some areas.

Fighting for ecological rights, for social justice for women, for minorities and the handicapped, promoting North-South cooperation and international solidarity are some effective ways to promote peace.

To create peace it is necessary to discard the psychological fallacy that virtue and righteousness are entirely on one's own side and evil completely on the other. People must stop projecting their own selfishness and faults on others with whom they are in conflict. People have to become objective and see their own qualities, merits, and faults as well as those of their competitors. The military must be trained not to see peace as a state of pre-war any more, and weapons manufacturers have to realize that peace does not necessarily mean bankruptcy, but could mean a period of readjustment and readaptation of their factories to the production of less lethal goods.

Another violence against peace comes from the fact that many rich countries have a greater interest in satisfying the consumer needs of privileged minorities in poor countries than the needs of the poor and starving majority.

The main reason the United Nations cannot in many instances stop armed conflicts between nations as well as civil wars is that most states still uphold the principle of national sovereignty; they believe themselves entitled to do whatever they want within their political jurisdiction and feel they can attack another state provided they can get away with it. In 1991, however, the Security Council of the United Nations did order the cessation of armed aggression when a combined U.N. force reconquered Kuwait from the illegal Iraqi aggression and occupation. It is vital that the United Nations act like this increasingly in the future.

Another obstacle to peace is the traditional belief that the more arms a country possesses, the more security it has. In the age of ballistic missiles and atomic weapons this is a very dangerous fallacy. Having atomic weapons might be a deterrent to an enemy's starting an armed attack against one's own country, but it might also terrify the enemy to act aggressively as a result of being overcome by panic. If the enemy also possesses atomic weapons, this could lead to a nuclear holocaust.

Another reason why nuclear weapons cannot eliminate war is that computer errors can confuse military experts, making them believe their country is being attacked and leading them to unleash a counter-offensive. Deterrence might eliminate war for a certain period of time, or even permanently, but does not create genuine and responsible peace. Disarmament is one of the preconditions of a genuine and responsible peace. This includes the elimination of atomic, chemical, and bacteriological weapons as well as of large quantities of conventional weapons, and calls for all governments to learn to trust each other in a mature and responsible manner.

Ideological differences must not lead to armed conflict. Rather, they should be solved by realizing that opposing viewpoints are often complementary. Nations and states who value only the rights and responsibilities of the individual must realize that countries and governments who value only the rights and responsibilities of the community and the state also have a valid point, even though both viewpoints are one-sided. Responsible, just, and efficient societies and governments value both individual and collective rights and responsibilities. Both are complementary and form a harmonious and integrated whole.

It is also important for people to realize more and more that survival of humankind as well as continuous human progress make it absolutely necessary today to think in terms of interdependence between different states and economies, rather than in terms of confrontation and conflict.

Environmental destruction is emerging as a major threat to international security and world peace. Historically, tensions and armed conflicts have been caused by struggles over land, water, and other resources. The desertification of large parts of Africa forced people to migrate and could lead to violence. Between 1940 and 1980 many countries have suffered water shortages, which also leads to disputes between nations. Maritime territorial zones and nations' fishing interests are another source of friction. All these environmental conflicts point to the absolute need for the eventual creation of a world government that will have the authority to allocate the resources of the world in an equitable manner among all nations.

The presence of nuclear weapons motivates people consciously and unconsciously to look for solutions that will avoid a possible nuclear holocaust. Ironically, this helps them to realize that war is both criminal and crazy. The danger of a nuclear holocaust will increasingly force people to choose survival. They will become more aware of the importance of God's help, and that it is crucial to develop a feeling of interrelatedness with all human beings and all life on earth.

In order to create a peaceful world it is also necessary that every person make it his or her goal to contribute to a peaceful world, in accordance with his or her interests and talents. This can be done by developing respect, appreciation, and understanding for individual, cultural, ethnic, religious, social, economic, and political differences and helping to build bridges of understanding and respect between them.

Creating a genuine and responsible peace also depends on creating economic conditions leading to moderate economic prosperity for all. The gap between the richest and the poorest and between the highest and lowest wage earner in any community must not be too big. Adequate social security must protect all citizens against the high cost of sickness and provide them an adequate income for old age and infirmity. People must be helped to fully develop their potentials through high quality, free educational services and then be motivated to make a contribution to society and the world. There must be full employment, and everybody must be helped and must help himself or herself to make a success of his or her life in a responsible, meaningful way. The death penalty must be universally abolished and there must be compulsory reeducation of delinquents and criminals toward personal, social, and moral responsibility. Family life has to be greatly valued and leisure activities should be responsible, enriching, and meaningful. It is also important that women play a bigger and more important role at all levels of corporate management, in non-traditional occupations, in government, and in the civil service.

The money governments will save by reducing their armies should be used to improve educational services, the health system, social security, universal medical insurance, and to help the development of poorer countries.

The creation of a lasting peace also demands that a relentless war must be fought against the real enemies of humankind—hunger, poverty, unemployment, sickness, ignorance, illiteracy, prejudice, discrimination, social and legal injustice, the death penalty, overpopulation, environmental pollution, indifference, heartlessness, absence of faith in God, lack of personal and moral integrity, lack of personal, social, and moral responsibility—and against any form of murder, unless it occurs in defense of one's life and the life of innocently aggressed people.

A colossal educational effort must be made by parents and educators to teach children, the young, and students to value peace and to make a contribution to bring it about. It is also the moral obligation of adults to continue for the rest of their lives to educate themselves to value peace and to make a contribution to create it.

### 9. Morally Outstanding Contemporary Individuals and Groups

The names of outstanding twentieth-century socially and morally responsible individuals and groups is incomplete. The humanitarians mentioned in this chapter as well as many others deserve the everlasting gratitude, love, and respect of every decent human being on earth.

The humanitarian individuals and groups are listed in alphabetical order.

## Examples of Personally, Socially, and Morally Highly Responsible Individuals

### Baba Amte

He has become an international symbol of protest for conservationists and environmentalists. The Baba's arguments against huge dam projects

41

in India, which were considered a remedy for power shortages and drought, have led politicians and administrators to change their views concerning development all over the third world. He convened a meeting of scientists and politicians and convinced them that big dams actually lead to destruction. He also championed the cause of the poor and oppressed in India. He won the United Nations Human Rights award.

## Norman Bethune

He was a brilliant Canadian doctor, specializing in pulmonary surgery. During the great depression years of the 1930s there were large numbers of unemployed in Montreal, just as in many other North American cities. At that time there was no Medicare or government subsidized, free medical service in Canada. The unemployed were especially hard hit as most could not afford to pay the doctors for medical treatment and most doctors would not treat them for free. Dr. Normal Bethune did treat them free of charge.

During the 1930s, he took part in the Spanish Civil War in the 1930s, serving as a physician on the side of the Republicans against the Fascists. He also served as a surgeon in Mao Tse Tung's army during its campaign against the Chinese Nationalist Army. He died in China during that war as a result of sepsis.

He said that he refused to live in a world that creates murder and corruption without lifting his small finger. He is revered in China as a great hero.

## Willi Brandt

He was West German Chancellor after the Second World War. During the war he fought in the Norwegian resistance against the Nazis. Before becoming chancellor he was mayor of West Berlin. As chancellor, he pursued a policy of reconciliation toward Eastern Europe and the former Soviet Union. He fell on his knees and cried during his visit to Auschwitz, where hundreds of thousands of Jews were exterminated during the war. He was also president of the Social Democratic World Association. He militated for world peace and received the Nobel Peace Prize.

## Gro Harlem Brundtland

She was the prime minister of Norway in the 1980s. In 1984 she was appointed chairperson of the U.N. commission on the environment. The commission produced the Brundtland report, which forced the issue of environmental global responsibility on the international agenda.

### Jimmy Carter

He was president of the United States from 1976 to 1980. Since his term of office, he has become extremely active in promoting humanitarian causes around the world. Among his goals are promoting free elections, fighting for the release of political prisoners, and showing farmers how to grow food. The Carter Human Rights Foundation supports the work of antitotalitarian groups around the world. Among his other projects are Global 2000, a collection of agricultural and public health projects in Africa and Asia, a task force for child survival, a juvenile health program for developing nations, and Habitat for Humanity, a volunteer group that builds houses for poor people in the United States and abroad. The former president participates as a volunteer in the house building project.

### Dr. Helen Caldicott

She has served as president of Physicians for Social Responsibility, an organization whose leaders won the Nobel Peace Prize in 1985. She wanted the world's 63,000 hydrogen bombs to be dismantled (only 1,000 will exterminate life on earth). She fought to stop the production of nuclear submarines and the use of uranium, with its danger of radiation and possible genetic mutation. She was the central figure of an Oscar-winning documentary, "If You Love this Planet."

### Madeline Cartwright

She is principal of James Blaine Public Elementary School, situated in a decaying Philadelphia neighborhood. Most of the children in the neighborhood grow up in abject poverty. In fact, 90 percent of Blaine's families receive some form of public assistance. Crack houses and young men selling dope are familiar sights for the children on their way to school. Cartwright brought hope, discipline, and involvement into the school, and succeeded in raising the children's attendance level considerably. Her tactics have made a difference. Despite an outward appearance of disrepair, the school is a clean scrubbed island, a safe zone in a violent world. One of her most important accomplishments was to get the parents involved in the school. She did this by asking the pupils to recruit their own fathers and mothers. She encourages the children to tell her their troubles. She believes that involvement in the children's lives prevents them from being abused.

The commitment to her students and her methods led to impressive results. The Merrill Lynch Company Foundation has selected 25 of her students for college scholarships.

### Dr. Pauline Cutting

She worked in 1986 as a volunteer British surgeon at Haifa Hospital in the Palestinian refugee camp in West Beirut. The hospital was hit by bombs, rockets, and tank shells, was short of medicine and equipment, yet it nevertheless treated scores of patients, many with terrible injuries. Dr. Cutting received threats of assassination, yet she continued to save lives under almost impossible conditions. She received the Order of the British Empire in July 1987 for her work in Beirut.

### Dalai Lama

He is the Buddhist spiritual leader of Tibet, who took exile in India when the Chinese communists took full, harsh control after an uprising in Tibet in 1959. He is a staunch fighter for religious freedom and rights.

### Terry Fox and Steve Fonyo

These two outstanding young Canadian men suffered from cancer, and each lost a leg through amputation. They decided to run from one end of Canada to the other, from the Atlantic to the Pacific, to raise money for cancer research. Terry Fox made it to Thunder Bay in Ontario where he became ill and died. Steve Fonyo reached Vancouver. Every year thousands of people continue their work, collecting money for further research.

### Anne Frank

This young Dutch Jewish girl died in a Nazi extermination camp in 1945. She wrote a diary in which she described her growing up into a young lady and stated—in one of the most beautiful statements ever written—that in spite of all the criminal inhumanity to which she and her correligionists were subjected by the Nazis, there is goodness in people, and that man is capable of good.

### Mohandas Karamohand Gandhi

He was the architect of India's freedom from British colonial domination. He urged India and the world to turn away from materialism and search for a new kind of brotherhood. He identified with India's pariahs, (also known as the untouchables, the lowest caste of people in India), who were deprived of most human rights. He believed that the struggle against British domination had to be a nonviolent one. Nonviolence was one of his main beliefs and philosophies. He further believed in democracy and social justice and lived a simple life of modesty and charity. He was assassinated in 1948.

## Martin Gray

He was a Polish Jew who escaped as a teenager from a Nazi extermination camp and fought in the Jewish uprising of the Warsaw ghetto and in the Polish resistance against the Nazis. His parents and siblings were murdered by the Nazis. He joined the Red Army in 1944 and worked for a while in Soviet military intelligence in Eastern Germany. He immigrated afterward to the United States, where he made a fortune in the antiquary business. He married a French Catholic woman whom he loved very dearly. They settled in Southern France, where he bought a house. She and their children died in a forest fire. He became very depressed after this tragedy, as this seemed to him the final blow after having first lost all his family in the holocaust, and he contemplated suicide. French friends persuaded him to help other depressed people. He decided to do so and donated a large portion of his money to help other victims of forest fires. He wrote two books, *The Book of Life*, and *In the Name of All of Mine*. His life story was made into a film in Hungary.

What is remarkable about Martin Gray is that he was a heroic, skillful survivor, who fought the Nazis, made a fortune after the war, but did not become infected by vindictive hatred nor corrupted by a lot of money. He maintained his humanitarian, philanthropic nature in spite of great tragedies in his life.

## Anatoly Grischenko

In 1986, at the age of 52, this Ukranian pilot flew over the nuclear plant at Chernobyl, for three days dropping wet concrete to bury the damaged and radiation-leaking reactor after its explosion and fire. He suffered radiation exposure as a result, which caused leukemia, leading to his early death in 1990. While performing his heroic and highly responsible mission he was fully aware of the risk involved.

## Paul Grueninger

He was the chief of a Swiss border town during the Second World War. He disobeyed government orders to bar fleeing German Jews from entering Switzerland, which saved the lives of 3600 Jewish refugees.

## Vaclav Havel

Havel, a Czech playwright, stood up to the despotic Czech communist regime for many years. He fought for truth and human liberty, went to jail for it, and in 1989 became the president of Czechoslovakia. He worked to end the lucrative Czechoslovak arms trade. He wants the politics of his country to be based on responsibility and morality. He would like to introduce morality into European and global politics as well. In an address before the U.S. Senate and House of Representatives, he said that the future of mankind depends on politicians acting in a morally responsible manner. One of his major themes is that individuals must take responsibility for their lives. He resigned as president in 1992, as Czechoslovakia will separate into two separate states: the Czech-lands and Slovakia. He will in all likelihood become the president of the newly formed Czech lands.

## Jaime Jamillo

He is a successful Colombian businessman from Bogota who made it his mission to rescue as many Bogota street kids as possible. Many of these children lead lives of crime and prostitution and are on drugs. They are abandoned by their parents and society and are in constant danger of being killed by Colombian death squads. Many sleep in the sewers of Bogota.

Jaime Jamillo and his wife Patricia formed the foundation "Children of the Andes." He bought six houses, which provide homes for 300 children. The children are weaned off drugs, sent to school, and are helped to find suitable employment afterward.

## Shulamit Katznelson

An Israeli teacher, she teaches Arabic to Israelis and Hebrew to Palestinians. She plays an important role in creating understanding between Israelis and Palestinians.

### Danny Kaye

The talented comedian, movie star, and accomplished symphony conductor was also a dedicated volunteer. For the last 34 years of his life he traveled the world to bring laughter to thousands of underprivileged children as official international goodwill ambassador for UNICEF (United Nations International Children's Educational Fund). U.N. Secretary General Perez de Cuellar called him a champion for children in every continent.

### Martin Luther King, Jr.

This American Christian minister was an important civil rights leader in the 1960s. He fought not only for black civil rights, but also for harmonious relations between people of different religions, ethnic backgrounds, and races. He died a tragic death at the hand of an assassin.

### Father Maximilian Kolbe

He was a Polish Franciscan priest who sacrificed his life at Auschwitz during the Second World to save another prisoner who had a family. He has been beatified by Pope Paul VI.

### Janusz Korczak

He was a Polish medical doctor and educator of Jewish origin. Before World War II, he founded Poland's first progressive orphanage. In 1942, the Germans ordered his orphanage closed, and all of the 200 Jewish children housed there were transported to the Nazi concentration camp Treblinka. He led them with dignity to the death camp, where all of them, himself included, died. His Catholic admirers wanted to help him, but he refused help, choosing to remain with his children until the bitter end. Forty-eight years after his death, both Poland and Israel claim him as a martyr and just man.

### Cardinal Paul Emil Leger

A Canadian cardinal, he resigned his job as archbishop of Montreal to take up missionary work in Africa. His mission and message were to help the sick, starving, and poor of the world. He helped the lepers in Cameroon and through the foundations he helped to create and the millions of dollars accumulated, he was also able to help the impoverished in many countries. He was a strong believer in ecumenism and as archbishop of Montreal he contributed to cooperation between Catholics and Protestants and better relations between Catholics and Jews. He died in 1991 at the age of 87.

### George Mantello

He was the first secretary of the El Salvador Consulate in Switzerland during the Second World War. He distributed Salvadorean citizenship papers without charge to Jews throughout Nazi-occupied Europe, especially in Hungary, thereby preventing some Jews from Budapest from being sent to extermination camps.

### Francesco Mendes

This forty-four-year-old Brazilian leader of a rubber tappers union fought to save the Amazon jungle from deforestation. He was shot dead in the late 1980s and became the world's first ecological martyr. He is credited with saving thousands of hectares of tropical forest from the bulldozer. He made enemies with land exploiters who tried to destroy the Amazon forests.

### Yehudi Menuhin

He is an American Jewish violinist and humanitarian, renowned the world over. Immediately after the end of the Second World War, he gave violin concerts for German audiences. He told Golda Meir, the Israeli prime minister, that she should do as much for the well being of the Palestinians as she did for the Israeli Jews. He is very involved in many humanitarian causes.

### Irwin Miller

He leads the way for the wealthy in working for public good. He is a multimillionaire who assembled a group of top American executives in 1963, after the Birmingham police attack on black children. Together with President John F. Kennedy, he convinced these leaders to fight segregation. They helped to desegregate many Southern cities. In 1989, in his late seventies, Miller turned his hometown of Columbus, Indiana into a series of experiments in racial justice, corporate health, and education.

### Father Rufino Niccacci

He was a Franciscan monk in Assisi, Italy, who organized the Assisi underground during the Second World War, saving the lives of more than 5,000 Jews. He was declared a righteous gentile by Israel, the highest Israeli distinction bestowed on a non-Jew.

### Raoul La Portiere

He was the mayor of a small village in France, who fabricated identification documents and border passes between 1940 and 1944, thereby saving the lives of close to 2000 refugees, mainly Jews.

### Anita Roddick

She is an Englishwoman who owns 600 beauty stores that carry only environmentally friendly products. In 1989 she received the United Nations award for environmental achievement. She returns some of the profits from her shops to poor countries through product development. In addition, she uses her shops to promote the cause of saving the whales, protecting rain forests, and ending the repression of political dissidents.

### Andrei Sakharov

He was a great humanist and humanitarian. A top Russian nuclear scientist, he became the most outspoken opponent of communist inhumanity and the best known Soviet dissident. He denounced the Soviet invasion of Afghanistan and championed the cause of human rights in the Soviet Union (for which he was imprisoned for many years). He won the Nobel Peace Prize in 1975 for his effort to limit nuclear testing and encourage multilateral disarmament. He was also a champion of the downtrodden and the persecuted in the former Soviet Union. He died in 1989 at the age of 68.

### Stephen Sanders

In 1990, Sanders, one of Vancouver's shrewdest and most successful real estate investors, signed over the titles of 23 luxury apartments he owned in downtown Vancouver (worth $170 million) to a charitable trust foundation. After allowing for mortgages, his gift was worth $110 million. Each year Sanders' foundation will grant many cosmic conscious awards of $25,000 to $30,000 to humanitarians in the third world. Sanders and his board will name the recipients. He will also give money to third world hospitals. One of his first projects was a orphanage in Sri Lanka. At the age of 55, Sanders stated that making a lot of money wasn't doing anything for him anymore. After donating the greater part of his fortune to charity and giving large amounts of money to his children, he decided that he and his wife could life comfortably on a yearly allowance of $40,000.

## Albert Schweitzer

He was a philosopher, theologian, musician, and mission doctor, who won the Nobel Peace Prize in 1952. He worked for a great part of his life as a mission doctor in Gabon, Africa. One of his most important values was reverence for life, which meant to him deep respect for people and all living creatures.

## Aristides de Sousa Mendes

He was the Portuguese Consul General in Bordeaux, France during the Second World War. He disobeyed the instructions of his government and issued thousands of visas to Jews to enter Portugal, thereby saving 30,000 lives. He lost his job as a result and fell into poverty.

## Maurice Strong

This influential Canadian businessman and public servant was the president of the United Nations' first environmental conference in Stockholm in 1972, and also of the Earth Summit in Rio de Janeiro in 1992. He promotes the ecological imperative that mankind must change direction to survive. He states that the threat to mankind's security from environmental pollution is at least as great a threat as the traditional danger of war.

## Chiune Sugihara

He was the Japanese Consul General in Kovno, Lithuania, who with his wife Yukiko, issued transit visas, which saved the lives of 25,000 Jews by enabling them to flee to Japan.

## Mother Teresa

She is a Catholic nun who founded the order of Missionaries of Charity. In 350 houses around the world the missionaries feed 80,000 families every day, teach 4,000 children, and care for 80,000 lepers. According to her, poverty is not just being without food; it is the absence of love. There are people even in rich countries who have no one. They are dying of hunger for love, especially the drunkards and drug addicts. In rich countries many people die of loneliness, being unwanted and unloved. For Mother Teresa, this is a much more bitter poverty than the poverty of being without food. Her missionaries give love and care to these lonely and abandoned people.

### Pauline Vanier

She was the wife of former Canadian Governor General George Vanier. She helped Jewish refugees from Nazism before World War II, at a time when Canadian government policy did not help these victims. She also helped veterans of the French resistance. After World War II she helped Jewish survivors of the holocaust. She visited prisoners and worked with Carmelite nuns in the poor districts of Montreal. After the death of her husband, she worked with her son Jean in France, helping retarded adults.

### Raoul Wallenberg

He was a Swedish diplomat who saved the lives of tens of thousands of Hungarian Jews during the last years of the Second World War by giving them Swedish passports. He also intervened with Nazi and Hungarian fascist leaders to prevent the massacre of Budapest's remaining Jews. He was arrested by the Soviets immediately after they entered Budapest in early 1945, and most likely died in a Soviet internment camp.

## Examples of Socially and Morally Highly Responsible Groups

### Teachers of America

A group of highly gifted American university students from all fields, including medicine and law, who decided in the late 1980s to do something about the low performance level of many American elementary and high school students in reading, spelling, mathematics, and science and who particularly wanted to help students in slums and drug-infected areas. The results obtained by these highly dedicated, practically idealistic young people, who interrupted studying for their chosen careers for one or more years, were close to miraculous. They brought up the performance level of most of their students to a level comparable with that of students in the best American schools.

### Medecins Sans Frontieres (Physicians Without Borders)

A highly dedicated group of European doctors who give free medical service in areas of the world ravaged by war, natural disasters, epidemics, and famine.

## Amnesty International

An international organization that fights against violation of human rights anywhere in the world. They fight against illegal imprisonment, torture, political assassinations, and all forms of oppression and abuse of human freedom and dignity. They sponsor an unjustly persecuted person or group, get people to write to the offending authorities, and have succeeded in freeing many political prisoners and saving many lives.

## Environmental groups fighting against the destruction of the planet

The best known environmental group is Greenpeace. Through energetic, courageous actions and initiatives, it fights against all forms of pollution of the environment and destruction of the earth's fauna and flora. Another crusading environmental group is Friends of the Earth. There are many more groups fighting to save the earth from environmental pollution.

## Groups helping the development of the Third World and Teaching East European Countries Market Techniques

There are groups like the Peace Corps and various other groups consisting of professionals and students who help in the agricultural, industrial, educational, social, medical, technological, and scientific development of the third world, many on a voluntary basis. There are also a group of retired managers who travel to East European countries to teach managers there free market managerial and administrative skills. In 1990, a whole class of M.B.A. graduates from a leading American university decided to go to Poland for a year, to teach Polish managers market managerial skills.

## Groups helping the children of the world

There are many groups and associations in North America and Europe who motivate people to make a monthly donation toward the welfare of a child in an underprivileged part of the world. This money helps the child to pursue his or her education and also helps to improve the socioeconomic conditions of the child's community.

## The heroic village of Le Chambon

The whole village of Le Chambon, south of Paris, consisting of 5000 Protestant Hugenots, risked their own lives during World War II to save 5000 Jews, whom they sheltered in their village and protected from the Nazi death squads in neighboring villages. When asked why they did it, they said it was a natural way to behave and referred to the biblical injunction of loving your neighbor as yourself.

### The women of Berlin who defied Hitler

Approximately 1000 German Christian women married to German Jewish husbands successfully blocked the deportation of their husbands to extermination camps in February 1943. At that time the Nazis decided to completely clear Berlin of all remaining Jews and to end the privileged status enjoyed until then by Jewish husbands married to gentile German women. The German women assembled outside the building on Rose Street where the Jews were held for transport to Auschwitz and blocked the street, making it impossible for the Nazi SS units to move the Jews out of Berlin. Even when the Nazis threatened to use their machine guns against the women they continued their fight to help and free their husbands by shouting: "Give us back our men. We want to see our men." After six days of protest, the Nazis finally gave in to the women and Goebbels ordered the release of the 1000 Jewish prisoners. Knowing the cruelty of the Nazis and their determination to kill every European Jew and to punish every Gentile who helped Jews, the heroic struggle of the German women on behalf of their Jewish husbands—and above all their success in forcing the Nazis to free their husbands—was definitely miraculous.

### 10. Remembering the Holocaust and other Genocides and Preventing their Recurrence

The term genocide refers to the extermination of social, religious, political, national, ethic, and racial groups. The word holocaust stands for the extermination of six million European Jews by the Nazis during the Second World War. The holocaust was similar to other genocides, which occurred before, during, and after the Second World War, but it was also unique in world history. It was unique because the totality of European Jewry was singled out for total annihilation. Killing Jews became the top priority of the Nazi hierarchy, even more important than the war effort itself. Toward the end of the war, when it was already evident, even to the Nazis, that the war was lost, they nevertheless continued to transport Jews to extermination camps—even before transporting their own troops to the front. The holocaust has also become a symbol of the irresponsible, criminal oppression and extermination of a minority by tyrannical, inhuman leaders and political regimes. In 1988, German Chancellor Helmut Kohl stated that the crime of the holocaust is without parallel in the history of humanity in its coldly calculating planning and its deadly effectiveness.

The horrifying, criminal irresponsibility and even insanity of the murder of six million Jews resided in the fact that Jews were murdered because they were Jews. Even the cruel Spanish Inquisition of the Middle Ages, which led to the expulsion and even burning at the stake of countless Jews by the Catholic church, persecuted Jews for what was considered a false religion, which did not permit salvation. Once converted to Catholicism, the Jews were accepted and the persecution stopped. The Nazis, however, did not give the Jews any chance to escape being killed. This totally inhuman and irresponsible attitude and behavior constitutes the epitome of evil.

To understand how the Germans, one of the most civilized people in the world, could submit to an insane, criminal genius like Hitler and execute his criminal orders and how even many German doctors carried out the murder of Jews in concentration camps, it is important to know that the Nazis considered the Jews an all-powerful source of evil in the world. They further had the demented belief that the Jews were a cancer within the Aryan body of Germany which justified their extermination, just as one extracts and eliminates a cancerous growth from the body of a patient to save his or her life.

Similar to delinquents, who will occasionally kill innocent bystanders in an indiscriminate manner in revenge for having been rejected or brutalized and physically and psychologically abused as children, the Nazis scapegoated the Jews because Germany lost the First World War.

Other reasons for scapegoating the Jews were the very harsh reparations imposed by the victorious allies on defeated Germany after their victory in the First World War, which resulted in catastrophic inflation as well as in mass unemployment, especially during the great depression. An additional factor responsible for the persecution of the Jews was the German authoritarian character, which was very often formed by brutal, insensitive fathers, resulting in submissive personalities who worshiped power and authority and despised human differences and minorities and were incapable of self-criticism and of criticizing authority. At a deep psychological level there was also a lot of envy of the Jews, especially because the Jews are considered to be God's chosen people. Knowing that they were wasting their lives, by having become hateful and glorifying war and brutish strength, the Nazis, who could not discharge this anger targeted instead the Jews.

Gwynne Dyer, in an article in the *Gazette*, quoted the German poet and writer Hans Magnus Enzensberger, who believes that Hitler's real purpose was the wish to die and to take everybody with him. At the end of his career, he said that the German people did not deserve to survive. It is clear that a criminally half-insane personality is profoundly destructive as well as auto-destructive and is a menace to everybody. Destructive leaders sometimes come to power in times of despair and hopelessness and collective humiliation. In order to avoid their coming to power it is vital that the justified yearnings of people for social justice, moderate prosperity, peace, and the opportunity to lead responsible, meaningful lives are satisfied. Otherwise, in despair and out of hopelessness, having nothing to lose, people can follow psychopathic killers like Hitler.

Social scientists Frank Chalk and Kurt Jonassohn state that the holocaust was perpetrated for ideological motives. The perpetrators admitted they did it and the survivors refused to remain silent. As a result of the holocaust, laws on human rights have been passed and there is an increased value and respect for human rights.

Other examples of twentieth-century genocides are the Turkish massacre of Armenians during the First World War, the murder of one million Cambodians after the Second World War by the Khmer Rouge, Stalin's assassination of millions of Soviet citizens, the killings of thousands of East Timorese in 1986 by the Indonesian military in Operation Eradicate, and the Nazi extermination of the Gypsies.

A very important positive precedent was created at Nuremberg after the end of the Second World War. Nazi war criminals were prosecuted and severely punished for crimes committed against humanity.

Life is ruled to some extent by the survival of the fittest. Yet, increasingly, the fittest, especially since the existence of nuclear weapons, are the peacemakers, the altruistic, cooperative, personally, socially, and morally responsible humanitarians. The holocaust was in a way a turning point, a tragic event at the crossroads between the end of an era and the beginning of a new one, a symbol of the past, of human bestiality, and personal, social, and moral irresponsibility as well as the beginning of the end of the moral dinosaurs of humankind, the warmakers and the worshipers of war. Like a flame, which flickers with increased intensity before it dies, the horrifying crimes committed by the Nazis represented a part of the final outbreak of total, complete inhumanity, evil, and social and moral irresponsibility.

It is very important that the holocaust be remembered every year. The Jews have chosen one day annually, Yom Hashoa, which falls shortly after Passover, to remember the Nazis' murder of six million innocent Jewish women, men, and children, slaughtered between 1939 and 1945. By remembering the death of these martyrs, the Jews also serve as a role model for the racial, religious, or national groups who were also victims of genocide, to also remember their innocently martyred fellow group members through ritualized ceremonies. The democratic government of West Germany apologized to the survivors of the holocaust and to the relatives of the dead. Remembering the holocaust is one way to prevent its recurrence.

It is also essential that high school students the world over are taught about the holocaust as well as about other genocides. The Ottawa board of education in Canada voted in 1988 to do exactly that, and ten percent of the material covered in senior level history and English courses will be devoted to either the holocaust or other genocides such as the Armenian genocide, the Ukrainian forced famine, or the Baltic massacres. This course helps students to understand the potential of irresponsible inhumanity in every group, as well as the social, political, economic, and psychological facts responsible for genocides. Above all, they learn how to create a socially, politically, economically, and morally more responsible world in order to prevent future outbursts of man's inhumanity to his fellow human beings. They also learn that they are individually and collectively responsible to ensure that this outburst of irresponsible criminal insanity does not recur.

It is vital to understand that members of the generation of the perpetrators of a genocide are individually and collectively morally coresponsible for the committed murders, because they were either indifferent to, or did not oppose, the committed crimes—even if they did not commit the crimes themselves. Insofar as following generations are concerned, those who were either children at the time of the committed crimes or did not live at the time of the atrocities, they are in no way responsible for the committed murders, but they are morally obliged and responsible for working harder than other groups to build a more peaceful, socially just, and socially and morally responsible world.

An extraordinary act of great courage, humanity, and social and moral responsibility occurred during the Second World War in German-occupied France, where the whole village of Le Chambon, south of Paris, sheltered and saved 5000 Jews from transportation to extermination in death camps. The residents of the village, 5000 in all, French Protestant Hugenots, did this at the risk of their own lives. The Nazi penalty for helping Jews was instant execution, yet they did it. Miraculously, both the 5000 Hugenots as well as the 5000 Jews survived. When asked after the war why they did it, the villagers said it was a natural way to behave, and referred to the biblical injunction of loving your neighbor as yourself. The people of Denmark also provided a beautiful example of collective social and moral responsibility. They thwarted the Nazi plan to deport all Danish Jews to extermination camps by smuggling an overwhelming majority of Danish Jews to safety in neutral Sweden over a short period of time. The Danish king, as a gesture of protest against the policy of the Nazis, wore the Star of David himself.

After the war, West Germany passed a law making it a crime for a subordinate in the armed forces to execute an order given by a superior officer if the order was morally irresponsible. This is a direct result of the holocaust, and a way to prevent subordinates from executing criminal orders, for example, killing innocent people.

To prevent the recurrence of genocides it is essential that people all over the world are educated to accept the value of individual and collective differences. Similar to a jigsaw puzzle, where every piece becomes indispensable to the total picture by virtue of its difference and distinctness, individual human and collective differences are similarly indispensable and enriching to the well being of society and the world.

It is also important for those countries where there is prejudice and discrimination against minority groups—whether on racial, ethnic, religious, or national grounds—to rectify that situation through the introduction of affirmative action measures, wherein some preference is given to talented and competent members of disadvantaged minority groups for admittance to university studies and to jobs in the public service.

To prevent further occurrences of genocides, people must be taught to accept human weaknesses, to tolerate ambiguity and ambivalence, and to develop compassion for the handicapped, the disadvantaged, and the downtrodden.

Parents and teachers must treat children and adolescents with respect and must not abuse them physically or psychologically. Punishment for infringement of regulations must not be brutal. Rather, such punishment should allow the child to understand why he or she is being punished and provide an opportunity for education in becoming personally, socially, and morally responsible. At all costs, parents and educators must prevent children from developing into adults with authoritarian personalities, who submit blindly to authority, hate and persecute people who are different and weak, and who have difficulty accepting ambiguous situations. Children must be educated to be humanitarian, internationally-minded, and to value human cooperation and solidarity.

Excessive, unjustified violence in T.V. programs, movies, and novels must be censored. The death sentence must be abolished globally and criminals must undergo compulsory reeducation toward personal, moral, and social responsibility.

There must be full employment and people must work in jobs which correspond to their interests, aptitudes, and personality traits, jobs that are useful and provide meaning and fulfillment.

All governments and societies must dedicate themselves to promoting the psychological, economic, and social well being of people as well as abolishing and outlawing all wars. They must strive to create a peaceful world under the authority of world government. All human beings have to realize that they are children of God, creator of the universe and of all forms of life.

The realization of the objectives stated above will guarantee that genocides will not recur.

## 11. Being Altruistic

Altruism is the need, desire, and moral and social obligation to help others, to promote their welfare. Based on the feeling of generosity, sympathy, love, and compassion, this concern with other people's welfare also satisfies one's own need for well being and self-esteem. It is highly fulfilling and rewarding to genuinely help others. Responsible altruism is both unselfish as well as enlightened self-interest.

Altruism fosters the development of responsible communities. It also helps people develop a responsible sense of power, which results from the use of personal talents out of a sense of moral obligation to advance the physical, psychological, social, economic, and spiritual welfare of others.

Helping others is beneficial to health. Research indicates that meaningful, altruistic, voluntary work leads to a lowering of blood pressure and also increases longevity in the helper.

There is a form of altruism which applies only to one's own group, whether national, cultural, or religious, and excludes help to people outside the group. I use the term responsible altruism as the moral, social, and personal obligation and duty to help every person, each member of the human family, who is in need of help. The biblical parable of the Good Samaritan is an ideal example of responsible altruism, which is also humanitarianism. People with a high degree of moral integrity and a well-developed feeling of self-esteem tend to be altruistic humanitarians, which is not necessarily the case with people expressing a more ethnocentric type of altruism.

Responsible altruism, as a moral obligation, must also include the rehabilitation of irresponsible delinquent people, who must be compelled to undergo reeducation toward social, moral, and personal responsibility.

Altruistic humanitarians, who at the risk of their own life rescued and saved Jews from certain extermination by the Nazis during the Second World War in Europe, acted according to deeply held moral values as well as by emotional attachment and identification with the victims. A moral sense of obligation to help others in danger as well as a social and often religious principle of justice and sympathy for innocent, unjustly persecuted victims are powerful motives to stimulate people to act in an altruistic, humanitarian manner.

Many people are unwilling to act in a responsible altruistic way to help others in distress, because certain segments of society don't attach value to altruism. Derisive terms like "do-gooders" or "bleeding hearts" illustrate this. It is therefore extremely important to educate people both individually as well as collectively to attach great value to altruism, as it ensures our survival.

The shameful and disgraceful incident in New York, where Kitty Genovese was stabbed to death in full view of many onlookers who failed to come to her rescue or notify the police, is a horrible example of social, moral, and personal irresponsibility. According to social psychological studies, the presence of onlookers in an area inhibits responsible action and intervention. Since the responsibility for helping the person or persons in distress is shared by everybody present, many people don't feel a duty to intervene and help since they believe others will do it. Furthermore, the fact that a lot of people don't act responsibly and don't help has a negative influence on the rest, who also abstain from rendering assistance. All this points to the absolute necessity for people to act as responsible individuals, irrespective of circumstances and the irresponsible behavior of others.

It is essential that laws are enacted to stimulate people to act responsibly and altruistically and to punish those who don't do so. People who don't care about others have to be educated, reeducated, encouraged, and, if necessary, even forced to help. An important decision was taken by the Minnesota legislature, which imposed on citizens the responsibility to provide aid to people in grave physical danger. If they witness such a situation and don't help, they are fined and legally pursued.

It is also important to reward those who show concern for others and act altruistically. Even though there are saintly people like Mother Teresa who help without thought of reward, most people require some social rewards and recognition for their acts of kindness from society.

A lot of young people have humanitarian, altruistic drives and needs and join international organizations like the Peace Corps in order to help humanity, to promote international understanding, to develop appreciation of other cultures, to strengthen peace, to become better people, and also to feel like citizens of the world. There are also professionals of all ages, including retired ones, who act as volunteers to help East European countries change to a market economy. They should be presented as role models by parents, educators, and other leaders to students as well as to all other people.

Exposing people to unjust suffering makes them more sensitive to the suffering of others and motivates them to perform altruistic acts. Witnessing the many African famine victims on television has created a worldwide sympathy for them and induced many people to make a contribution to alleviate their misery.

People everywhere should be educated to feel responsible for the well being of others. This need to help must include our fellow human beings anywhere in the world who are victims of discrimination, war, hunger, sickness, illiteracy, unemployment, or any form of social injustice or discrimination and must take the form of a personal involvement and commitment to correct some of these injustices and misfortunes. Doing so will help us develop a greater feeling of human solidarity as well as a feeling of authentic, responsible human power. In their warped and distorted sense of values, criminals believe that kindness, goodness, and altruism are signs of weakness. In reality they denote genuine human strength.

It is also essential that society and the media give more publicity to acts of altruism. Society must value responsible, altruistic, compassionate, humanitarian people. They must become well-known and put up as role models.

## 12. Understanding Responsible Freedom

Freedom is an absence of restraint, an opportunity to do as one pleases. Freedom can be personal or collective. An example of collective freedom is that of a nation enjoying civil and democratic liberties. Freedom also means absence of oppression or tyranny. There is also inner freedom, which refers to the ability to think without outward constraint or pressure.

The positive aspect of freedom refers to freedom from oppression or tyranny. The negative aspect is exemplified by the perpetration of crimes or the gratification of harmful desires (taking narcotic drugs). Negative personal liberty is also exemplified by the license to abandon one's family and to put personal or special interests ahead of the general common good.

Responsible freedom is the realization that freedom has limits. It must not infringe upon another person's rights. One is responsibly free when one respects others as well as oneself and when one responds simultaneously to other people's needs by satisfying them as well as responding to and gratifying one's own needs.

Responsible freedom is more than absence of restraint. It implies acting spontaneously in a socially and morally just manner. Responsible freedom goes beyond liberty from control to the obligation to think and do the socially and morally right and just thing.

Human progress can be seen as the emancipation and attainment of a greater degree of decency and social and moral responsibility as well as an advancement of responsible freedom.

Responsible freedom occurs through the synthesis of two vital virtues and values—freedom and responsibility. It is the ideal as well as practical compromise between liberty and duty. The bible gives us a beautiful example of responsible freedom: Moses, who freed the children of Israel from Egyptian slavery, gave them the ten commandments, and then led them to the promised land, Israel.

The other side of the coin, irresponsible freedom, is exemplified by some drivers who see being forced to take an alcohol test, if they are suspected of driving while intoxicated, as an infringement of their freedom. This is totally irresponsible; freedom definitely does not mean the right to kill while drunk. Another example of irresponsible freedom is seen in the case mentioned in the last chapter of the people watching Kitty Genovese being savagely stabbed to death in New York in 1969 without coming to her help or notifying the police. Cutthroat competition, where a ruthless businessman drives a competitor into financial ruin, is another example of irresponsible freedom. So is hate literature, intended to vilify certain individuals or groups, or discrimination against others on the basis of race, ethic origin, age, sex, religion, or nationality. Yet another example is the excessive portrayal of violence in movies and television, catering to and exploiting people's vilest and most primitive instincts to make money. Allowing the free purchase of guns, without very stringent regulations and controls, is another example of irresponsible freedom, as is the production and distribution of pornographic material with its degradation of women and violence against feelings.

The list of responsible freedoms must be enlarged to include freedom from ignorance, from indifference to suffering, and from poverty throughout the world. Responsible freedom must also include the spontaneous obligation to fully develop one's potential and to become personally, socially, and morally responsible.

It is my firm belief that responsible freedom can help humankind to abolish war and bring about progressive, reformatory, and, if necessary, nonviolent revolutionary changes. These changes can and must enable people to live in harmony with God, their fellow human beings, nature, and with themselves, creating a world order based on a world government and on generalized social, economic, political, psychological, and spiritual well being.

## 13. Being Compassionate

Compassion is a noble, altruistic, sensitive feeling of pity for the distress, suffering, misfortune, misery, or unhappiness of fellow human beings associated with the desire to help or spare. It creates a responsible blend of solidarity, sympathy, and principled love between people. Responsibly mature and humane people feel compassion for the poor, the unemployed, the sick, the handicapped, the emotionally troubled, and for the victims of crime and all kinds of injustice and discrimination. It is genuine human strength and power to feel compassion for the underprivileged and the underdog. Compassion is both humanistic and humanitarian and a compassionate person, when meeting people who suffer, will be inclined to say "there but for the grace of God go I."

It is a moral duty to feel compassion for people who suffer, to want to help them to cope with and overcome their problems, social handicaps, and difficulties. One must sympathize by principle with victims of all kinds of misfortune. Sometimes one might feel disgust or mild revulsion when faced with a person whose face or body has been severely mutilated by a hereditary condition, sickness, or accident. Yet one must by principle feel and express one's compassion in a sensitive way. This is a form of responsible love. Some of Hitler's followers saw him as a man without compassion and generosity. Compassion, together with generosity and social and moral responsibility, as well as genuine faith in God, the creator of the universe, of humankind, and of all living creatures, is what makes us truly human.

## 14. Doing One's Best

It is both a psychological and a moral necessity to do one's best. Psychologically it helps us to develop and use our potential. At the same time it is also meaningful, rewarding, and fulfilling. It also promotes excellence and denotes a high degree of conscientiousness, which is an important moral quality.

By doing our best, we are respectful of others as well as of ourselves. It also strengthens the feeling of duty and obligation and motivates us to bring out the best in ourselves.

We should do our best only if it is in the pursuit of a noble, humanitarian, altruistic cause or in the discovery of truth, the creating of beauty, the spread of responsible faith, or in any endeavor destined to make life more pleasant and meaningful for others as well as for ourselves. We should also do our best when working within the social system and executing a task given by our superiors, provided the result of our work does not cause harm to others, to society, to the world, and to the environment.

Finally, doing one's best also has an effect on the behavior of those around us as it tends to stimulate and motivate them to do likewise.

## 15. Loving by Principle

There are various forms of love: parental, filial, love for a friend or spouse. All these forms of love involve feeling and expressing genuine affection for the loved person. There is also love for people we respect and admire—teachers, benefactors of society and humankind, heroes, doctors, statesmen, etc. Then there is love for God, for humankind, for country, for a just, responsible, and valuable cause, love of beauty, love of truth.

This chapter deals with additional forms of love that go beyond the obvious and familiar ones mentioned above. Such forms are love by principle or *agape*, which means the responsibility, obligation, and duty to treat another or others, whether it be a person or a group, with dignity, respect, compassion, understanding, and justice. A father or mother might or might not feel genuine affectionate love for their child. Teachers may or may not love some of their students. Doctors and other professionals may or may not feel authentic sympathy for some of their patients or clients; they might even dislike some of them. Yet, regardless of whether there is genuine sympathy or love, it is the duty of parents, spouses, teachers, and professionals to love their children, spouses, students, patients, and clients by principle. A parent might feel more sympathy for one child than for another, yet moral responsibility demands that the parent do his or her utmost to treat both children with the same degree of respect and justice, to become aware of the lack of affection for the one child, and to strive to develop sympathy and compassion for that child through a combined effort of intellect and willpower. Feelings tend to follow intentions and ideas. Teachers as well as all categories of professionals and all people helping and serving others must make the same effort.

It is obvious that one cannot force oneself to genuinely love an enemy toward whom one feels hatred, instinctive antipathy, or dislike, yet a sense of moral responsibility obliges one to understand the enemy, to be objective, and, if necessary, even to be helpful. It is through love by principle that the human condition can be changed and improved and a greater degree of harmony, cooperation, and solidarity can be established between people.

To love by principle must also include love for oneself and for the whole human race as well as for animals and plants. One must feel responsible for others and for oneself, ready to promote their material, spiritual, social, and psychological well being as well as one's own. One must also help people and oneself realize their potential. Love by principle implies that we love not only our neighbor but every human being on earth.

It is also one's obligation to love God for having given us life, for having created all the beautiful things in the universe, and for endowing us with the necessary potential and talents to become empowered by working in cooperation with him to create a harmonious, peaceful, moderately prosperous, and relatively pollution-free world.

The reason why it is not enough to love only with one's emotions is that love can turn to indifference or even to hatred. That is an additional reason to love by principle, and people should and must be educated to do it. Emotional love should be strengthened and complemented by love based on moral, social, and intellectually responsible principles.

In the case of enemies who have harmed us or people we love, moral responsibility asks us to understand the reasons for their behavior, feel pity and compassion for them for having made a mess of their lives—in some cases even wasting or ruining them. If possible, one should even help the enemy who harmed us to become rehabilitated and reeducated toward personal, social, and moral responsibility. This would be a step toward creating a better world. Responsible love by principle also implies cooperating with others. Management must cooperate with employees and unions, nations must cooperate with other nations, people must cooperate with other people and with God.

The reasons for the relative absence of love in the world—especially during most of the twentieth century—are manifold. Among the main reasons are the cult of narcissism, the exclusive identification of love with sexuality, the excessive competitiveness prevalent in the economic and even in the social realm, the exaggerated contemporary cult of materialism and consumerism, the reemergence of historical and traditional hatreds between different nationalities, religions, races, linguistic, and ethnic groups, as well as the excessive disparity and gap between the haves and have-nots all over the world.

Loving others by principle can contribute to introducing good will into the world and can help transform our planet into a place of human cooperation, responsibility, and solidarity.

## 16. Developing Responsible Reverence for Life

It is very important that people develop the conviction that all life is sacred, that human beings are part of all of life, including animals and plants, and that there is a common ground between all living creatures. Furthermore, people will have to become increasingly responsible for every living creature.

In order to eliminate and outlaw killing, people will have to be educated and educate themselves that no person has the right to inflict suffering and death on other living creatures except in cases of self-defense, or from the necessity to kill some animals and plants in order to eat, and the need to avoid the overabundance of one species of animal at the expense of other species. Other justified reasons are the necessity of using some animals for scientific research in order to find a cure for sicknesses, and the required extermination of harmful organisms like insects, bacteria, or viruses, which endanger human, animal, or plant life.

Albert Schweitzer, the great humanitarian doctor, philosopher, and theologian, realized in an inspirational manner that people can only establish a harmonious relationship with other human beings as well as with all living creatures through "reverence for life." This profound feeling of reverence and solidarity with all of life is highly salutary and is at the basis of responsible morality as well as of genuine universal peace.

It is a paradox of history that life was very cheap in past centuries, when there were fewer people on earth. People were sentenced to death and executed for offenses like petty theft, which in most civilized countries today would be punished by a sentence that is neither too harsh nor leads to a long deprivation of freedom. In contrast, at present, when the human race is threatened by a population explosion, there is an urgent and absolute need to value the sacredness of every human life and of all life in general. All killings of people, unless done in self-defense, must be eliminated and outlawed. This prohibition against killing human beings must include the abolition of war and the abolition of the death penalty.

It is also important to outlaw hunting for pleasure and sport as it induces cruelty and insensitivity to life. Both cruelty and insensitivity concerning the lives of other living creatures anesthetize the human spirit to feeling compassion for life and diminish the motivation for individual and collective survival.

## 17. Developing Solidarity with Humankind

Solidarity means to be linked together in a common cause or a community of interest. It also means joint liability. Above all, it connotes human interdependence, as well as the obligation of human beings to help each other.

Traditionally, the majority of people in a given country, nation, or community developed solidarity on the basis of belonging to the same ethnic, national, religious, or linguistic group, and by expressing hostility against minorities. Often a whole country would develop solidarity by hating a neighboring country. This was and unfortunately still is the case in the event of war. There is solidarity among allied nations fighting a coalition of hostile states and hostility directed against the enemy states. All this has to change radically, as humankind is faced with the danger of a nuclear holocaust, population explosion, destruction of the environment, potential calamities, and disasters which threaten the very survival of human beings on our planet. It becomes therefore increasingly imperative for all human beings to develop a worldwide solidarity with mankind. This can and must be achieved by feeling hatred against the many common enemies of mankind—poverty, unemployment, curable and incurable sicknesses, prejudice, discrimination, exploitation of human beings, all forms of social injustice (racism, sexism, ageism, ignorance, intolerance, illiteracy), lack of integrity and lack of faith in God, all forms of violence including wars, torture, physical, psychological, and sexual abuse.

Solidarity can and should also be developed through the belief that mankind is most likely alone in the universe. Most probably, there is no intelligent life anywhere else in the universe outside our planet. This feeling of loneliness will definitely contribute to the creation of solidarity with all of humankind. Faith in God, the creator of the universe, and the awareness that all human beings on our planet were created by him, fosters the feeling of belonging to the world human family, and promotes interrelatedness and solidarity.

It is also important to develop solidarity with all decent, responsible people in the world. Abolition of the concept of class struggle and war also fosters human solidarity. Following the pioneering example of Germany and the Scandinavian countries, a close cooperation, mutuality of interest, and solidarity must develop among entrepreneurs, managers, industrialists, businessmen, and white and blue collar employees, and professionals. All employees in an enterprise should have some input concerning decisions in the production of goods and services, and there should also be some form of profit sharing. This harmonious cooperation and solidarity disagrees with the Marxist class struggle as well as with the confrontation between unions and management common in much of North America, which foments social strife and unrest.

Personally, socially, and morally responsible people should not feel solidarity with societies that discriminate against or scapegoat innocent individuals or minorities.

Envy, jealousy, rivalry, and competitiveness divide people. Just as every piece of a jigsaw puzzle, by virtue of its distinctness and difference, is indispensable to the total picture and pattern, so people must develop a mentality that looks upon every person as belonging and being indispensable as a result of his or her uniqueness and distinctness to the community, nation, state, and mankind.

It is imperative on a global scale that people in the economically prosperous nations of the world feel solidarity with people in poor, developing countries. This can be facilitated by using the concept of the common good and mutual interest of mankind. Helping the Third World is also very beneficial to the industrialized countries of the world. People must be educated to realize that the well being of every human being is dependent on the well being of every other person. People must learn to feel responsible for each other and to each other.

In the hierarchy of moral values, the unity and solidarity of the human race and loyalty to humankind must emerge as being superior and more important than national loyalties. National loyalty and solidarity is important, provided it is subordinated to loyalty to and solidarity with mankind.

Many war veterans feel guilty about harm done to innocent civilians of an enemy country during war. On a profoundly moral level these guilt feelings testify to the existence of an unconscious solidarity among people of the world. These feelings of solidarity have to be integrated into the conscious personality so that they can become a part of the total personality. The many decent people who feel outrage and sadness about innocent victims of war, hunger, and injustice anywhere in the world are often, without being consciously aware, already citizens of the world. Mankind must create a world government in the form of the "United States of the World." This world government, based on worldwide human solidarity, must eventually become a reality.

### 18. Understanding Enemies

Totalitarian regimes tend to dehumanize their enemies and opponents by depriving them of their humanity and by ascribing inhuman, utterly distorted, and false characteristics to them. The Soviets considered the landowning peasants, whom they dispossessed of their land and famished, as pigs, while the Nazis considered their Jewish victims, whom they murdered, as parasites. In both cases the oppressors and executioners lost their humanity, while the victims preserved theirs. Similarly, nations at war totally dehumanize their enemies and in the process lose their own humanity. One must distinguish between unprovoked, aggressive wars started by power-hungry, megalomaniac dictators and defensive wars waged in response to unprovoked attack. However, even where one side defends itself against a cruel aggressor, there is a tendency to exaggerate and to deprive the aggressor of any redeeming human quality.

It is obvious that we cannot love an enemy whose intention is to destroy us, yet it is our duty to understand his reasons and motives as well as the special circumstances that have shaped him to become what he is and as he is. This kind of understanding and empathy must also be applied to hostile groups. One must go further and try to detect good qualities even in enemies. By doing this one might eventually succeed not only in defusing the hostility against the enemy but also in seeing the inimical group or the antagonist as fellow human beings worthy of one's understanding and empathy.

This responsible attitude of understanding and empathy toward enemies would go a long way toward improving antagonistic interpersonal relationships and also those between hostile groups. It would also contribute to creating a more objective and peaceful social and international climate.

## 19. Knowing to Whom One Owes the Highest Loyalty

Loyalty and allegiance are beautiful and highly positive values, provided one takes into account to whom or to what one owes one's loyalty and allegiance. To be loyal to a group of criminals or anti-humanitarian oppressive dictators is morally irresponsible. Avowed allegiance and loyalty should be given only to responsibly decent institutions, groups, and leaders whose aim it is to promote the welfare and well being of all people, irrespective of race, religion, sex, ethnic origin, nationality, and age.

It is also extremely important to be aware and choose wisely and responsibly to whom one owes the highest allegiance and loyalty and that all other loyalties are harmonious, compatible, and subordinate to that highest allegiance. The highest loyalty should and must be to God, the creator of the universe, of mankind, and of all life on earth. This should be followed by loyalty to humankind as well as to individuals.

This level of responsible social, moral, and personal loyalty goes hand in hand with a commitment to support the self-determination of nations and groups in a spirit of responsible freedom, and to promote international worldwide solidarity and the eventual creation of the United States of the World. It further includes a dedication and commitment to fully develop one's aptitudes and talents and also to help other people to develop their potential as well as to make a contribution to creating a peaceful, moderately prosperous world, free of major sicknesses, hunger, poverty, illiteracy, unemployment, prejudice, oppression, and wars.

Supreme loyalty to God, mankind, and to individuals would strengthen faith in God, promote the development of human solidarity, and foster responsible individual growth—three important conditions for creating and building a better, more responsible, and humane world.

## 20. Developing Integrity

Integrity means to be whole as well as to have uprightness of character and to be honest. It is psychological as well as moral. Psychologically it means to develop and unify one's intellectual abilities, one's feelings and emotions, and one's intuitions, perceptions, and sensations. It also means to integrate qualities of the head with qualities of the heart. Morally and ethically, integrity means to be decent and honest and to act in harmony with one's principles and values, provided they are humanitarian. Acting in accordance with prejudiced, discriminatory, racist ideals might denote a certain degree of honesty, but it cannot be called acting in a manner either morally responsible or showing moral integrity, since racism is morally and ethically extremely irresponsible.

It is important that people try as much as possible to develop psychological as well as moral integrity. Schools, corporate and government institutions, and society as a whole should foster, advocate, and encourage the full development of qualities of the head as well as of the heart in their employees and the people they serve. According to Michael Maccoby, corporate North American institutions encourage the development and use of qualities of the head in managers and executives—qualities like initiative, cooperativeness, self-confidence, and coolness under stress. However, they downplay the development of qualities of the heart—compassion, generosity, sensitivity, and idealism. The same applies to administrators and bureaucrats in the public service and in government in general, who don't value sensitivity and genuine feelings and emotions too highly. Yet it is is of the greatest psychological, moral, and social importance that all people develop and use qualities of the head and qualities of the heart. The well being of individuals and of society as a whole depends on it. Interestingly enough, a majority of people in Western democracies are attaching increasing importance to the necessity that political, business, social, and religious leaders act in accordance with the principles of personal and moral decency, integrity, and responsibility.

It is also important to be aware that personality consists of both conscious and unconscious traits. It is a lifelong psychological and moral obligation to become increasingly aware of one's unconscious ideas and feelings through intellectual and emotional insights, and to integrate them into consciousness; this leads to the integrity of personality. Carl Jung emphasized the necessity of people integrating unconscious thoughts and feelings by making them conscious and the importance this has for the well being of individuals as well as of society as a whole.

Increasingly, it must become one of the main objectives of responsible people to develop both psychological as well as moral integrity.

## 21. Building Bridges between Generations

There has always been conflict between people of different generations. However, this conflict is more intense and acute nowadays than in the past. Today's young people are generally better informed and educated than their parents. This produces tension and even envy and rivalry in some families, especially in those where parents have difficulty accepting the intellectual and educational superiority of their children.

There are also contemporary factors—the increased rate of divorce, the decline of community spirit, the increase in poverty, unemployment, homelessness, the population explosion in many parts of the world, the increased tensions and violence of modern living—which also contribute and lead to alienation and conflict. Deep down many adolescents and young adults hold their elders responsible for the mess the world is in and they feel overwhelmed with the almost superhuman task of finding solutions to the many problems of society and of the world that awaits them when they reach positions of command.

In spite of these social and global challenges, every young adult must still cope with such life problems as earning a living and becoming a productive member of society, getting married and raising a family.

Many young people have difficulty identifying with parents or political, social, or moral leaders as role models. The increased rate of divorce leads to breakdown in communication in many families, and the declining degree of social and moral responsibility and integrity in many public figures and social leaders—as well as their inability to come to grips with many important world problems—explain why fewer young people today than in previous generations respect and look up to these leaders.

Wrong and irresponsible values are also responsible for the existing alienation between the generations. The excessive preoccupation with the acquisition of material goods, of material success, the exaggerated competitiveness which permeates all facets of modern life, preventing the development of altruism, solidarity, and cooperation, the overvaluing of the head at the expense of the heart (hindering many people from remaining idealistic, compassionate, and generous)—all of these things make it very hard for the young to deeply respect and love their elders. The factors just described make it equally hard for the middle-aged and elderly person to develop the necessary insight, empathy, and sympathy to understand adolescents and young adults.

In spite of these almost insurmountable obstacles to genuine understanding and harmony between the generations, there is nevertheless reason for hope. People live longer today and are relatively healthier than in past generations. Many people reach old age relatively secure financially. It is important that the elderly of today use their retirement years to continue to develop their personalities, their integrity, their wisdom, to further their education, and to continue to use their experience and skill to be socially useful as well as improve the world. By doing this, they will be an inspiration to the young, who will look forward to their own old age as a period of continuing development, usefulness, and dedication to the community, to individual people, and to mankind. Today's young people must realize that the immensity of the challenges confronting all of us will almost certainly incite many people to rise to the occasion and successfully meet these challenges and find satisfactory solutions to the many problems troubling humankind. Most people use only a part of their potential throughout life. The many challenges presently facing humankind will stimulate many people of all ages to develop their potential to the maximum.

Life's meaning is only profound and responsible if people who now live realize that they owe an immense debt to people who lived in the past and that they have a personal, social, and moral responsibility to future generations to ensure the survival of mankind.

The old and the young of today need each other more than ever before in human history. Responsible cooperation and mutual respect between the two groups must increasingly become a social and moral imperative and reality.

## 22. Overcoming the Evil of Indifference

In March 1964, a young woman, Kitty Genovese, was stabbed to death in a New York parking lot in full view of 38 people who witnessed the murder from their apartment windows. No one intervened to help her against her assailant, or called the police. This utterly irresponsible behavior can be explained by the fact that when in a crowd, people tend to project their responsibility on others, believing that others will help. Besides this diffusion and projection of responsibility, another explanation of this irresponsible behavior might have been the fear of appearing foolish, or being criticized, or cowardice. Whatever the explanation, the evil, selfish, indifferent behavior was totally irresponsible. One must act in a small or large group as if one were alone, doing one's best according to the responsible dictate of one's conscience.

The indifference to the extermination of the Jews by the overwhelming majority of German people during the Hitler regime was another inexcusable example of extremely irresponsible indifference. When one is indifferent in the face of evil one becomes a silent accomplice in perpetrating evil. The cowardly and irresponsible indifference of very large parts of the civilized world to the plight of the European Jews facing extermination from the crazed, criminal Nazis—which made it almost impossible for the endangered Jews to find refuge in most countries—indicates that at certain periods, irresponsible indifference to suffering and persecution can be almost universal.

In order to understand the evil of indifference, it is important to know that there are many children who would prefer to be abused and mistreated by their parents rather than being ignored or treated with indifference. Being treated with indifference warps and cripples the personality of a child.

In a television interview, Elie Wiesel, winner of the Nobel Prize for Peace, spoke of the evil of indifference. I think he is absolutely right. Indifference is silent violence, equally, or almost equally, as irresponsible as any other form of physical or psychological aggression and violence directed against other people or against oneself.

It is essential that people develop genuine interest and concern for the wellbeing of others, of humanity, and of the world.

## 23. Forgiving Responsibly

The personal, social, and moral responsibility to forgive is often thwarted by the urge to avenge a suffered offense or injustice. Revenge is based on hatred and is also quite often self-destructive. A person filled with vindictive hatred is not only unhappy but also endangers his or her mental, emotional, and physical health.

On the other hand, however, committed crimes and injustices must be righted before a victim forgives a persecutor or aggressor. The wrongdoer must first admit that he or she has done wrong and regret it. Then a price must be paid for the wrongdoing. The most responsible way for the offender to pay for the committed offense is to undergo reeducation and to become a personally, socially, and morally responsible person. This reeducation toward personal, social, and moral responsibility must go hand in hand with helping the offender gain insight into his or her personality and to understand the psychological reason for the transgression. The offender should and must also apologize to the victim and repay his or her debt for the committed offense by being obliged to work for a while voluntarily for the social welfare of society and of the victim.

After the rehabilitation of the offender, it is the duty of the victim to behave in a personal, social, and morally responsible manner and to forgive. While one should not forget a suffered injustice, one nevertheless has the obligation to forgive a wrongdoer who has redeemed himself or herself socially and morally.

## 24. Understanding the Benefits of Responsible Guilt

Some psychiatrists today see only the crippling, paralyzing effects of guilt and consequently hold the wrong belief that all guilt is neurotic, unhealthy, and bad. They simply reflect the outlook of a hedonistic, selfish, consumer society unwilling to experience any form of pain and suffering. Since feeling guilty is psychologically painful, many people reject any form of guilt. When people behave irresponsibly, it is perfectly normal to feel guilty. It indicates that one has empathy for others. Feeling guilty, when this is indicated and appropriate, leads to atonement and making amends for the wrong committed. It also leads to ethical and moral improvement to avoid repeating the same irresponsible behavior. Therefore, feeling guilty for having behaved irresponsibly and immorally is highly responsible. However, the guilt one feels must not be too intense psychologically but should be strong enough to produce feelings of regret and remorse as well as a responsible improvement in conduct.

It is imperative that one distinguish between neurotic guilt, when a person who has mixed-up values feels guilty even for healthy, normal thoughts, feelings, or behavior, and responsible guilt, which is socially, personally, and morally salutary.

There is moral pain and shame caused by a bad conscience, which leads a person to set right what has been done wrong. In the moral realm we can experience in the present a pain engendered by past action that seems to us reprehensible. To the extent that we try to forget or ignore our past actions, we might feel guilty of bad faith, of breaking covenant not only with others or with God, but with our own nature as well.

Therefore, it is extremely important that people not forget or repress past irresponsible behavior. The acceptance, admission, and remembrance by many Germans of the crimes against the Jews committed during the Second World War, their willingness to atone and become rehabilitated through the considerable reparations paid to surviving Jews and to Israel, is a pertinent example of the value of responsible guilt in human redemption and moral improvement. It is also very relevant in this context to mention the remarks a German journalist made in a televised discussion on German unification in June 1990: Because of the terrible crimes committed at Auschwitz, the Germans have to work harder than any other nation to build a better and more peaceful world.

Other forms of responsible social and moral guilt are the feelings of many people in wealthy countries who feel guilty for having so much, while other people in many parts of the world or even in their own country have very little. Responsible people also feel guilty when they feel that they can do little to change the cruelty, injustice, exploitation, inhumanity, and irresponsibility prevalent in so many parts of the world. People also feel responsible guilt for not living in accordance with their most noble ideals, for not using their talents to improve the world, and for not developing more personal and moral integrity and wisdom as well as their hearts.

If properly understood, accepted, and integrated, responsible guilt can be a powerful energy motivating us to become personally, socially, and morally more responsible.

## 25. Disobeying Morally Irresponsible Orders

To obey authority is virtuous and responsible when it is justified and reasonable and does not violate humanitarian and moral guidelines of conduct.

Psychologically, the authoritarian personality is submissive to authority and worships the strong, irrespective of whether the worshiped person is morally responsible. The authoritarian person is profoundly ambivalent, hates the weak, submits to the strong, and commits sometimes irresponsible acts toward what he or she calls inferior people, whose ethnic origin, nationality, race, or religion is different from that of the majority. His or her attitude toward authority is one of unquestioning, servile, blind, submissive obedience. This is an irresponsible attitude and form of behavior.

The Nuremberg war crimes trials, following the end of the Second World War, demolished for the first time in world history the "follow orders" defense. The defense of the Nazi war criminals that they were only following orders when they committed their monstrous crimes against humanity was rendered irrelevant and irresponsible. They justly paid the price for their morally irresponsible crimes. Today the German army asks every new soldier to be aware that it is criminal to obey a morally irresponsible order given by a superior. In other words, it is the soldier's responsibility to disobey a morally irresponsible order.

In January 1992 a panel of judges convicted two former East German border guards for killing their fellow countrymen who tried to flee to freedom in West Germany. The judges told the guards that they had a duty to disobey the communist government's unjustified shoot-to-kill policy along the Berlin Wall. One guard was sentenced to prison for three and a half years for manslaughter, while the second guard received a two-year suspended sentence for attempted manslaughter. The judge, Theodor Seidel, said that not everything that is legal is right and just, and that the legal maxim of the East German communist regime deserved no obedience. Judge Seidel further said that the lesson of German history is that each person must use his conscience and decide to refuse to obey immoral commands. This is extremely important, as many people tend to obey orders whether or not they are moral. The psychologist Stanley Milgram did an experiment in which people off the street were asked to administer electric shocks as ordered by a white-coated authority figure, who was actually a bogus. Sixty-five percent of the experimental subjects administered extremely dangerous electric shocks. Our culture has failed to inculcate internal controls in actions that have their origin in authority: Many people behave in an immature and irresponsible manner when following orders given by authorities. People have to learn from an early age to oppose evil commands from authority figures and to feel and assume coresponsibility for the wellbeing of others.

In another important experiment, psychologists Zimbardo, Haney, and Banks did a simulation of prison life at Stanford University. In only six days they changed typical university students into abusive guards and servile prisoners. The two groups of students, originally similar, changed within a week. Prisoners became passive, dependent, and helpless. Guards enjoyed their power and the responsibility to resist sadistic feelings weakened. Torture became routine. This indicates that many people internalize the image that authority is repressive and abusive. When in a position to exercise authority they behave as they think authority is and behave irresponsibly. That is why it is crucially important that people learn from as early an age as possible to identify authority with decency, common sense, sensitivity, justice, competence, and above all, social and moral responsibility.

Studies on authoritarianism reveal that the willingness to submit to authority and the need to dominate others are the result of education. Until the end of the Second World War, German educational values stressed blind submission and obedience to authority. We know the catastrophic consequences of these wrong and inhuman values. In post-Second World War West Germany, students were encouraged to talk among themselves and to appreciate democratic values. In a 1971 study, in which students of various nationalities had to state their opinion of the statement "The people in power know best," 18-year-old West German students disagreed more strongly than other nationalities with this statement. West German students also scored high on tolerance and civil liberties.

Supreme examples of justified civil disobedience were given by Gandhi and Martin Luther King, Jr., who opposed unjust laws by nonviolent protest. Whether they protested against and opposed racial segregation and discrimination or political domination and subjugation, their examples of nonviolent protest were highly moral and responsible.

It is also important to mention that quite a few irresponsible war criminals, Adolf Eichmann being the chief example, appeared to observers to be average and normal, family men, without any outward signs of sadism and brutality. Nevertheless, their inhuman, criminally insane values, their extreme authoritarianism, their contempt for humanity, and absence of compassion and moral responsibility made them depraved and wicked monsters. Their servile following of totally irresponsible moral orders was not only evil in the extreme and utterly contemptible, but also unsurpassed in the annals of history in its total absence of moral responsibility.

### 26. The Responsibility to Future Generations

One of the reasons why a large number of people are not more altruistic is that they have neither faith in God, nor do they lead fulfilled, meaningful lives. Consequently, they see no reason why they should improve the world and hand over a better place to future generations. Their selfish philosophy of life is best expressed by the saying, "Après moi le deluge" (After me, the end of the world).

It is essential that apart from leading fulfilled, responsible lives—and developing profound faith in God, which provides meaning and continuity—people realize that in order to immortalize themselves they must leave a legacy to future generations in the form of a relatively intact environment with as many natural and energy resources as possible, a relatively peaceful world, and a more responsible world order. Steps must also be taken—on a worldwide scale—to slow and eventually control the threat of a global population explosion as well as to eliminate hunger, poverty, unemployment, illiteracy, major sicknesses, wars, child slavery, and all forms of human exploitation and discrimination.

We must see our generation as a bridge between the past and the future and inspire the next generation with the sense of mission, purpose, and faith to continue the individual and collective job of making the earth, with God's help, a better, more responsible, and more peaceful place.

## 27. Exercising Efficient and Morally Responsible Leadership

There are all kinds of leaders—business, industrial, community, political, military, educational, moral, and spiritual. Parents also exercise leadership in their families. One of the main functions of any leader is to lead, control, and guide a group, an institution, or an organization, as well as to make decisions alone or together with others.

A successful leader must be efficient. He or she must satisfactorily meet and realize the objectives of the institution he or she leads and must also satisfy the needs of the people who work for him or her, as well as motivating them to do their best.

Governments endure only as long as they respond successfully to challenges. When well-meaning but weak leaders fail to act swiftly and effectively to come to grips and cope with serious challenges that arise, an evil alternative can present itself and the weak, indecisive leader might be replaced by an unscrupulous, strong leader, sometimes even by a dictator. An efficient and responsible leader must be both strong as well as humanitarian. It is the uppermost duty of any responsive and responsible society to choose competent, efficient, strong, mature people as leaders, who are guided by personal, social, and moral responsibility. Responsible leaders are responsive to other people's legitimate, positive needs. They don't dominate or oppress, but respect those they lead. They set goals, but are also receptive and accept input from the people.

Plato believed that rulers and kings had to be philosophers; he even coined the term philosopher-king. Wisdom is an eternal and absolutely indispensable human virtue. At present, when the world is threatened by nuclear holocaust (even though the danger is much smaller since the dissolution of the Soviet Union than it was during the cold war years), by pollution and destruction of the environment, by overpopulation, and a myriad of other problems, it is absolutely essential that leaders in all fields of human endeavor possess wisdom. They must be able to harmonize and synthesize contradictions and oppositions, know intuitively which values lead to human survival, progress, and wellbeing. Besides brilliant intelligence, they must also possess qualities of the heart such as idealism, compassion, altruism, and generosity. They must also possess personal and moral integrity and must be capable of making judicious decisions as well as having a responsible and enlightened vision concerning ways to improve a situation, an institution, society, the world, and the human condition.

James MacGregor Burns believes that there are two types of leadership: transactional and transforming. Transactional leadership deals with the task of administering a company or institution. Transforming leadership, which is rarer, yet vitally important, is based on man's need for meaning and purpose. The transforming leader is concerned with the techniques of the educator, the mentor, the value shaper. He or she is an innovator, reformer, pathfinder, and responds to the need of transcendency in people. Transforming leadership is exercised when inspired, responsive leaders mobilize psychological, political, social, and moral resources in their followers, satisfying their needs and solving their most pressing problems. Transforming, responsible leadership occurs when leaders and followers raise one another to higher levels of motivation. It is elevating, ennobling, and uplifting. Responsible, transforming leadership becomes moral by raising the level of human conduct as well as the ethical aspirations of the leader as well as the led.

Moral leadership transforms the conscious and unconscious aggressive tendencies and energies of people into powerful forces to fight such real human enemies as poverty, unemployment, racial, national, ethnic, or religious discrimination, sicknesses, illiteracy, and wars. It inspires people to act in a humanitarian, altruistic, generous, and compassionate manner. Inspiring, responsible leaders must be practical idealists. They must believe that society and the world can and must be improved. Outstanding political leaders are genuine statesmen and also psychotherapists, especially when they use moral responsibility and encourage people to face and accept the truth. Gorbachev helped the people of the former Soviet Union to become aware of the terrible crimes committed by the Soviet regime during the rule of Stalin, just as the German chancellor Konrad Adenauer encouraged the Germans to accept responsibility for the crimes committed by the Nazis against the Jews.

There are types of leadership styles and modes that correspond to three different personality structures. Harold Leavitt views the leadership process as an interaction of three leadership variables: pathfinding, decision making, and implementation. Pathfinders are visionary innovators, highly intuitive. President Kennedy was a pathfinding president. Professional managers who use, sometimes exclusively, the rational approach are decision makers. Finally, Japanese managers are implementers. In common with teachers, psychologists, social workers, and salesmen, implementers most enjoy—and are most effective—working with people. It is very rare for one person to be at the same time a pathfinder, a decision maker, and an implementer. A successful business enterprise or a well-led institution is blessed to benefit from the harmonious interaction of these three types of leaders.

One of the reasons why political leaders don't often behave in a morally responsible manner is that in a democracy they owe their elected position to the majority of voters who voted for them. In order to satisfy the majority they must be attuned to what unites most voters. Unfortunately, this is quite often the lowest common denominator. Faced with the reality of responding to and satisfying the will of the majority (who often act exclusively in their own self-interest—as in the case of people of a prosperous country who favor a drastic reduction in the number of immigrants and political refugees it will allow to enter), it is the moral duty of leaders not to be led by voters but to educate them to social and moral responsibility.

Leaders in any field and especially political leaders exercise a great deal of power. The psychologist Rollo May said that people who don't have power or don't want to use it condemn themselves to lives of frustration. There is nothing negative about exercising power, provided that one realizes that there is also some degree of genuine and responsible human power in such moral qualities as decency, humanitarianism, generosity, integrity, idealism, social justice, and altruism.

It is also true, however, that many people, when they exercise too much power over others, become puffed up with their own importance. Their values become self-serving, and they become corrupt. It is also important to realize that psychologically insecure power holders, whether executives, teachers, parents, or politicians, when they believe that they control another person's behavior, tend to devalue the intelligence, success, or skills of that person. That is why genuinely responsible and responsive leaders motivate and encourage others to develop fully and do their best. By doing this, they not only bring out the best in others, but they also create a climate of harmonious cooperation and mutual respect.

Authoritarian leaders attach too much importance to status, power, and their role in a hierarchy. They are people who look up to those who are highly placed in the hierarchy and look down on those with a low position. They have identified with the established hierarchical structures of society and are determined to preserve it. They tend to submit to authority figures, are intolerant of ambiguity, and see things only in terms of white and black, often prejudiced against minority ethnic, national, or racial groups. They tend to have a cynical outlook, believing that in order to produce, people have to be coerced, controlled, and threatened. Through their attitudes, beliefs, and practices, authoritarian leaders manifest contempt for people as well as an absence of moral responsibility.

The journalist Christian De Brie states that in order to preserve their positions of power many political, social, business, and industrial leaders all over the world are periodically tempted to block and obstruct people's aspirations to peace, dignity, social justice, and the search for happiness. These irresponsible leaders have difficulty accepting change and are not attuned to the profound social, political, technological, and industrial changes transforming our age. Many political, industrial, and social leaders in the industrialized world as well as in developing countries are corrupt.

Themes like violence, survival of the fittest, excessive competition, conquest, exaltation and praise of wealth, of material success, indifference to social justice and harmony dominate many of the movies, television, and radio programs in many parts of the world, indicating an absence of social and moral responsibility in the cultural leaders responsible for the production of these programs.

Psychologist Michael Maccoby has given psychological projective tests to American executives. The given responses indicate that some of the most creative top executives expressed self-contempt in their answers, which they attribute to their failure to develop their hearts and to respond to the needs of others. Among the qualities of the heart which corporate managers did not develop—partially because they are not valued by corporate culture—are: sensitivity, honesty, integrity, compassion, generosity, altruism, and idealism. It is absolutely essential that corporation executives as well as government bureaucrats develop not only qualities of the head but also qualities of the heart as well as their social and moral conscience.

It is unfortunate that political candidates in a democracy have to compete in an election, often in the most cutthroat type of competition against their opponents. This type of electoral competition often leads to contests replete with slurs and below-the-belt blows, robbing the candidates of their dignity. It is unnatural to expect two opponents who have participated in mutual character assassination during an electoral contest to genuinely respect each other once the election is over. Besides, this type of contest debases and leads to contempt for politicians, which is very regrettable and bad, as the improvement of the world depends to a large extent on dignified politicians with a good sense of personal, social, and moral responsibility.

Many of the problems confronting the world will be solved when efficient as well as wise and morally, socially, and personally highly responsible people occupy positions of leadership in the areas of politics, the military, business, industry, education, culture, religious, and social and community organizations.

It would be very beneficial for the evolution of the world toward more social justice and social and moral responsibility if the political, military, business, industrial, educational, moral, and spiritual leaders of every country would meet for a few weeks to dedicate themselves to the realization of these objectives and to discover the most suitable means to implement them. A world university dedicated to the task of transforming the world into a socially just and socially and morally responsible place would have to be created and would be the ideal meeting place for such a gathering. The relatively short duration of the convention would make it possible for the leaders to attend and would also allow, once the sessions are over, for a new group of leaders to start their studies and deliberations. The meeting of leaders from different countries and different areas of human activity would widen their horizons, make them more universalistic and globally oriented, and would enhance their spirit of cooperation. It would definitely have an impact on their ability to improve the world toward an increased degree of personal, social, and moral responsibility.

It is also very important to be aware that the victorious leaders of the allied nations in the Second World War learned from the mistakes of the triumphant leaders of the First World War. The winners of the First World War imposed extremely harsh conditions on the losing side (Germany, Austria-Hungary, Turkey), which not only humiliated the pride of the losers but also bankrupted their economy and was to some extent responsible for the emergence of Hitler. The allied winners in the Second World War, however, were much wiser and more responsible. Through the generous Marshall Plan, the Americans made it possible for war-ravaged Western Europe, including West Germany, to rise from the ashes and to attain unprecedented levels of prosperity. A similar responsible approach, combined with reeducation, permitted Japan also to reemerge from total defeat and ruin to become one of the world's leading economic powers and financial giants. This change in attitude of the allied leaders in the Second World War constitutes an important step forward for humankind on the road to replace vengeance and retribution with reeducation to democracy and increased personal, social, and moral responsibility.

## 28. Knowing that Aggression Has Psychological and Social Causes

This chapter deals with individual as well as with collective negative aggression. One could even call it destructive—for such is the harmful consequence of negative aggression. In North American society, the word aggressive has a positive connotation as well, meaning to be vigorously active and assertive. Companies who are looking for a salesperson sometimes ask for an aggressive person. Positive aggression, especially responsible assertiveness is an important quality which contributes to success in a competitive market economy.

Destructive aggression connotes an unprovoked attack (one individual against another one, for example) or an encroachment (the intrusion upon the possessions or rights of another). This book deals elsewhere with war, another manifestation of destructive aggression, and the duty to end all wars.

Violence is a form of destructive aggression, characterized by an abusive exercise of power, causing injury or death. Physical, psychological, and sexual abuse are examples of violence, which can manifest itself in the form of verbal degradation of others, corporal punishment of children by parents, marital violence, intimidation, bullying, rape, exploitation, slavery. Excessive drinking, smoking, taking narcotic drugs, or committing suicide are also manifestations of destructive aggression and violence, which are self-destructive (directed toward oneself). Often this can be caused by conscious or unconscious guilt feelings, originating from delinquent thoughts or behavior or from not living responsibly and responsively. Not living responsibly and responsively can take the form of not realizing one's potential, of not living according to the best and most noble in oneself, of giving in too much to the demands of parents or other authority figures (choosing careers or marital partners to suit them rather than oneself). Aggression directed against oneself leads to depression and to other psychosomatic sicknesses. A person with sadomasochistic tendencies is cruel toward others, as well as toward himself or herself, and derives pleasure from this sickly behavior. The underlying unconscious wish underlying a suicidal impulse is often the desire to kill or hurt another person. Hitler and Napoleon were two political leaders who started suicidal and aggressively destructive military campaigns against Russia, with no realistic chance of winning, considering Russia's immense size and superior number of people. These aggressors were eventually defeated.

Irresponsible aggression can in some instances be nonviolent, as in the case of a passive-aggressive person, who can treat others in a dissimulated friendly manner, but who nevertheless cheats or betrays them, or a parent who rejects or ignores his or her children, or an employee who expresses his or her displeasure for a detested job by coming late to work on a regular basis.

There is no scientific proof whatsoever that destructive, unprovoked aggression and violence are instinctual or inherited. In most mammals, aggression directed against animals of the same species does not aim at killing, destroying, or torturing, but merely serves as a warning. The psychoanalyst Sigmund Freud, as well as animal psychologist Konrad Lorenz, were wrong to believe that failure to express aggression is unhealthy. Aggressive people tend to be more stressed and prone to heart sickness than non-aggressive ones. Freud was also wrong to believe that venting aggressive emotions made people less aggressive. The exact opposite is true. Expressing violent emotions or behaving violently makes people more violent and aggressive.

Destructive aggression and violence are induced by psychological and social factors. Child abusers and other violent criminals have often been victims of abuse or rejection by their own parents. They repeat the suffered abuse by hurting their own children or by taking vengeance against innocents. The "spare the rod and spoil the child" argument of parents or educators who believe in corporal punishment is both wicked and foolish. It tends to lessen the sense of self-worth of children, teaches them that violence is the best response to difficult situations, and that the world is cruel, violent, and unjust. It also forces children to submit blindly to authority and creates hostile, vindictive, ambivalent, and unhappy people, prone to despise, exploit, and abuse the weak, minorities, and subordinates.

Aggressive and violent behavior against others can be a response to frustration, to fear and anxiety, to inferiority feelings, to a suffered injustice, humiliation, or degradation (having lost one's job, for example). Destructive behavior might also be induced by the failure of a person to have developed his or her potential or to find responsible meaning in life, to live in moderate prosperity, to work in a fulfilling job, or to have a happy marriage and family life. False beliefs and values as well as prejudice also cause destructive aggression and violence. Many innocent women were burned at the stake in the Middle Ages because of the crazy and criminal belief that they were witches. Likewise, anti-Semitic slander led to the holocaust. Torture is another form of malicious violence. Prostitution and pornography are two other forms of violence, which cause personal degradation and loss of self-worth, and are an onslaught against feelings, decency, and integrity.

Emotionally socially and morally responsible and mature people are to a considerable degree less violent and destructive than immature, irresponsible people.

In 1986 a group of eminent social scientists, psychologists, and natural scientists issued a statement in Seville, Spain, declaring that it is scientifically incorrect to believe that we have inherited a tendency to make war and behave violently from our animal ancestors. Animals don't wage war. Neither war nor violence is genetically programmed or inherited. Violence and selfishness are created by faulty education and negative social forces. They also concurred that status within human groups has been achieved by the ability to cooperate and fulfill social functions. War or violent behavior is not caused by instinctual motivation. The way combatants are trained exaggerates violent traits, which were, in turn, transmitted to the majority of people when asked to support the war effort.

Scientific studies have indicated that the death penalty does not deter potential killers. Many of them have an unconscious or even conscious desire to die and use killing people as a means to fulfill this desire, especially in countries where the death penalty is not yet abolished or was reinstated.

A very good proof for the sound and responsible belief that violence is caused by psychosocial factors rather than by biological ones, can be found in the fact that the United States has a murder rate 50 times higher than that of New Zealand, which is also an English-speaking, multicultural, urban, frontier-based society. New Zealanders have the same endocrine system, but they don't kill each other. The answer lies in the fact that New Zealand does not have the slums, the high percentage of poverty and unemployment among inner-city residents as the United States has. New Zealand is a capitalist country but also a welfare state.

Other causes of violence are: divorce, a large gap in wealth and income between rich and poor, heartlessness and excessive competitive values of society—especially of the market economy and of corporate culture—too much emphasis on material values and on excessive consumption, a high rate of unemployment, and the excessive portrayal of violence in films and television programs.

Contrary to popular belief that overcrowded cities cause aggressive and violent behavior in their residents, Hong Kong and Tokyo, which are as overcrowded as Mexico City and New York, have a far lower rate of crime. This is because they have a relatively low level of unemployment and of poverty, and the vast majority of people live in relative comfort and dignified conditions.

The twentieth century has not only witnessed the crimes of Hitler, Stalin, and of many other dictators and tyrannical, criminal regimes, it has also seen the birth of nonviolent rebellions as exemplified by Gandhi's successful, nonviolent revolt against British colonial rule in India, as well as the relatively bloodless removal of communist dictatorships in Eastern Europe and the former Soviet Union. What a miraculous advancement of humankind in the direction of social and moral responsibility.

## 29. Valuing Responsible Sacrifice

Sacrifice means giving up something cherished or valued for the sake of something else. An example is the student who temporarily gives up his or her recreational or leisure activities to concentrate exclusively on studying in order to become a professional. Sacrificing immediate pleasure for long-term responsible goals is an illustration of responsible sacrifice. The young mother who decides to stay at home for a few years in order to bring up her baby and by doing so abandons the pursuit and advancement of her professional career for a while, allowing her to be exclusively with her child when she is most needed emotionally and psychologically by her baby, is another example of responsible sacrifice.

It is vital that people become aware of the important goals in their lives and learn to temporarily or permanently sacrifice less important objectives in order to be able to realize their most essential aims.

People should and must also be educated and encouraged to give up to some extent their selfishness, excessive competitiveness, their lust for power and fame in order to become more altruistic, generous, and compassionate. Similarly, groups of people, nations, and states should and must learn to responsibly sacrifice some of their exclusive authority and jurisdiction for the greater common good of humankind. A world government in the form of the United States of the World can only come into existence if individual states give up some of their national jurisdiction, just as the European states have to sacrifice some of their exclusive jurisdiction and independence in order to form a united Europe or a European community.

Traditionally, leaders of states and governments did (and still do) have the right to declare war and sacrifice the lives of their people in fighting the war, for causes which very often did not justify armed conflict and loss of life. Autocratic rulers like Napoleon, Hitler, and many others used people as cannon fodder and sacrificed them irresponsibly for national conquest and aggrandizement.

One should only sacrifice oneself in very exceptional circumstances when one acts in a heroic, generous, and altruistic manner to save others from certain death.

Human solidarity also necessitates that prosperous people sacrifice some of their wealth and share it with materially less fortunate people, individually and collectively. This sharing should take the form of sharing jobs to fight unemployment, sharing wealth, resources, and knowledge, or enabling immigrants and refugees from overpopulated areas of the globe or from dictatorial countries to come to prosperous, relatively underpopulated democratic countries.

Sacrifice done in a responsible manner enhances personal and collective wellbeing and strengthens peace and genuine human solidarity.

## 30. Overcoming Prejudice and Discrimination

Prejudice is a preconceived judgment or opinion formed before a thoughtful examination of the pertinent facts, issues, or arguments. It is mostly unfavorable or derogatory, often resulting in hatred or dislike for a particular group, nationality, race, or religion. There is also positive prejudice, however, where preconceived favorable opinions are formed and expressed. As favorable as positive prejudice may superficially appear, though, it nonetheless constitutes a distortion of facts and of truth, as it is either an exaggeration of a favorable quality or the application of the outstanding qualities of an individual or of a few to an entire group.

Prejudice leads to stereotyping, where one attributes qualities or characteristics to a person that typify a particular group. In extreme cases, prejudice and stereotyping lead to discrimination, violence, and to the extermination of individuals and even of a whole ethnic, national, racial group—as happened during the Second World War when six million Jews were killed by the Nazis.

Ancient Greeks called strangers barbarians, which connotes the idea of a primitive, inferior, brutal culture and civilization. This arrogant attitude justified conquest, discrimination, and war in the minds of the ancient Greeks. To some extent, even today many people in many parts of the world still tend to have this attitude. This form of discrimination and dehumanization is due to some extent to an often unrecognized fear of strangers, but also to a projection of one's own primitive, irrational, cruel, and violent instincts on others.

Some social psychologists and psychoanalysts believe that prejudice, racial hatred, intolerance, and discrimination against minorities or other groups is caused by an authoritarian personality. Psychologists attribute this type of personality (evident in the Fascists and Nazis) to faulty upbringing. The child who is forced to submit blindly to authority, who is cruelly punished for the slightest disobedience and insubordination learns to respect only brutal force and has contempt for all kinds of weaknesses and differences. This includes minorities and outside groups. Social psychologist Thomas Pettigrew, however, opposed this idea. He saw good egalitarian whites in the United States who believed in segregation. He correctly concluded from this that prejudice is not simply a matter of personality or of attitude but is rooted in social institutions and history.

In order to change prejudice, attitudes as well as social institutions must change. Once institutions like schools, workplaces, and neighborhoods encourage contact between blacks and whites, attitudes of prejudice and discrimination tend to change, leading to an increased acceptance of blacks and to better integration into white society.

It is important to understand that even people who think that prejudice is wrong may feel some prejudice. It is very important that political, social, religious, moral, educational, and business leaders condemn prejudice. As a result, even though many people will still feel some form of latent prejudice, they will control it, will not express it, and, as time passes, these people will become more and more tolerant.

Another effective way to combat prejudice is to have people of different racial, ethnic, national, and religious groups work together in a team to attain and achieve a common purpose. For example, people belonging to different groups could play on the same team in a sports contest or unite in solidarity to fight to improve the quality of life in their neighborhood, city, or country.

It is essential that personal and social attitudes as well as the structure of society change, in order to control and overcome prejudice, stereotyping, and discrimination. Responsible education starting as early as possible in life has the power to make a major contribution to considerably weaken prejudice, stereotyping, and discrimination. Exposure to other cultures, races, religions, and worldviews, as well as learning that human differences are enriching and indispensable can help immensely to instill tolerance and sympathy. The best example of the indispensability of differences is provided by a jigsaw puzzle, where every piece by virtue of its difference is an essential part of the total picture and pattern. Similarly, every person, as well as every cultural, national, and religious group is, by the very fact of being different, indispensable to the wellbeing, solidarity, and harmony of humankind.

### 31. Understanding that Forgiveness Requires Rehabilitation of the Offender

Responsible forgiveness is not forgetting, but understanding why a person or a group committed a crime or behaved wrongly. Responsible forgiveness requires that the person or the group who misbehaved or committed a crime be helped either through friendly persuasion or—when this fails—through force to undergo personal, social, and moral reeducation and to pay reparation to the victim or victims for the committed offense.

While is it natural and normal to hate a wrongdoer, especially if the victim was physically, economically, psychologically, socially, or morally hurt, hatred is nevertheless mentally, emotionally, and physically very damaging to the person who feels and experiences it. The feeling of hatred can be somewhat weakened or even overcome and transformed if the victim attempts to understand why the offender or offenders acted as he or she or they did. In some cases hate can be overcome through understanding and empathy and be transformed into compassion for the transgressor.

A good example of collective social and moral rehabilitation is that of West Germany which, paid billions of dollars in restitution to the Jewish survivors of the holocaust and to the relatives of the victims as well as to the state of Israel after the Second World War. While it is extremely hard for survivors of the holocaust or the relatives of the innocently slaughtered to forgive and not to feel hatred and hostility against those who committed the crimes and also against the Germans who did not protest against the murders, the material reparations paid by Germany to surviving victims and to Israel as well as the acceptance of guilt and sorrow by many Germans who were born after the Second World War, the visits made by young Germans to Israel, the twinning of some Israeli and German cities, and the mass demonstrations in Germany against hatred of foreigners and antisemitism will nevertheless in the long run lead many Jews to responsibly forgive the Germans.

The important thing to remember is that responsible forgiveness helps the offender to become personally, socially, and morally rehabilitated and responsible, the victim to transform hatred into understanding and sometimes even compassion, and society and the human community as a whole to become more just and socially and morally more responsible.

### 32. The Responsibility for Animals

Many dogs, cats, rabbits, monkeys, and other animals are used for medical research in the twentieth century, enabling people to live longer and healthier lives. Many of the diseases which have been conquered—mumps, measles, polio, diphtheria, and smallpox, for example—were contained by the use of animal research. Animal research also played an important role in the control of diabetes. Furthermore, intravenous feedings, radiation therapy, and chemotherapy for cancer and anesthetics were tested on animals.

Unquestionably animal research has resulted in a lot of benefits for humankind. It has also benefited other animals. A vaccine for rinderpest, a virus that kills millions of cattle, was developed through research on animals. The vaccine is now used by the World Health Organization on millions of cattle in Africa.

It is important that people become responsible and abstain from inflicting cruelty and unnecessary pain on animals, to kill animals only if necessary for nutritional purposes and only in such numbers as to ensure the survival of the species.

Hunting for sport and pleasure should be mostly prohibited and allowed only where there is an overabundance of animals (interfering with agriculture or the wellbeing of people) and if it contributes to controlling their number. It is similarly cruel to kill animals for their furs, especially if the furs are only used for fashion or beauty. This only exception would be in the case of people like the Eskimos, who inhabit remote, extremely cold polar regions of the world. Garments made of the pelts and furs of animals are the only ones they have to protect themselves against the cold. Killing animals for fun, sport, or fashion brutalizes and makes people cruel and insensitive to suffering and death. The killing of elephants or other endangered species for valued parts of their bodies should also be banned.

It is also essential that research be made less painful and that the number of animals used for research should be considerably reduced. Scientists should also continue to look increasingly for alternatives. Guinea pigs are no longer used to isolate the tubercle bacillus; this has now been replaced by the use of culture methods.

The suffering of food animals must also be alleviated. The British and Swedish parliaments have enacted minimal protection for food animals, including legal requirements that they be provided more room to move around. This provision would make life more agreeable and less stressful for them. All states should enact similar laws protecting food animals.

Becoming gentler and more compassionate toward animals is an important step in the evolution of people to greater kindness and moral responsibility.

# CHAPTER FOUR

# *Philosophical Responsibilities*

### 33. Developing a Wise and Responsible Philosophy of Life

A WISE AND RESPONSIBLE PHILOSOPHY OF LIFE MUST BE BASED ON a profound understanding of genuine and vitally important needs and values as well as on sound moral and ethical principles. It must be anchored in faith in God and humankind as well as in wisdom and in the belief and conviction that in spite of selfishness, ethnocentrism, tendencies to dominate and exploit other people, propensities toward excessive material acquisitiveness, territorial conquest, extreme competitiveness, cruelty, indifference to suffering and wars, human beings long for and are capable, if properly educated and motivated, to become responsible, altruistic, compassionate, and humanitarian.

One cannot live an authentically successful life without a wise and responsible philosophy of life. Such a philosophy serves as a guiding principle in one's life journey. It gives courage and hope, helps solve personal and social problems, and allows people to maintain their personal and moral integrity.

Research has shown that people who trust others and unify this confidence with their philosophy of life are less deceived by others than cynical people. The cynic's utter distrust of others and absence of the redeeming quality of faith in the ultimate triumph of good over evil causes him or her to be deceived more often than a trusting person. His or her cynicism turns into a self-fulfilling prophecy. A wise and responsible philosophy of life has to be both realistic and idealistic. It must also combine the intelligence and qualities of the head with the intelligence and qualities of the heart. A good illustration of a wise and responsible philosophy of life is the belief that in spite of all the ugliness and evil in the world, there is nevertheless a lot of beauty and goodness as well.

A wise and responsible philosophy of life, while acknowledging the importance of the material needs and aspects of life, nevertheless attaches great importance to ideas and ideals, as well as to spiritual and moral needs and values. Above all, a wise and responsible philosophy of life helps people to lead well balanced, mature, complete lives and enables them to develop their personalities and talents, to become responsible spouses as well as good parents, to make a valuable vocational or professional contribution in accordance with their interests and aptitudes, and to contribute to the solution of many world problems as good citizens on a local, national, and global level.

## 34. Valuing Truth

The dictionary defines truth as the state or character of being true in relation to being, knowledge, or speech; conformity to fact or reality, to rule or ideal or to the requirements of one's being or nature.

The basic interest and preoccupation of a scientist is the pursuit and discovery of truth, which goes together with an attitude of objectivity and great value attached to factual evidence.

Holding untrue and distorted beliefs is highly irresponsible and can have catastrophic and horrible consequences. The Nazis who falsified history and truth and who believed that the Jews were inferior, evil, and a misfortune who had to be extirpated from German society, were able to brainwash even many doctors and turned them into accessories to the criminal slaughter of countless innocent Jewish victims.

It is not only important that one is true to ideals but also that these ideals are based on truth and are also uplifting, noble, and humanitarian.

Shakespeare's adage, "To thine own self be true," has considerable psychological validity and is not only the basis of authenticity but even a good recipe for mental health and even for vocational success and satisfaction. Related to the choice of a trade or profession, it means making one's choice on the basis of one's real and genuine interests, aptitudes, values, and personality traits.

The biblical saying that the truth shall make one free is also very meaningful. It makes one free of falsehood and illusions. In the long run, only ideas based and founded on truth conquer and triumph.

## 35. Understanding, Developing, and Using Wisdom

The dictionary defines wisdom as the power of true and right discernment as well as conformity to the course of action dictated by such discernment. It also means good practical judgment, common sense, and a high degree of knowledge.

Being wise means to understand that in spite of all the world's cruelty and ugliness there is also a lot of goodness and beauty in the world and in people. Wisdom is a result of the synthesis of the intelligence of the head with the intelligence of the heart. It is also the ability to see both sides of an issue. In addition, it is also the result of the integration and harmonization of psychological faculties like logical reasoning, intuition, feeling, and perception. It is also fundamentally a profound knowledge and awareness of and respect for such essential values as kindness, love, compassion, integrity, honesty, personal, social, and moral responsibility, peace, moderate general prosperity, full employment, health, unpolluted environment, worldwide human solidarity, world government, social justice and social security, personal and human rights and freedoms, responsible human differences, reverence for life, beauty, truth, faith, dedication, commitment, and happiness.

In spite of the fact that wisdom is not always appreciated and valued by some people, it is nevertheless a most important quality, and essential to helping humankind to find efficient and responsible solutions to the many problems confronting the world. It is also vital in promoting harmonious interpersonal, intercultural, and international relations as well as in finding responsible meaning and happiness in life. Wisdom is a faculty which, if properly valued and fostered, can grow and develop throughout life. It must become the responsibility of all people to develop wisdom throughout life and to use and apply it in everyday living as well as in solving the many problems of society and of the world.

## 36. Developing a Responsible and Wise Worldview

The word worldview is a translation of the German word *Weltanschaung*, an opinion and belief concerning the nature and the origin of the world and man's relationship to it. It is obvious that people's worldviews differ. What is important to understand, however, is that a responsible and wise worldview has to consist of a synthesis of the best and most positive beliefs and opinions concerning the nature of the world and man's place and role in it.

Considering the extraordinary complexity and beauty of the world, and knowing scientifically that human beings have developed through an evolutionary process from more primitive forms of animal life, it is highly responsible and wise to believe that both divine creation and evolution played a part in the creation of the world and human beings. God created the world and human beings through a combination of planned creation and evolutionary process. Chemically, man's body consists of substances found in the inanimate world. Biologically , human beings have many similarities with animals. Through their reasoning human beings understand the functioning of the world and of the universe. It should and must become increasingly man's task to work together with God by being on the same wavelength with him and to take the initiative to continue to evolve psychologically, socially, morally, and spiritually. Human beings should and must view and consider themselves individually and collectively as God's partners and coworkers engaged in transforming the world, in accordance with biblical prophecy, into an earthly paradise, where there will be as little pollution of the environment as possible, where there will be no wars anymore, and where people will live in moderate prosperity and in solidarity and harmony with each other.

Increasingly, human beings would have to view and consider themselves as custodians of the world created by God, responsible for the care and preservation of the environment, to ensure that the world is not destroyed by nuclear holocaust, by sicknesses, or by overpopulation. People have God's creative spark to become personally, socially, and morally responsible, to lead healthy, peaceful, fulfilled, and responsible lives, and to create a peaceful and moderately prosperous world. This presupposes a social, moral, political, and religious evolution toward the creation of a world government ruling over what should best be called "the United States of the World."

## 37. Pursuing Responsible and Long -term Goals

Behavior is goal directed. This has been corroborated by experiments conducted with American and Israeli soldiers. When they knew their point of destination and the length of their march through deserted terrain, they endured the ordeal much better, even though they had to march for longer periods of time than fellow soldiers who were kept in ignorance as to the destination of the march. Helping people to choose responsible short-term as well as long-term goals, and encouraging, motivating, and supporting them to realize their objectives and ambitions is a characteristic of competent leaders, parents, educators, and counselors.

The importance of reaching short-term goals is evident. What is less well known is that many American business managers sacrificed long-range goals for the sake of short-term profits. Many industries planned for short-term profit and expansion, even at the expense of polluting the environment in the long run. Similarly, in democratic societies, politicians have a tendency to gratify the immediate wishes of the people by ignoring long-term imperatives. To a certain extent, the spectacular expansion of the Japanese economy is due to a concerted effort of politicians and business people to pursue long-term goals.

Choosing responsible long-term goals also implies the use of ethical, moral means to realize these objectives. The saying, "The end justifies the means" is morally irresponsible. Quite a few authoritarian, dictatorial, tyrannical regimes, whether of the extreme right or extreme left, achieved some degree of prosperity, full employment, and a more egalitarian society by wiping out large groups of people, whether the upper or middle classes or people of different political convictions or ethnic, racial, or religious backgrounds. In spite of having achieved some positive results, these tyrannical, despotic regimes, by having used morally irresponsible and criminal means, have ethically corrupted their countries and have transformed them into living hells.

Selecting responsible long-term goals and developing the skills, motivation, and perseverance to reach and realize them is an individual as well as a collective task. Sometimes the goal is so far in the future that it can only be realized by future generations. The vitally important objective—creating a politically, socially, and economically united world in the form of a world government, for example—which today is only a dream, vision, and hope, will nevertheless become a reality in the future. The many international agreements in the ecological sphere, in communication, transportation, the emergence of the European community and also of free trade and common market blocks point to the fact that the world is slowly inching toward a greater degree of internationalism. However, even if the collective goal of creating a world government will not be realized in one's lifetime, it must nevertheless continue to be envisioned, planned, and pursued, since the long-term survival of humankind depends on it becoming a reality.

On an individual level, examples of lifelong responsible goals are: to become personally, socially, and morally more responsible; to develop personal and moral integrity, wisdom, compassion; to strengthen the interest to learn new things; to value increasingly truth and beauty; and to fortify one's faith in God and humanity and to love others as well as oneself.

### 38. Valuing a High Quality of Life

Human wellbeing and a high quality of life depend on economic prosperity, yet there are economically prosperous countries that do not value the quality of life and human wellbeing too highly. The United States, with the highest Gross National Product in the world, scored 19th among the nations of the world on the Human Development Index. This index , created by the United Nations, combines life expectancy, literacy, and purchasing power. Millions of poor people in the United States have no access to quality medical service, and there is a relatively high rate of infant mortality among the poor.

In addition to the criteria mentioned above, a responsible measure of human wellbeing and of the quality of life must include such things as a very low level of poverty and unemployment, providing free high quality medical service for everybody, as it is done in Canada, providing free elementary and high school education for all as well as giving the opportunity to every talented student to attend college and university. There also must be social justice for women, such as equal access to high ranking and high paying executive and professional jobs and equal pay for equal work. Also, the difference between the richest proportion of the population and the poorest one should not be as high as it is in the United States. In addition, a country which values a high quality of life and human wellbeing must have a low level of crime, little drug addiction, a limited percentage of divorce and mental sickness, and a high degree of cooperation, solidarity, and community spirit. A country which promotes human wellbeing and a high quality of life must have a government that attaches importance to the protection of the environment, to the promotion of peace in the world, to the lowering of military spending, and to helping the third world develop economically and socially.

It is unacceptable that 77 percent of the people of the world earn only 15 percent of its income. A more just and equitable redistribution of income must take place peacefully and responsibly among the people of the world.

The U.N. Development Report of 1991 states wisely and responsibly that lack of political commitment and not of financial resources is the main cause of human neglect in the world.

It is essential that governments become more caring and committed to the promotion of human wellbeing. Also, rich countries must give a much higher percentage of their Gross National Product than they now do to foreign aid in order to help the developing world to develop economically and socially. This would have a very favorable effect on the human wellbeing and the quality of life of people in the third world, as well as in the prosperous regions of the earth.

### 39. Valuing Pluralism

The dictionary defines pluralism as a social condition in which disparate religious, ethnic, and racial groups are geographically intermingled and united in a single nation, as in the United States. The term is also used in the context of pluralistic society and pluralistic culture. Pluralism is further used to cover a variety and diversity of opinions and viewpoints.

95

Valuing and promoting pluralism must become both an individual obligation as well as the duty of society, the government, and the state.

Valuing different opinions, outlooks, and beliefs is a virtue, provided they are morally and socially responsible, which means that they must exclude prejudiced and scientifically false views as well as opinions which advocate war, violence, exploitation of other people, and hatred of and indifference toward other individuals or groups.

It is the responsibility of educators, as well as of all moral and political leaders, to advocate, promote, and value cultural, social, religious, and political pluralism. Having high regard for human differences and integrating these differences into a meaningful, coherent, connected social entity whether at the local, neighborhood, or provincial, national, or worldwide, global level is absolutely vital and indispensable for the creation of a peaceful, responsible world based on social justice, moderate prosperity, and psychological, social, and spiritual wellbeing for all people. Similar to a jigsaw puzzle, where every piece is indispensable by virtue of its difference to the total pattern, pluralism is absolutely necessary and indispensable to the wellbeing of humankind.

## 40. Valuing Integral and Responsible Humanism

According to the dictionary, humanism is a system or attitude in thought, religion, etc., in which human ideals and the perfection of human personality are made central, so that cultural and practical interests rather than theology and metaphysics are the focus of attention. Humanism puts human beings at the center of interest.

Secular humanism is usually and generally atheistic, denying the existence of God. While often generous, helpful, and tolerant, secular humanists believe only in scientific truth and refuse to believe in the supernatural or the miraculous intervention of God in human affairs. In contrast, responsible, integral humanism, while accepting the importance of human beings and the need for their personal, collective, social, and moral improvement, also accepts the reality of the existence of God both as an immanent and external force. Human beings are only whole and have integrity if they develop faith in God and work together with God and their fellow human beings to improve society and the world. Responsible, integral humanism stresses harmony with God, with nature, with humankind, and with oneself.

Many people today no longer have faith in the capacity of governments to find solutions to the many problems confronting them. Also, faced with the realization of the immensity of space, the billions of galaxies and the comparable smallness of the planet Earth, they tend to feel insignificant, alone in the universe, and helpless. Yet, by acquiring the faith in the existence of God, the creator of the universe, and by seeing themselves as God's coworkers in improving human nature and creating a more just and peaceful world, they can develop the necessary confidence, courage, and determination, in solidarity with other human beings, not only to solve the many problems confronting them today but also to acquire a feeling of pride and importance in being human.

Greek humanists stressed intellectual and aesthetic development, harmony, and balance. Chinese humanism, as taught by Confucius, endeavored to establish a harmonious earthly city. It stressed sympathy or fellow feeling and attempted to develop cultivated gentlemen—reasonable, tolerant, mellow, and humane. It also emphasized man's obligations rather than his rights. In this respect, it can still serve as a partial model today. Responsible, integral humanism stresses both the obligations and the rights of human beings. It is also tolerant of differing philosophies, religions, and political ideologies, provided that they too tolerate differences and respond to people's needs to live in peace and harmony with God, nature, their fellow human beings, and with themselves. The Roman humanists were tolerant of other beliefs, except for the God-believing religions of Judaism and Christianity. Since both Judaism and Christianity are highly responsible religions seeking to improve human beings morally and spiritually, the Roman intolerance of these two religions was wrong and barbaric. That is why responsible humanism has to be integral, stressing the cooperation between human beings and God, their duties and freedoms, and their full intellectual, emotional, psychological, spiritual, and moral development. Responsible, integral humanism emphasizes the full development of qualities of the head—the ability to take the initiative, pride in performance, pleasure in learning something new, flexibility, openmindedness—as well as qualities of the heart—compassion, generosity, idealism, loyalty, sense of humor, spontaneity, independence, and honesty.

Humanistic psychology stresses personal growth, self-development, self-actualization, and development of human potential, and attaches importance to values, feelings, and subjective experiences. This must be combined with the highly responsible realization of the extreme importance for human wellbeing of faith in God and altruistic cooperation with other human beings.

Integral, responsible self-actualization is not achieved through egotistical, selfish, narcissistic, excessive preoccupation with self, but through altruistic, compassionate involvement with and commitment to responsible social and moral causes, leading to a better, more peaceful, more humane and just world.

## 41. Thinking Globally and Assuming Global Responsibility

The many problems confronting us that deal with the survival of humanity—outlawing war and creating lasting world peace, controlling the global population explosion, and protecting the environment—make it imperative that people all over the world start to think globally, develop worldwide solidarity with fellow human beings, and assume responsibility for events anywhere in the world. Environmental disasters like the one at Chernobyl have made all of us aware that atomic catastrophes and pollution don't respect geopolitical borders and affect people in countries far away from the site of the accident. Similarly, the ongoing population explosion in many parts of the world also affects the survival and wellbeing of people everywhere. Sicknesses like AIDS, which spread from country to country and from continent to continent with extraordinary speed, also demand that we expand our area of interest and protective concern to include the whole world.

The existence of an immense arsenal of devastatingly powerful nuclear weapons also makes it more necessary than ever before to create an international political world order in the form of the "United States of the Human Family," embracing all existing states of the world. This world government must dedicate itself to the abolition of war and to the creation of global peace, to controlling the population explosion, to creating global industrial and agricultural conditions that will allow for generalized, global moderate prosperity without destruction of the environment, and to the creation of social, psychological, cultural, spiritual, and political conditions that will foster and promote the general wellbeing of people in the world.

All this will require a revolution of thought that will induce people to develop a profound solidarity with fellow human beings all over the world, to see themselves as citizens of the world, to accept God's supreme authority as ruler of the world, and to become aware that human beings as individuals and as collective groups can and must make a difference and must become empowered to transform the world into a place of peace, of solidarity among all people, and of generalized welfare.

## 42. Seeing the Total Picture

There are two sides to many, if not most, issues and conflicts, and it should and must become one's responsibility to understand both sides of an issue or a conflictual situation and to see the total picture. One should also develop the capacity to see individuals as being part of a larger community, just as in a jigsaw puzzle every piece is an indispensable part of the total picture. This type of responsible thinking also enables one to see states as part of the world community of interdependent nations and ensures human survival.

It is also important to become educated and continuously educate oneself to see the positive as well as the negative side of every situation or controversy, just as it is essential to understand the positive qualities as well as the faults of people. This requires an objective, unbiased, open, insightful, and observant attitude. It makes for fairness in interpersonal relationships, helps to defuse enmity between people by enabling them to be aware of and even appreciate qualities in opponents and competitors and to understand their opinions.

The understanding and the tolerance of responsible opinions and viewpoints that are different from one's own is not only enriching; it also creates a social climate of openmindedness and receptiveness essential for the functioning of a responsible community, relatively free of serious and severe social conflict.

With the help of faith and an optimistic outlook, one can see even in setbacks and in personal tragedies opportunities for personal development toward becoming wiser, more compassionate, or simply learning from one's mistakes. By asking oneself what the blessing in disguise is of an unhappy situation or occurrence one trains oneself not only to see the total picture but also to transform adversity into triumph and to live successfully in spite of everything.

Finally, one should also train oneself to count one's blessings and to thank God for all the beauty and goodness in the world and to do so in spite of all the evil and ugliness which are also a part of the reality of the world.

### 43. Believing in Responsible Progress in Spite of Everything

Progress implies the notion of advancement, movement toward an improved, better, more complete state or condition. Responsible progress leads to an improved human condition on a local, national, and global level, that manifests itself through more social justice, general improvement in the standard of living, better health for all people as well as a longer life, quality education, and adequate social security. Responsible progress also means more democracy and a society more responsive to ethical and moral values and norms of behavior.

In spite of the existence in the world today of famine, poverty, widespread sicknesses, exploitation of people, prejudice, and ethnic and national wars, there are nevertheless more people today who live longer, healthier, more prosperous, fulfilled lives than at any previous time in history.

Historical progress occurs to some extent similar to the shape of a spiral. In a spiral there is constant progression, yet it also includes regression to a previous state, yet always on a higher level. In other words, historical progress occurs through dialectical oscillations between opposite sides, reverting periodically to past stages, yet always on a higher level. The conservative wave, which swept much of the Western world from the beginning of the 1980s into the 1990s, following many years of liberalism, was in a way similar to past conservative periods, yet also very different. In the conservative period of the 1920s, there was no social security legislation protecting the unemployed, the poor, and the sick, whereas the conservative years of the end of the twentieth century contain and incorporate all the socially protective mechanisms that were developed during and after the great depression of the late 1920s and 1930s.

Belief in responsible progress in spite of everything necessitates a strong, profound faith in God and in in humankind. In spite of Germany's regression during the Nazi period to monstrous barbarism, West Germany has undergone a fantastic transformation since the Second World War into a freedom-loving, highly democratic, prosperous, responsible country. Belief in responsible progress in spite of everything necessitates having the faith that in spite of setbacks, humankind will advance to the stage where it will create a united world, in the form of the "United States of the World," and that conditions of universal peace and moderate general prosperity for all as well as protection of the environment and social, psychological, and spiritual wellbeing for everybody will eventually prevail in the world.

## 44. Understanding the Need for Responsible Change

Change is the law of life. People grow older, eventually die, and others take their place. But change, which occurs at all levels of human activity, is not always positive. Responsible change results in progress and in the improvement of existing conditions, accomplished without the use of destructive violence.

Change can occur through evolution, which is a gradual progressive transformation, and through revolution which occurs suddenly, more spontaneously, and more explosively. Both forms of change are necessary. Quite often, had the establishment considered and acted upon the grievances of unsatisfied groups and carried out necessary reforms, much tragedy and violence, as well as many upheavals, could have been avoided. There was a lot of violence and bloodshed during the French Revolution of 1789 and during the communist revolution in Russia in 1917, whereas the removal of communism in Eastern Europe and Russia in the late 1980s and early 1990s occurred with very little violence and loss of life. This points out how necessary it is for governments and authorities to respond to popular grievances which are justified and to effect responsible change in the form of enlightened, efficient, and humanitarian reforms.

Western democracies, with a few exceptions, are characterized by nonviolent conflicts and civilized controversy between divergent factions and opinions. These conflicts are solved mainly through compromise and responsible reforms.

As we discussed earlier, it is helpful to view historical change as similar to the developmental growth of a spiral, where there is a recurrent return to a previous state, yet always on a higher level. Cyclical economic, social, or political transformations often follow this spiraled form of progress. As we saw, in the 1980s, the United States experienced a return to conservatism, yet it was different from the conservatism of the late 1920s when there was no unemployment insurance, no old-age pensions, and no other form of social insurance against sickness, work-induced invalidism, or other forms of social or personal calamities. The conservatism of the 1980s preserved much of the highly responsible social policies developed immediately before, during, and after the Second World War, but it did so in a manner that reduced government intervention and expenditures to some extent. The return of a part of the Jewish people to the ancestral, biblical land of Israel and the rebirth after 2000 years of the State of Israel is in a way a return to the past, yet in a highly modern form. It incorporates and resuscitates the past in a highly progressive, evolutionary, modern way.

Responsible change is a positive improvement of a situation, which occurs with the least amount of destruction and which is based on the integration and absorption of the best from the past. A certain amount of destruction in any form of change is unavoidable. An old house must first be demolished before building a new one on the same spot. Responsible change is similar to architectural renovation, where the old structure is either restored in a modern form, or some parts of the old construction are preserved—perhaps in the form of a facade—and integrated into a highly contemporary structure.

Positive and responsive change is based on the obligation to improve the social, political, and economic system by rendering it more efficient, more socially just, more responsive to the human needs for personal development, social security, worldwide peace, a pollution-free environment, moderate prosperity, fulfilling work, a healthy, long life, and psychological and spiritual wellbeing.

Responsible reform at all levels of human activity must be effected through the cooperation of various levels of government, of institutions and corporations, and of the overwhelming majority of responsible and decent individuals.

## 45. Valuing Responsible, Positive Conservatism

The dictionary defines conservatism as devotion to the existing order of things and opposition to change. It has applications in politics, religion, culture, and in everyday life.

European conservatism is more pessimistic about history than American conservatism. It views man as inclined to be cruel and often behave criminally, and holds that the institutions of law and politics are fragile. It is not a positive or optimistic outlook. If people are overwhelmed by poverty, disease, hunger, war, and ignorance (as was the case in the past in many parts of the world and still is today), then of course they will be hostile and will try to destroy the existing order. Faith in responsible progress leading to an improvement of social, material, and psychological conditions is the best antidote to negative, pessimistic conservatism. On the other hand, responsible, positive conservatism attempts to preserve only the best from the past. This refers to protecting the environment, and preserving valuable cultural, artistic, and architectural monuments, buildings, and artistic treasures. Valuable responsible, educational, social, political, and religious institutions must also be preserved, but at the same time periodically reformed and improved. Likewise, beautiful and highly meaningful eternal values such a honesty, loyalty, duty, commitment, dedication, integrity, love, respect, social justice, dignity, truth, beauty, faith, idealism, and sacrifice must be perpetuated.

Responsible conservatism is aware that responsible progress is absolutely necessary, as the existing order must be improved at all costs. The best from the past can only be preserved if one discards what is irresponsible and replaces it with more responsible ideas, values, or institutions, better suited to help humankind live in peace, harmony, a moderate level of prosperity, and enjoying psychological, social, and spiritual wellbeing.

## 46. Using Reason to Serve Truth, Love, and Peace

Reason and logic are very highly valued. Most people believe that reason is not only one of the highest human faculties (if not the highest), but that all the problems of the world could be solved—including the creation of a peaceful, cooperative, prosperous world—if the majority of human beings would be guided by this sensible quality.

To a great extent, reason is based on logic and on analytical and synthetical mental processes as well as on inductive and deductive thinking. In deductive thinking one makes inferences from premises to arrive at a conclusion. It is absolutely essential that the premise be both true and humanitarian, which means that it must be based on love and benevolence. If the premise is untrue and based on hatred of people, the result, in spite of logical reasoning, can be totally irresponsible and tragic. Hitler's hatred of the Jews was presented in a rational manner, yet it was based on the false and foolish premise that the Jews were an inferior race, an evil group, of great danger to humankind. Nazis, including some doctors, further believed that the Jews were a cancer in the body of mankind. Similarly, if people believe that aggressive, destructive, warlike behavior is due to an instinctual, unchangeable, permanent, innate component of personality, then no matter how judicious, logical, or commonsensical their reasoning, the final conclusion that there will always be wars is inevitable, even though this is an utterly pessimistic, totally false, and highly irresponsible opinion and judgment.

Responsible reasoning concerning human behavior must be based on the faith that people can mature and change to become socially, personally, and morally responsible as well as on the scientific, truthful evidence, based on research, that destructive, violent, warlike human behavior is not innate but socially and politically conditioned.

Reason should and must be increasingly used to promote love and respect for human differences, to foster harmonious, cooperative relations with others, and lead to a wise, penetrating, insightful, and sensitive understanding of human nature and of people. Reason together with love and human solidarity must increasingly rule the world and transform it into a peaceful planet.

## 47. Valuing and if Necessary Rewriting History

History is hardly valued today, and not much of it is taught in most American and Canadian schools. In some other parts of the world, especially in totalitarian countries, history is taught in an untruthful, distorted manner, corresponding to the ideology and worldview of the dictatorial, oppressive regime. The American philosopher George Santayana said that people or societies who ignore history are bound to repeat it. History shows us the continuity and evolutionary development and progress as well as the setbacks and failures of societies, states, and of culture and civilization. Ignoring or distorting history can have disastrous consequences. If a person represses or ignores his or her past or fails to remember and understand past yearnings, aspirations, ideals, values, feelings, and desires, that individual is somewhat weakened and lacks the necessary integrity and psychological strength to cope successfully with life. Similarly, nations and humankind as a whole must, in order to master the many problems with which they are confronted, understand and remember their past history. By caring for the past, we are also setting an example for future generations, which will motivate them to imitate our responsible sense of continuity and to become likewise interested in our struggles, triumphs, and defeats.

It is essential that we become aware, as history shows us, that there is progress, often in spite of everything. Notwithstanding many setbacks and many problems, humankind and individuals are far better off today in terms of prosperity, education, and overall quality and length of life than in the past. The best of every past civilization and culture has survived and forms the basis of and has been integrated into modern society and institutions. Democracy, which was invented by the Greeks in antiquity, when it applied only to free men and not to the many slaves that existed in their city-states, has conquered huge parts of the world today and will become increasingly in the future the ruling form of government all over the world—in an improved and even more responsible form.

In order to understand progress and evolution throughout history, in spite of setbacks and reverses, let us return to the image of the spiral. In a spiral, there is a forward movement, followed by a backward one, which gives the impression of a continuous repetition, yet there is a progression nonetheless, because the backward movement or repetition of a past stage occurs on a higher level, so there is evolution. And this evolution to continuously higher levels also incorporates the past windings of the spiral. In just such a way, civilizations advance to higher and higher levels by reverting back to and at the same time integrating the past. The Renaissance in the Middle Ages reverted to the Greek and Roman humanism of antiquity, to their celebration of the beauty of the human body, as well as their classical form of literature, poetry, and architecture. But the Renaissance artists used more sophisticated means to portray human beauty than the artists of antiquity and also integrated the wisdom and faith of biblical characters and of the bible into their art.

The rebirth of Israel as a political state after 2000 years of Jewish dispersal among the nations of the earth, as well as the retransformation of the desert into fertile land, as in biblical times, is another example of the applicability of the law of the spiral to historical events. Modern Israel is a sophisticated Western state, yet in many ways it constitutes a resurrection of the past. The resurrection of Hebrew, the language of the bible, from a language used only for prayer to one which is used in daily conversation as well as in scientific research is another illustration of the applicability of the law of the spiral to historical events. In ancient times Hebrew was the spoken language of the Hebrews, then it became a dead language (with the exception of its use in prayer). After 2000 years it again became the spoken language of the people of Israel. The conservative wave which swept many parts of Europe and North America in the 1980s and the first part of the 1990s seemed superficially like a throwback to the conservative age of the 1920s. Yet, in the 1980s and 1990s, the conservative governments have accepted and integrated many of the social accomplishments of left-of-center liberalism and social democracy: social welfare, unemployment insurance, universal medical insurance, workmen's compensation, and old-age pensions.

Hegelian dialectics, or the change from a situation or condition called thesis to its opposite, antithesis, followed by a synthesis or fusion of the two opposites, can also be used to help us understand progress in history. The synthesis between capitalism and a socialistic society, one being the thesis and the other the antithesis, is a responsible market-directed economy with a social conscience and responsibility, namely a social democratic or liberal welfare state.

It is crucial to bear in mind that traditionally the teaching of history in high schools was an almost uninterrupted succession of wars, military leaders, kings, emperors, and conquests with relatively little time being devoted to the study of past cultures and civilizations. This tendency has to be understood in the light of the reality that war was and still is considered to some extent—even though less than in the past—an honorable institution. Increasingly, this has to be debunked. Unless they are waged in justified self-defense, wars should and must be considered delinquent undertakings. The role of military leaders should be downplayed and humanitarians as well as people in the fields of science, technology, art, literature, religion, music, medicine, law, teaching, and others who contribute to helping people improve their health, to live meaningful, responsible, fulfilled, enlightened, productive, happy lives, and promote peace and human solidarity should be considered the real heroes of humankind. The crucial contribution made by women in all fields of human endeavor must also be valued and mentioned. History must be rewritten in order to reflect the suffering, the loss of health, and the loss of life caused by wars. More emphasis must also be placed on teaching the lives of ordinary people who lived in the past. The influence of irresponsible leaders in starting wars should also be stressed, as well as the role played by irresponsible territorial conquest. It is also important to study the exploitation of women and children and of indigenous people in Africa and Asia by colonial powers, and the history of slavery and the extermination of American Indians.

History must also emphasize the slow but gradual, unconquerable evolution and triumph of such noble and responsible ideals and values as democracy, responsible freedom, social justice, human solidarity, truth, beauty, faith, integrity, decency, peace, international cooperation, world-wide moderate prosperity, and personal, social, and moral responsibility. The creation in the twentieth century of such international humanitarian organizations as UNICEF (Untied Nations Children's Fund), UNESCO (United Nations Educational Scientific, Cultural Organization), World Health Organization, Amnesty International, Medecins sans Frontieres (Physicians Without Borders), must also be mentioned. The creation of the above-mentioned international humanitarian institutions and many others indicates an irreversible long-term trend and evolution toward responsible international solidarity and cooperation and social and moral responsibility; pointing the way to the eventual emergence of a united world under the rule of a world government.

History must also teach the evolution of the respect for various human rights and responsible freedoms as well as the social and moral responsibility of governments and of society to grant them.

History must also point out the great importance of the belief in God, the creator of the universe, and the progressive and continuing growth and transformation of faith among the people of the world. Organized religion and faith in God played an important role in overcoming communist rule in Eastern Europe and the former Soviet Union in the late 1980s and early 1990s.

There are religious historians and moral philosophers who believe in revealed truth and absolute values, while others believe that revelation is progressive. It is my belief that there is no contradiction between the two viewpoints, and that they are complementary. An example is the biblical commandment, "Thou shalt not kill," which is an absolute injunction, valid for all times and applicable to humankind as a whole.

Since antiquity, this injunction has been legislated by practically all civilized states and applies to any murders, except the killings committed by soldiers against enemy military forces in times of war and to the people sentenced to death and executed for having committed a crime. In the second half of the twentieth century, most Western democracies have completely abolished the death penalty. Unfortunately, some of the United States have reintroduced the death penalty. Even so, it is my conviction that in spite of temporary setbacks in some places of the world, there is an unstoppable evolution toward the universal abolition of the death penalty. Considering the danger to the survival of the human race, war in an atomic age has become utterly outdated and suicidal. This means that with God's help, sooner or later wars will be outlawed and eliminated, and the biblical injunction not to kill will have attained one of its objectives—to abolish universally one of the worst forms of killing people. These two examples illustrate how an absolute moral value evolves throughout history and how through gradual, progressive revelation and insight, combined with social and moral responsibility, any form of murdering human beings will in time disappear from the face of the earth.

It is also important in this context to mention the colossal contribution made by the biblical prophets to personal, social, and moral responsibility. They developed a rational and responsible theory of history. They refused to accept fate as the explanation of historical events and introduced human character and behavior as playing an important part in shaping and influencing history. They believed that human beings have to learn through suffering to become just and righteous and that they are responsible for good and evil. They also demanded that the rulers of the earth serve a higher law than that of the state. They believed fervently in a universal God and that life on earth is meaningful. They also believed that the divine purpose in history can be fulfilled only be a community. Their idea of community has to be enlarged to include the community of the worldwide human family; sooner or later this has to become a political reality through a world government having authority over the "United States of the World."

Karl Marx is the most prominent social, economic, and political philosopher who believed that history is controlled by immutable and unchangeable laws. Together with Friedrich Engels he interpreted history through the doctrine and law of dialectical materialism. They saw history from a small perspective, only concentrated on one aspect of reality, and failed to realize the importance of psychological, spiritual, and moral values. They were also blind to the reality of God. In cooperation with

God, and through responsible freedom and responsible self-determination, as well as through personal, social, and moral responsibility and a responsible vision of the future, people can create bloodless revolutions, as happened in Eastern Europe and the former Soviet Union in the late 1980s, to improve society and the world.

A further role and responsibility of history is to portray the political evolution from city-states to national states to associations between states, as exemplified by the birth toward the end of the twentieth century of the European union, the East Asian trading bloc, and of the North American Free Trade Agreement. It is also important to emphasize both the positive and the negative sides of nationalism. The solidarity of citizens and the love of their country is admirable, provided that it does not degenerate into chauvinism and includes solidarity with and love of other countries as well. The traditional we-and-they dichotomy which united people within a country against outside enemies is gradually changing, and must do so, to an even greater extent in the future. What must also develop is a worldwide solidarity against the common enemies of humankind—disease, poverty,war, unemployment, persecution of innocents, torture, illiteracy, and absence of faith in God, the creator of the universe.

The creation in the twentieth century of international organizations such as the short-lived League of Nations, followed by the United Nations at the end of World War II, constitutes an important step toward a greater degree of international political, social, and moral responsibility. The United Nations, in spite of its many failings, has succeeded to some extent through its various agencies in promoting and supervising peace, fighting hunger, sicknesses, and illiteracy in many parts of the world, as well as preserving important cultural sites and monuments of mankind. The United Nations does not yet have real authority to stop wars or to prevent criminal governments from persecuting their own citizens. Preventing wars, imposing peace, and protecting the individual and collective rights of all people of the earth must eventually become the responsibility of a world government having authority over all the states of the world.

History must also teach the gradual development of individual and collective rights and freedoms. The failure of communism can be attributed to a large extent to its utter disrespect for individual rights and freedoms. Despotic monarchies have been replaced by constitutional ones, military dictatorships in South America have been replaced by democratic regimes. This is of tremendous importance as democratically governed states do not wage wars against each other. There is also a continuous worldwide trend toward increased individual and collective empowerment of people and toward an increase in their social and political responsibility.

History must also mention the extraordinary scientific and techno-logical progress in the nineteenth and twentieth centuries which helped to cure many sicknesses, considerably prolonging the average life span of people and reducing the hours of the work week, allowing workers to devote more time to their families and to leisure activities. Progress in technology, especially in the fields of communication and transportation transformed the world into a global village and made travel to foreign lands accessible to an increasing number of people. Scientific and technological progress has also greatly improved the standard of living of most people in the Western world and even in parts of the third world.

Finally, it is essential to understand that for the first time in history, after the end of the Second World War, the Nazi war criminals responsible for crimes against humanity were prosecuted and sentenced. The victo-rious allied nations, representing the conscience of the whole human race, punished the Nazi evildoers for crimes committed against humankind. This points to the evolution of humankind toward a higher level of personal, social, and moral responsibility.

One can compare the evolution of humankind with the growth of an individual from infancy to maturity. As a person moves toward adulthood and maturity, he or she assumes more and more responsibilities at work, within the family as well as within the local community. Similarly, humankind must mature to a level where it assumes full responsibility for the many problems threatening its survival as well as for creating a more socially just, peaceful, and moderately prosperous world.

## 48. Appreciating and Honoring Genuine and Responsible Heroes

Traditionally, throughout most of history, the heroes who were most glorified and honored were military leaders or rulers of states, whether kings or emperors, famous for winning battles, defeating enemies, and expanding the territory of their kingdoms or empires through military conquest. Very rarely in the past were people honored for qualities such as courage and fortitude displayed in situations other than battles. Some of the people mentioned in the bible, especially the prophets who had the courage to stand up and protest against moral decadence, corruption, and false beliefs, who preached righteousness and obedience to God's laws, were authentic, true heroes. It is the bible's undying, outstandingly supreme merit to honor these moral and spiritual giants.

There are thinkers at present who believe that we live in an age of the antihero, an age of mediocrity, with no real appreciation of human greatness. This might be partially true, yet it is much better than the past (and sometimes still present) glorification of selfish, partially irresponsible people whose fame rests either on military exploits or on accumulation of huge fortunes, often acquired by the use of unscrupulous methods.

The real, genuine, and responsible heroes of the human race are the courageous men and women who have advanced human knowledge, decency, and social justice in spite of great adversity, difficulties, and often danger to their own lives. People who have dedicated their lives to helping the downtrodden and the underdog, to promoting truth, love, genuine faith in God, kindness, and compassion deserve our gratitude and it is our responsibility to honor them.

It is also our responsibility to honor people who display responsibility and courage by saving others from life-threatening situations. We must also appreciate and honor the handicapped, who display courage by leading relatively normal lives in spite of adversity. They also are genuine and responsible heroes.

Any person who uses his or her talents to help make our world a better, more decent, more peaceful place is a courageous, genuine and responsible hero. The Good Samaritans of the world who help the underprivileged and exploited to regain their human dignity and to lead relatively normal and useful lives are genuine role models as well as responsible heroes. They must be honored and immortalized. One example among many others—and probably the best—is the extraordinary humanitarianism and philanthropy of Mother Teresa.

## 49. Accepting Suffering as Part of Life

One must first differentiate between unavoidable and avoidable suffering. Death of family members or of friends, accidents, personal experience of failure, and all sorts of disappointments are unavoidable and cause suffering that sooner or later affects every human being. On the other hand, there are avoidable forms of suffering caused by irresponsible behavior, like injury owing to reckless driving, drinking excessively, or taking drugs unnecessarily. Suffering can also be divided into normal and neurotic. Normal suffering occurs when one feels guilty for an immoral and irresponsible deed that one has committed, whereas self-destructive, masochistic, self-depreciating thoughts, behavior, or feelings that are harmful to personal functioning and psychological as well as physical wellbeing are neurotic in nature.

Contemporary Western culture and society, especially in North America, does not educate people to tolerate and experience the painful feeling of suffering, even in situations where it would be justified, appropriate, and healthy. People are not encouraged to mourn and grieve with a certain degree of intensity and for a longer period of time, even though emotionally and psychologically it would be salutary and beneficial to the bereaved person. Many doctors prescribe and encourage the taking of sleeping pills and antidepressants even when the malaise or discomfort is minor. There is a lot of publicity, especially on television, stimulating people to take sleeping pills even when they have minor difficulties falling asleep. There are healthier and better ways to help people overcome minor sleeping problems. Enduring pain and discomfort is a natural part of life, and people who can endure and tolerate a certain amount of pain and suffering are usually strong people, capable of feeling and expressing joy as well as love. To a great extent, the taking of narcotic drugs is due to the incapacity of many people to tolerate frustration, disappointments, sadness, and anger.

While many people become cynical, insensitive, vindictive, and intolerant as a result of having suffered abuse, neglect, rejection, or other forms of injustices in childhood or as adults, a minority becomes literally ennobled by these unhappy experiences. They become more understanding, empathetic, and compassionate toward other people who have undergone similar experiences.

It is very important for society to teach people to accept unavoidable suffering as part of life, and to help people to express grief more openly: to allow boys to cry when in pain or sad, to discourage the taking of drugs for minor physical or psychological discomfort. Society must emphasize and value qualities like endurance, fortitude, sympathy, love, and compassion; qualities that become strengthened through a positive attitude toward unavoidable suffering.

### 50. Viewing Opposites as Complementary

People have traditionally looked at opposites as being antagonistic or inimical. While this is true in the case of a criminal intending to commit an aggression against an innocent victim, it definitely is not true in the case of opposite personality traits or ideas. Opposites have to be viewed as being essential parts, completing each other, as indispensable components and elements forming a whole. In some successful marriages, where one partner is a gregarious extrovert and the other is rather introverted, the two mates are attracted by their oppositeness, satisfying each other's needs to function as a strongly united couple. The introverted spouse with his or her depth of feelings strengthens the emotional ties between the two marital partners, while the extroverted person contributes to the social life of the couple.

111

It is equally important to view opposing differences of opinion as different, complementary, and enriching. Just as a coin has two sides, there are at least two sides to most polemical issues. A synthetic mind looking for truth, understanding, and reconciliation will responsibly try to understand both sides and to arrive either at a synthesis or at a compromise between the opposing opinions, ideally incorporating the best, most truthful, and responsible elements of the two contrary viewpoints into a broader, more complete point of view.

Marxist philosophy tends to view the evolution of history as a result of a conflict between classes of society, where a thesis tends to lead to, and is followed by its opposite, an antithesis, which will eventually be transformed into a synthesis consisting of the most important elements of the two opposites. The trouble with this viewpoint is that it is mechanistic and fatalistic, believes that progress occurs only through violent struggle and war, and must result in the wiping out of the opposition. This is not a responsible view, even if this analysis and description is partially accurate historically. The two conflicting social classes—the landowning or entrepreneurial capitalists and the workers or employees—should never be engaged in a violent struggle. Both management and entrepreneurs and owners on the one side, and blue collar, white collar, and professional workers on the other, must cooperate with each other and resolve their differences either through arbitration or through responsible, effective negotiations. Viewing both sides as complementary and indispensable to the successful functioning of an enterprise contributes to efficiency as well as to harmony and social responsibility.

### 51. Valuing Responsible Liberalism

The dictionary defines liberal as characterized or inclining toward opinions or policies favoring progress or reform, as in politics or religion. It further connotes being broadminded and not intolerant or prejudiced. Liberals advocate the modification of laws and institutions in accordance with changing conditions.

Within the Protestant religion, liberalism advocates latitude in scriptural interpretation and doctrine, as opposed to fundamentalism. Unitarians are a good example of religious liberals. Reform Judaism, which places more emphasis on moral values than on ceremony and rituals, is another example of religious liberalism. Religious liberals tend to believe that religious revelation is gradual, progressive, and continuous. Responsible religious liberalism, even if it is in some way close to secular humanism, will nevertheless stress faith in God as an essential virtue and an indispensable value.

112

Responsible liberalism, whether in politics, education, economics, or in other fields is based on a synthesis and compromise between conservatism and reformist radicalism. It tries to maintain the essential values from the past by adapting them to current circumstances. Responsible liberalism means to be tolerant and to oppose fanaticism without being licentious and without lacking in moral restraint and responsibility.

In economics, unrestrained liberalism, as opposed to responsible liberalism, is represented by laissez-faire—the theory that the state should exercise as little control as possible in trade and industrial and labor relations, and not interfere in the fierce competition between business and industrial corporations. In other words, laissez-faire does not impose any restrictions on competition. Laissez-faire, as described above, is rather extreme and is socially and morally not too responsible. An economic system based on the laws of the market, on private ownership, competition, and profit, is very efficient in terms of producing the necessary goods to satisfy the demand of consumers. It is, however, also important that governments to some extent regulate the economic process in order to prevent fierce and unscrupulous competition and the creation of industrial cartels and monopolies.

In the fields of childrearing and education, liberalism is often associated with permissiveness. It is increasingly accepted that in order to develop into psychologically, socially, and morally mature and responsible adults, children need love, understanding, and respect as well as discipline. Parents and teachers must stimulate the development of potentials and talents as well as set limits. Discipline combined with love builds character and allows a child to develop a sense of personal, social, and moral responsibility, enabling him or her to withstand peer pressure to experiment with drugs, to drink excessively, or to engage in promiscuous sex. A responsible liberal education will also punish children for wrongdoings or transgressions, but always in a nonviolent manner. Punishment must not humiliate the child, but help him or her to become personally, morally, and socially more responsible. This can be achieved if the reason for the punishment is well explained to the child.

In spite of its tolerance, responsible liberalism nevertheless advocates censorship of printed material, movies, and television programs that portray excessive, unnecessary violence, written or produced only to increase its appeal to the basest and vilest instincts of the public. Responsible liberalism also advocates censorship of pornographic material—the portrayal of sex done only to titillate and which is a form of violence directed against feelings. Finally, responsible liberalism also censors any form of incitation to racial, ethnic, or religious discrimination through the use of printed material, film, television programs, or radio broadcasts.

## 52. Being Guided by Responsible Values

The dictionary defines value as the desirability or worth of a thing and as something regarded as desirable, worthy or right, as a belief, standard, or moral precept: the values of democratic society, for example. Psychologically, values are very meaningful to people who invest them with emotional energy. The thing valued can be an object such a a house, an action such as offering to help others, a state of body or mind such as health or wisdom, an idea, a personal quality such as courage or sensitivity, or a social abstraction like justice or democracy. When one speaks of placing a high value upon a particular idea or feeling, one means that the idea or feeling exerts a considerable force in instigating and directing behavior.

The German philosopher Spranger considers values as evaluative attitudes. According to Spranger, the value orientation of a person forms the basic type of personality of a person. There are six different personality types: the theoretical, whose main interests are the pursuit and discovery of truth; the economic, whose main preoccupation is usefulness and practicality; the aesthetic whose main values are beauty and harmony; the social, who is characterized by love of people; the political, who is interested in power; and the religious, who is guided by faith and most appreciates cosmic unity.

There are socially and morally responsible values and irresponsible ones. Examples of responsible values are: intelligence, wisdom, courage, perseverance, legal and social justice, compassion, love, altruism, generosity, loyalty, commitment, respect, consciousness, democracy, humanitarianism, faith, beauty, usefulness, responsible freedom, practical idealism, responsible reform, and responsible continuity. Examples of irresponsible values are: chauvinism, bigotry, hate, dictatorship, oppression, slavery, treason, exploitation, war, hedonism, egoism, anarchy, cowardice, laziness, deceit, and injustice.

The reason for adopting personally, morally, and socially irresponsible values might be due to a hateful personality, to adverse social and political conditions, or to ignorance and inability to distinguish between responsible life and welfare furthering values and irresponsible, destructive ones, especially if the bad values happen to be fashionable. The present era can be characterized by a state of confusion in many people's minds as to which are responsible and which are irresponsible values. The popularity of violence in films and television programs and the

114

prevalent cult of selfishness and excessive consumerism exemplify this confusion. It requires moral strength and wisdom to be guided by responsible values. Delinquents are an example of the espousal of irresponsible values as well as the confusion of values. They primarily value violence, force, and power, and consider love, affection, and honesty as weaknesses. Deluded, scientifically false, and untrue beliefs coupled with prejudiced hatred against the Jews explains why many Nazi doctors murdered Jews in concentration camps. To them the Jews were an enemy and a cancer that the national Aryan body of Germany had to extirpate. This shows how important it is to have sane, truthful beliefs and socially and morally responsible values. Similarly, some Soviet psychiatrists valued blind obedience and conformity to totalitarian communism more than truth and allegiance to the Hippocratic medical oath to do the best they can in the best interest of their patients. Some of them diagnosed as schizophrenic people who criticized the communistic system and placed them in mental hospitals. Some U.S. psychiatrists during the Vietnam war treated any rebellion against orders or refusal to kill as pathology. It is a testimony to the existence of profound humanitarianism and of human solidarity within the majority of decent people when they hesitate to kill during war. The only time when killing the enemy during a war should be condoned is in a war of self-defense against a criminally despotic tyrant, bent on conquering and destroying morality and civilization, as was the case during the Second World War, when the democratic world had to stop Nazi Germany in its quest to conquer the world.

It is also highly irresponsible for a society to sacrifice innocent individuals in the interest of the collectivity, as is practiced in many tyrannical, totalitarian countries. Totalitarian despots deceive the people when they pretend that the welfare of the collectivity is protected when innocent individuals who are falsely accused of crimes against the state are destroyed. The so-called crime usually consists of criticizing the government, which is an accepted right in any democratic country.

While all socially and morally responsible values are important, one person cannot espouse them all. The important thing is to develop the wisdom to appreciate responsible values and live according to those values that best suit the aptitudes, interests, and personality of the individual. It is also vital to develop a hierarchy of values and to integrate lower values with higher ones. For instance, sexual needs should be integrated with love for one's spouse within a marital relationship. Love for one's nation and country should be integrated with worldwide international solidarity, with considering oneself a citizen of the world, and advocating and promoting world government. Earning a salary should be integrated with doing productive, useful, meaningful, and fulfilling work.

It is very important to know by what criteria to evaluate the merit and responsibility of a value. The best criteria for evaluating values are to judge them by their economic usefulness, their degree of social justice, their adherence to truth, their beauty, their faith in god and humankind, their universality and promotion of psychological, physical, social, moral, and spiritual welfare, and by their respect for individual and group differences. Responsible values are incompatible with killing and murdering people, except in self-defense, with physical and psychological abuse of others, with prejudice and oppression of others, as well as with insensitivity and indifference to people's legitimate needs. Responsible values are based on respect for every decent person as well as for his or her opinions and beliefs, regardless of whether one agrees with them or not.

The process of educating people to appreciate and espouse responsible personal, social, and moral values must start early in life. Parents and teachers should be living examples and role models to children and adolescents of decency, commitment, faith, compassion, conscientiousness, courage, moral strength, personal and moral integrity, wisdom, maturity, and dedication to improve society and the world. Children and adolescents should be taught to recognize, appreciate, and espouse responsible personal, social, and moral values. They should also study the teachings and lives of highly responsible social and moral leaders. The process of embracing responsible personal, social, and moral values must continue throughout life. Adults should strive to become better, more genuine, and more altruistic human beings, more appreciative of truth, beauty, and social justice.

Young people start off with a natural appreciation of beauty, but in the process of growing up in an industrialized society, they lose this appreciation and resign themselves and become indifferent to much of the ugliness of modern life. Appreciation of beauty becomes less important in their lives. This can have catastrophic results, as many Americans are willing to live with the ugliness of pollution, slums, decaying inner cities, and the increasing numbers of homeless people. By continuing to value beauty throughout life, we will also be more inclined to fight pollution and slums and to improve the social situation of the homeless.

Some philosophers and psychologists argue whether values are absolute and eternal or relative, changing, and only valid for a certain period of time, to be replaced by other values more in harmony with a new epoch. I believe that both ideas have some validity and are complementary. Certain values like faith, love, truth, beauty, justice, loyalty, decency, integrity, as well as personal, social, and moral responsibility are absolute, independent, and not related to any historical period. In this sense they are timeless and eternal, but they also vary in accordance with the customs and beliefs of any given epoch. Many people do not find any relevance and validity today in the ten commandments given by God to Moses in biblical times. These people are wrong. The injunction to believe in and worship the supreme and only God, the creator of the universe, forms the basis and eternal hope for eventual worldwide human solidarity and peace in a united world under the authority of a world government. The injunction not to kill must also become an absolute and universally respected precept, as it is the practically ideal foundation of human solidarity and of the abolition of all wars, whether internal or international.

Values are also simultaneously universal and objective as well as related to the specificity of a culture or subjectivity of individual people. There are objective criteria of beauty, yet what people like varies from individual to individual. For instance, some people will admit that a certain person is handsome, yet might say that it is not the kind of beauty they like. It is also important to notice that while three of the great religions of the world, Judaism, Christianity, and Islam, are monotheistic and worship the same God, the creator of the universe, yet the way he is worshiped varies in accordance with cultural differences and historical traditions.

It is vitally important to understand that responsibility to God, humankind, and individuals is the basis of a more humanitarian and harmonious culture and civilization. The values of personal, social, and moral responsibility are the foundation upon which a peaceful, united, and socially just world can and must be built.

## 53. Understanding Responsible Self-Determination

To some extent, individuals as well as collectivities have the power to determine the course of their lives. People as individuals and groups are not only determined by their genetic make-up, their heredity, environment, upbringing, the culture and values of their respective societies, but also by the period in history in which they live. But they also have a certain degree of free will to create their future. The opposite of self-determination is fatalism, determinism, and utter dependence on and submission to blind social, biological, psychological, historical, and religious forces, all of which lead to helplessness and powerlessness of peoples. Understanding one's heredity, upbringing, the mores of society, the Darwinian laws of the survival of the fittest, and history gives one a certain degree of freedom to self-determine the course of one's life.

Total submission to God also leads to passivity, helplessness, and fatalism. In biblical times it was God who chose people; in our time it must be people who choose God, to participate as a coworker and partner with man to rule and improve the world. Studying the bible and having an enlightened and personally, socially, and morally responsible vision concerning the desired form of society and the world gives us the goal, end, and objective toward which our efforts must be directed. Our vision of people, society, and the world must be based on decency, personal and moral integrity, personal, social, and moral responsibility, faith in God, responsible and full human development, peace, social justice, elimination of war, complete absence of killing, abolition of the death penalty, not too wide a gap between rich and poor, full employment, absence of poverty, respect for human dignity and differences, absence of prejudice, discrimination, human exploitation and oppression, responsible and full development of human potentials through education, moderate prosperity and medical social insurance for all, and other forms of social welfare to ensure that no person is homeless, abandoned, or abused. The vision must also include the rehabilitation and reeducation of delinquents and criminals to personal, social, and moral responsibility.

Two main trends compete to shape the post-cold war world. One is the move toward uniting nations in economic groupings like the European community, while the contrasting trend consists of separating existing nations into smaller ethnic and national groups, as in the former Soviet Union, Yugoslavia, and Czechoslovakia. Some political scientists believe that this splitting up of former national states into ethnic components is a necessary turmoil accompanying the birth of a genuine world order, no longer dominated by large nation-states but composed of regional associations of smaller countries.

Responsible ethnic self-determination based on the idea that every group with a common ancestry, history, language, and culture should have its one state was supported by Woodrow Wilson at the end of World War I, and in 1945 the United Nations accepted the self-determination of ethnic groups to encourage the dismantling of exploitative colonial empires. The miraculous political rebirth of the state of Israel is a pertinent example of a group with a common ancestry, a common distant history, and a common religion, self-determining itself and reestablishing a national state after 2000 years of dispersal.

Responsible individual and collective self-determination makes an invaluable contribution to a more socially just, peaceful, moderately prosperous, united, and cooperative world, in harmony with God and nature.

### 54. Finding Genuine and Responsible Meaning

Human beings find meaning in many activities and enjoyments. Genuine, responsible meaning, however, is to be found only in activities which are useful to others as well as to oneself in a humanitarian, beneficial, altruistic manner that promote psychological, social, economic, moral, and spiritual wellbeing. Loving others as well as oneself, being kind, generous, and altruistic is both highly responsible as well as genuinely meaningful. Responsible, genuine meaning is also derived from developing and using one's potential in productive, creative, innovative actions and deeds, which are socially useful or contribute to uplifting people philosophically, spiritually, culturally, aesthetically, and morally. Responsible genuine meaning is also derived from appreciating and valuing beauty, goodness, truth, psychological and moral integrity, human solidarity, and faith in God.

Genuine, responsible meaning is also found in actions by institutions or governments that meet human needs for moderate material prosperity, peace, social justice, full employment, socialized medical insurance, and adequate old-age pensions, for receiving free or affordable high quality education in accordance with potentials and abilities, as well as for protection of rights and freedoms, and of the environment.

Finding genuine, responsible meaning is both subjective, depending on personal interests as well as objective, depending on universal criteria. Experiencing genuine, responsible meaning is also humanitarian. Hitler's or Stalin's or any dictator's tyrannical oppression or extermination of people with different viewpoints looks and appears meaningful to their adherents and followers, yet are definitely not responsibly meaningful. Disrespect of others, prejudice, extermination, exploitation, any type of killing or destruction of the environment are devoid of moral responsibility as well as of genuine, responsible meaning.

# CHAPTER FIVE

# *Educational Responsibilities*

### 55. The Lifelong Duty to Become a More Responsible Person

TO A GREAT EXTENT, THE MORAL DEVELOPMENT OF A CHILD occurs through incorporation and introjection of parental commands and values. By doing this the child develops a primary conscience or superego. As a general rule, a child (and the adult the child later becomes) feels guilty if he or she does not listen to or follow the dictates of the primary conscience. As the introjection of parental demands and values occurs at a very early age, a certain part of a person's primary conscience remains unconscious throughout life, which means that the person is largely unaware of the power the primary conscience or superego plays in his or her life.

When parents are mature, firm, consistent, sensitive, compassionate, and loving with their child, the chance is very good that the child will develop into a psychologically healthy, emotionally mature, balanced, and sensitive adult. Trouble arises, however, when parental or other authority figures are delinquent, neurotic, or psychotic. Their actions and values can be cruel, antisocial, unethical, confused, ambiguous, and contradictory. Children or students of such troubled, unhappy people can become delinquent and insensitive themselves or feel guilty when doing a normal thing like earning a living or getting married.

It is important that people become aware of their values and beliefs received from their parents and teachers. If the values and beliefs are social, decent, humane, practical, responsive, and above all responsible, they should be preserved and retained. However, if the values and beliefs are immature, hostile, cruel, prejudiced, and confused, they must be discarded and replaced with positive, humanitarian, responsible, true-to-life values. Even those people who had mature, responsive, humanitarian, emotionally mature parents and educators, who inculcated positive and responsible values and codes of behavior, must further develop their consciences by increasingly valuing integrity, authenticity, personal,

120

social, and, above all, moral responsibility, as well as universalism and humanity. The conscience developed through one's own moral and ethical efforts can be called secondary conscience. Really happy people are those whose primary conscience is in harmony with their secondary conscience.

The task to become a better, more decent person, more genuine, with a greater sense of personal and moral integrity, as well as a high sense of personal, social, and moral responsibility, must be pursued throughout life. In this sense, one can truly say that one of life's most important goals should and must be the responsibility to improve as a human being, a task that has to continue until the end of one's life.

## 56. Educating Children and Adolescents to Responsibility

The education of children and adolescents toward personal, social, and moral responsibility has to be done by parents and teachers supported by society and by the whole community. It is the responsibility of society to ensure that parents and teachers help children and adolescents to develop their intellectual, emotional, social, and moral potentials as well as their aptitudes and special talents, and that they are not abused physically, emotionally, sexually, or psychologically. Adequate foster parental care must be provided to those children whose parents, because of sickness, immaturity, alcoholism, drug addition, or delinquency are either incapable or incompetent to responsibly bring up their children. Those parents who lack the necessary skills, or who because of personal emotional or psychological problems or poverty, cannot responsibly educate their children or cannot provide the minimum of material goods necessary for their proper development must receive courses in child education and how to understand and relate to adolescents, and, where necessary, receive the proper material aid.

The entertainment industry should and must stop producing visual and musical texts that portray excessive, totally unjustified violence, sexual abuse, and pornography. Similarly, toy guns and military equipment should be produced less and less, and video games simulating the annihilation of people should be prohibited. Television programs, films, comics, toys, visual games, popular musical songs, and books for children and adolescents should be entertaining as well as educational, furthering the youngster's intellectual, emotional, social, and moral development. Social, political, business, educational, and moral leaders must become exemplary role models, who inspire and stimulate children and adolescents by their virtue, experience, competence, commitment, practical idealism, and personal and moral integrity, to develop into personally, socially, and morally responsible adults dedicated to and capable of improving the world. It is especially the responsibility of educational leaders—and society must help and support them—to be aware of their duty to be role models to the young and to do everything within their power to lead both responsibly successful as well as virtuous and dedicated lives, and to preserve their practical idealism, which is the best guarantee that they will not suffer from burnout and become demoralized and cynical.

A beautiful, inspiring example of dedicated, practically idealistic teachers was set in the early 1990s in the United States by a group of gifted students from the fields of teaching, medicine, law, and business, who formed the association "Teachers for America," and gave one or two years of their lives to teach youngsters in disadvantaged slums on a voluntary basis. The outcome of this highly responsible effort was highly successful.

It is unfortunate that teachers are not highly valued in the United States. This is partially due to an exclusive belief in pragmatism. The saying, "He who can does and he who cannot teaches," exemplifies this unhappy belief in exclusive pragmatism. In addition, the anti-intellectual climate in the United States is to some extent responsible for not showing teachers the degree of respect they deserve. It is an absolute obligation to respect and value both intellectual activity as well as teachers, and to make it possible for them to earn adequate salaries, making it unnecessary for them to take a second job in order to make ends meet. It is essential that teachers have a high degree of self-esteem and self-respect and that they can devote a great deal of their energies to the important task of teaching, which is not possible if they have to hold a second job.

In order to educate children to become generous, empathetic, and compassionate, it is important that parents help their children to under-stand how others feel, to encourage them to help people in need and with problems, and to give them courageous, compassionate people with a well-developed sense of personal, social, and moral responsibility as role models. Parents must treat children with respect, understanding, love, and firmness of purpose. Children must be helped to feel good about themselves and must develop a great deal of self-esteem. They must also learn to tolerate frustration. They should be encouraged to compete, but to do so in such a way that they don't lose respect for their rivals. They must also be encouraged to have faith in God, love for humankind, to develop wisdom and fortitude. Loving parents discipline their children in order to help them accept limits, and should only punish them for wrong behavior or infractions of rules. The punishment must not be cruel, must not humiliate or abuse the child, and the reason for the punishment must be explained to the child.

Parents must believe that destructively aggressive behavior is socially and morally wrong and must teach this to their children. Children have to be told about the consequences of hurting others and must be helped to become sensitive to the suffering and pain of people, while parents must be role models of honesty and personal, social, and moral responsibility to their children. They must have sympathy for the deprived and for people who are different, and should not place a wall between themselves and other groups. Children must also be educated to become cooperative, caring, and responsive to the positive, responsible, vitally important psychological, social, and moral needs of others.

Parents must also stimulate the curiosity of their children and encourage them to develop their imagination in a creative, responsible, and constructive manner. A further obligation of parents is to praise their children when they do their best at school, when they perform duties like doing household chores, when they show skill in a craft, playing a musical instrument, writing a poem, or in sports. This helps the child to develop the feeling of being competent and capable.

In some parts of the world, mothers inculcate in their sons uncaring behavior patterns. Boys in Central American families, for example, are not taught to help out with household chores, while girls are taught to help their brothers. Boys get everything done for them. In a certain way, women take vengeance against the injustices perpetrated against them and for being transformed into second-class citizens by making their sons passive, violently aggressive, and macho playboys. This should not be allowed. It is important to educate both girls and boys to care for others, to assert themselves, as well as to think of themselves as having equal human value.

The responsibility of a mother toward her child starts from the moment she is pregnant. Drinking alcohol or taking cocaine while pregnant has a negative influence on the unborn child's physical and mental development and state of health. After birth the parents must teach the infant that by responding to his or her crying and to the need to be fed or comforted, his or her behavior has an effect on others, who respond in an altruistic fashion. Through this process the child learns to trust others as well as to become as responsive and responsible as his or her parents. It is essential to understand what happens when parents fail to satisfy vital needs of the child. Deprivation occurs when parents are unavailable or distant, rarely cuddling a crying baby or expressing interest in the infant's development. As a result, the child fails to develop a sense of emotional security. Deprivation also occurs when the child fails to receive emotional rewards for curiosity, growth, and accomplishments. Another form of irresponsible parental behavior is rejection of the child, which often leads to teenage delinquency. Deprecating the child, which is psychological abuse, is also highly irresponsible. Some parents constantly deprecate a child. Denigration of an achievement that falls short of perfection is also psychological abuse. Abused children not only fail to develop self-esteem and confidence in their abilities, but also have difficulty empathizing and developing sympathy for the distress of others.

Teachers have a very important task to teach children not only to read and write (as well as mathematics, science, geography, and one or two foreign languages), but must also help to develop their specific talents, stimulate their curiosity about different ethnic, religious, national, and cultural groups, awaken their sense of responsibility to preserve the world's environment, to be interested in local and international events, and, above all, to motivate them to continue to learn throughout their lives as well as to make a contribution to improve the world and the human condition. Educators must also teach students the necessary skills that will enable them to make a living, and encourage them to keep in shape through daily physical exercise and sports activities. Students must also be taught efficient studying methods and through competent vocational and career counseling sessions learn to understand and become aware of their interests, aptitudes, talents, personality traits, values, and aspirations, and integrate them in a suitable vocational or career choice. They must also be taught social skills and encouraged to develop a high sense of personal, social, and moral responsibility.

Parents and teachers must understand the phenomenon of adolescent rebelliousness, which is a necessary stage in growing up to become independent and mature, and help the adolescent to channel it into a peaceful and responsible contestation of social injustice, pollution, unemployment, prejudice, and international conflicts. Likewise, the idealism of adolescents to better the world must be valued, and the adolescent must be taught to keep this precious personality trait for the rest of his or her life.

Schools must also teach students nonviolent values and solutions to problems. Nonviolence must become institutionalized. Students must learn that conflicts and disagreements can be solved in nonviolent ways through discussion and compromise. Parents as well as teachers must not use corporal punishment as a form of discipline, as it brutalizes and humiliates, and leads the child to view the world as cruel, where physical violence prevails and is the way through which the strong and powerful authority figures settle conflicts. As a consequence, the child will become brutal, authoritarian, and will view violence as natural. The responsible way for parents and teachers to discipline a child is to apply the principle that when the child transgresses rules, it must suffer the consequence. The child has to know the expected rules of conduct, and parents must explain the reason for the punishment. Children should even be asked what punishment they would recommend if they were in the position of the adult. The punishment must not humiliate the child but teach him or her that a price has to be paid for transgressing expected rules and codes of behavior.

Teachers must continue the efforts of parents to help to develop in their students qualities of the head—logical, analytical, and synthetic reasoning abilities—as well as qualities of the heart—compassion, generosity, sensitivity, and idealism. Schools should and must also give courses on sex education, which must not only consist of information on anatomy, but must also deal with personal identity, human interrelations, emotions, feelings, respect for the other sex, and, above all, personal, social, and moral responsibility. Students should get information on the use of contraceptives and should be informed of the risk of contracting sexually transmitted diseases, including AIDS, and how to avoid becoming infected. They should also learn their responsibility to prevent teenage pregnancies, as teenagers generally lack the maturity to raise children in a responsible manner.

To a great extent, learning should occur through a cooperative effort between teachers and students and between students themselves. Every student should be allowed to learn at his or her own rhythm and according to his or her own learning style, which becomes possible through the introduction of computers and other teaching aids. Every student of average intelligence must as a minimum successfully complete high school. What distinguishes bright from less bright students is not the capacity to learn but the rate of learning.

It is important that students become familiar with the greatest literary, poetic, musical, artistic, and philosophical creations of humankind.

Teachers must preserve at all cost their practical idealism throughout their lives; being idealistic is the best way to prevent burnout. Teachers must also serve as role models of integrity, competence, and personal, social, and moral responsibility to students. In order to make this possible, it is necessary that society value teachers more than it does at present, and adequately compensates them. These two conditions will contribute to motivate some of the brightest, most practically idealistic, and personally, socially, and morally responsible students to select teaching as a profession. Fulfilled, inspiring teachers not only instill in their students a sense of wonder about life and the world, but also help them to hope and to become optimistic concerning the future of human-kind, as well as strengthening their faith in God and in man's capacity to improve the world in spite of problems and difficulties.

Teachers should also advocate academic excellence and encourage moderate competition to help students to achieve it. Educators must also believe in the value of positive expectation and apply it by expecting their students to succeed. As indicated in the chapter on positive expectation, research has shown that expected success turns into a self-fulfilling prophecy and leads to successful performance. The educator who expects the student to succeed will encourage him or her more. The student, in turn, sensing this, will do his or her best, in order not to disappoint the teacher, to fulfill the teacher's expectation. Combined with cooperative learning and helping every student to progress at his or her own rhythm, positive expectation is another powerful method to help every student become an academic success.

It is also important to ensure that every student becomes a success, and that not too much importance is attached to grades. What is important is what every student has mastered. Some minor importance has to be attached to grades, especially good grades, as a reward of mastery. Helping every student to become an educational success would instill in students a love for learning and would help them to be less envious, to feel more capable, and to develop a greater degree of confidence in their abilities.

It is also extremely important that young people develop practical idealism and preserve this vitally important quality of the heart throughout their lives. It helps to preserve their practical idealism if they take as role models outstanding people who practiced in their own lives what they thought, wrote, and advocated, and by doing so made a contribution to a better world. A beautiful example of such a role model is Albert Schweitzer, the twentieth-century theologian, philosopher, and physi-cian, who believed in and wrote about reverence for life and devoted his life to work as a medical missionary in Gabon, Africa.

Teachers must also promote a new environmental ethic and encour-age students to contribute to solutions, by fighting pollution and environ-mental degradation. For example, they could encourage students to participate in a campaign to motivate people, either by telephone or by going from door to door, to fight pollution through reuse and recycling.

Students should also help motivate people to make greater use of public transportation and to participate in keeping cities clean.

When a child or teenager commits a crime, parents—and in some cases even teachers, friends, and relatives—should and must be held accountable. This would induce parents, teachers, friends, and relatives either to influence in a positive way a troubled, frustrated, potentially violent youngster, or inform people (such as policemen) who could prevent the committing of a crime or of the occurrence of antisocial behavior, which could have tragic consequences. The old motto of, "One for all and all for one," is an excellent principle of personal, social, and moral responsibility and of human solidarity, which encourages an individual to work for the common good and society to care for the wellbeing of every individual. In Los Angeles in 1989, a 37-year-old mother of three became the first person to be arrested and accused under a new California law that holds parents responsible when their kids go bad. Her son was accused of raping a 12-year-old girl. She is charged with failing to exercise reasonable care, supervision, protection, and control of a child. A magnificent precedent. Every country in the world should take California as an example and pass similar laws. It contributes to motivating parents to do their best to educate their children responsibly. The California law should be extended to include teachers, as well as friends and relatives. Of course, teachers, friends, and relatives are in most instances not as close to the child and teenager as are the parents, and should not be arrested, but in the case of a crime committed by a child or teenager, they should be reprimanded for having shirked their responsibility to counsel and control the youngster. This would instill in a growing number of people an increased sense of responsibility for the wellbeing of youngsters and would contribute to the creation of a personally, socially, and morally more responsible society.

The state of Maryland has been the first in the United States to introduce in its high schools an obligatory public service assignment for students. Students have to do a few hours a week of social and community work, helping disadvantaged people and the elderly. One educator said that the purpose of this is to teach the students skills and not necessarily to feel good. But one student interviewed on television said that the social activities make her feel content. I think that the program is admirable and should be started by all schools in the United States, all over the Western world, and even all over the globe. It would teach students not only social skills, but also develop their hearts, their compassion, empathy, and sympathy, would develop their sense of personal, social, and moral responsibility, their responsiveness to human and social needs, would

127

make them feel important and needed, capable of making a difference, improving the world, and making it more human. It would teach them the importance of voluntary community work, which is a great blessing, would help to bridge the generational gap between the young and old, as well as the gap between rich and poor. It is also a powerful way to eliminate to some extent crime from urban communities, strengthen human solidarity, and implement the blessed biblical saying that we are our brother's keeper.

## 57. Eliminating Illiteracy

Illiteracy, the inability to read and write, is a major psychological educational and social problem and misfortune. There are 950 million illiterate adults in the world. Basic illiteracy means a total inability to read and write. Functional illiteracy occurs when a person might know the letters and be able to read and write at a rudimentary level, but not sufficiently to function at a satisfactory level in society. The term functional illiteracy applies to those individuals whose reading and writing skills have not progressed beyond the level of a second year high school student. There are also cases of bright people who, owing to learning disabilities like dyslexia or other incapacities, also experience some difficulties in reading and writing.

The cause of illiteracy can be psychological, physiological, social, or economic. Some children do not learn to read and write because they are mentally retarded, or because of already mentioned learning disabilities, which might be caused by physiological or perceptual factors. A lot of illiteracy is caused by poverty, by an absence of sufficient schools and teachers in the third world, by child exploitation and slavery, by unmotivated children affected to a great extent by poor educational methods and philosophy, and by the existence of many disillusioned and burned out teachers and educators all over the world. Many children in many parts of the world—industrialized as well as developing—spend more time watching television than reading or doing homework. Considering the mind-dulling effect of much of television programs (with the exception of high quality educational programs), it is not surprising that one-third of the functionally illiterate Canadians are high school graduates. The same percentage of functionally illiterate people most likely also exists in the United States and in some other industrialized countries, not to mention many third world countries, where the percentage of functional illiteracy is much higher.

Illiteracy condemns people to unemployment, to jobs of inferior, poor quality, and to low wages. As the economy becomes more and more dependent on highly sophisticated technology, illiterates and other poorly educated people are bound to suffer more and more misery and psychological humiliation and pain. Besides, not being able to read and write is a terribly irresponsible waste of human potential and talents. It isolates people from vital sources of learning and prevents them from communicating properly with others.

It is essential that governments, community leaders, educators, and parents do the utmost to ensure that all children and adults throughout the world become literate. Behavioral techniques of positively reinforcing progress in learning, as well as the use of educational software programs, which allow each child to progress at his or her speed, rate, and level of learning, are highly effective and successful and enable even some mentally retarded children to acquire some degree of literacy. It is never too late to become literate. Adults of any age can be taught to read and write. It is also the responsibility of every illiterate person to motivate himself or herself sufficiently to seek help, and to learn to read and write.

## 58. Reeducating Criminals to Responsibility

Criminals must pay for their crimes, yet the punishment must not be the death penalty. Condemning criminals to death dehumanizes society and transmits the message that the most responsible elements of society use vengeance to punish offenders. Society must be socially and morally superior, more humane, and more responsible than criminals and must always give them an opportunity to rehabilitate themselves through reeducation and obliging them to do altruistic, voluntary community work. Besides, it is doubtful whether the death sentence acts as a deterrent to the criminals. Statistics don't prove that the death sentence deters other criminals from committing crimes. Unconsciously, some criminals kill because they suffer from unrecognized guilt feelings for past transgressions, for which they unconsciously or even consciously believe they must die. They sometimes kill, or commit another serious crime in order to be punished or even to die. Criminals should and must pay for their crimes by losing their freedom temporarily or for good, depending on the nature, seriousness, and severity of the committed crime, and by having to submit to reeducation toward personal, social, and moral responsibility and by being obliged to do altruistic, voluntary community work.

Recent tendencies in some Western countries to oblige the delinquent to pay restitution to the victim, as well as to do community work, are a step in the right direction. Besides being obliged to become altruistic by doing voluntary altruistic work, the delinquent must also be enabled to work and to use a great part of his or her earnings to compensate the victim or the victim's relatives.

The length of an offender's loss of freedom should depend on the seriousness of the committed offense. The criminal must be reeducated to understand that it is emotionally, socially, and morally mature and responsible to do good, even if for a while (or for good) he or she has to be forced to do so.

It is socially and morally not too responsible that juveniles who commit atrocious crimes like murder, rape, or hurting others physically, psychologically, or financially receive light sentences for their crimes. They should and must be deprived of their freedom at first totally and later partially by being obliged to work for the betterment of society and the world by fighting pollution, cleaning the environment, helping the elderly, the handicapped, the homeless, and by keeping other juveniles from committing crimes.

The reeducation of the criminal must be intellectual, emotional, social, and moral. Criminals must be motivated to develop some intellectual and emotional insight into the reasons they committed their offenses, as well as to understand their personalities and the local and national social conditions, so that they can see the link between these factors and the committed offenses. They must also be helped to realize and avow that they acted immorally and irresponsibly and must regret, feel sorry, repent, and apologize. The criminal must become decriminalized and transformed into a decent and compassionate person. In order to achieve this, it is essential that the penal system abstain from humiliating or abusing the offender through the use of physical or psychological violence. Psychological coercion to help a criminal become personally, socially, and morally responsible is neither a form of humiliation, abuse, nor of psychological violence, and is essential to achieve this practical and idealistic objective.

Developing and accepting feelings of guilt for the committed offense is an important step toward personal, social, and moral responsibility. The intensity of guilt must not be devastatingly crippling, yet strong enough to help and induce the offender to repent and change for the better. It is also essential that the experts, who reeducate the criminal to responsibility, believe in the power of positive expectation. In spite of his or her bad past, the delinquent can and must become a decent, responsible person. Society must believe that he or she can change to become a responsible person and must have the faith to expect this transformation, while the delinquent must also contribute to his or her rehabilitation with perseverance and cooperation. Behavioristic techniques using positive reinforcement, as well as group psychotherapy, are also useful to help in the offender's reeducational process.

Society has the moral right and the obligation to reeducate criminals, providing it does not degenerate into brainwashing, done through electroshocks or through the administration of certain drugs. Teaching the delinquent that he or she acted wrongly, that the purpose of life is to be and to do good, that compassion, love, sympathy, social, moral, and personal responsibility are superior to hate, to destructive violence, and to all other types of crimes, is an effective way to reeducate the delinquent to become a decent human being.

It is also important to understand the many reasons that lead to criminal behavior. Many delinquents were neglected, rejected, abandoned, or physically or psychologically abused by parents, parental substitutes, or by educators. Some become delinquents owing to poverty, unemployment, alcoholism, and addiction to drugs. Drug addiction often leads to prostitution or theft, in order to enable the addicted person to get enough money to buy the desired drugs. Some delinquents, especially the ones rejected by one or both parents in childhood, or the ones who were brutally abused physically, sexually, or psychologically, retaliate vindictively and sometimes indiscriminately against innocent people, often strangers, by causing them serious harm. The criminal often blames everybody for the rejection and mistreatment he or she suffered. This fact is vitally important, indicating the stake society as a whole and every citizen has to ensure that every child is brought up in a responsible, loving manner, and that poverty and unemployment are eliminated. Otherwise, no citizen is safe from crime.

Criminals who value power exclusively and excessively must learn that compassion, kindness, sensitivity, and love are sources of genuine human power.

The bible tells us that God rejoices more about one sinner who becomes reformed than about the conduct of ten men who never sinned. Many a medieval saint was a sinner in his or her youth. If properly helped by society, many a delinquent person can become rehabilitated, even to the extent where he or she becomes a role model to other delinquents and a promoter of personal, social, and moral responsibility.

# CHAPTER SIX

# *Health and Scientific Responsibilities*

### 59. Leading a Relatively Healthy and Long Life

WHILE IT IS UNFORTUNATE THAT A CERTAIN PERCENTAGE OF PEOPLE are born with inherited sicknesses responsible for certain physical and mental handicaps, a far greater percentage of people contract unnecessary illnesses, shorten their life span, and even if not sick are not in top physical or mental shape. It has been scientifically proven that good physical health habits have a positive influence on mental health and productivity—and vice versa: Good psychological, social, moral, and spiritual attitudes, beliefs, habits, and practices favorably affect physical health as well as the quality and quantity of performance.

To remain relatively healthy and prevent sickness it should and must become a person's duty to eat a healthy diet, avoiding animal fats as much as possible and not eating too much red meat, to consume a lot of fiber, vegetables, and fruits. The consumed milk and cheese should be low in fat content. Proteins should be obtained primarily from poultry, fish, and tofu. One should eat only whole wheat bread. Smoking must be totally eliminated and alcohol should be consumed only in moderate quantities, if at all. Physical exercise, consisting of aerobic activity, muscle building, and stretching, is an absolute must. Besides keeping the body healthy and increasing fitness, physical exercise also has a positive effect on mental processes and on a person's general feeling and wellbeing.

It is also important to distinguish between positive stress, which is stimulating, and negative stress or distress, which must be controlled and eliminated, as it can lead to sicknesses. Being humiliated at one's job by being underused or by not being appreciated for a valuable contribution can be as negatively stressful or distressful as working excessively for prolonged periods without taking a vacation. On the other hand, working

132

hard at what one enjoys and finds meaningful can be invigorating and health-furthering.

To remain healthy and live a long life it is also important to have a mission or a purpose in life or a socially or morally responsible cause to which one dedicates oneself.

It is also important that one keep informed about health issues and sicknesses by reading medical books and health magazines. One must also have a mature and responsible attitude toward doctors. One must neither accept unquestioningly all their opinions, nor avoid consulting them and ignoring them. Doctors should be viewed as very important consultants, but the final decisions concerning one's health should be made by the patient after having received one or more medical opinions. It is important to have regular checkups and take all the necessary preventive tests. Some tests could detect cancerous cells in some organs at a very early stage and the cancerous growth can be extirpated before it spreads any further.

There are various forms of oriental meditations that induce profound relaxation. Praying to God and developing a profound faith in him also have a very positive effect on one's health. People who pray tend on the average to live longer and be healthier than those who don't. Being altruistic, generous, and compassionate by doing meaningful, socially responsible voluntary work also has very salutary effects on one's health and longevity.

Good, genuine personal relationships with one's spouse, children, other family members, friends, coworkers, neighbors, and people in general are also health-furthering and prevent sickness. It is also important to remain idealistic in a practical sense throughout life and to avoid becoming cynical in spite of all the disappointing experiences one has had. Losing one's ideals is often the cause of burnout, and becoming cynical can lead to heart problems and sickness.

## 60. Providing Universal Medical Insurance

According to a 1990 study by the World Health Organization, 600,000 people worldwide are infected by AIDS, 3 million die yearly of smoking-related conditions, 2 billion are infected with the hepatitis B virus.

In the poorest countries, six out of seven children are not vaccinated, nine out of ten people have no access to clean water. Every 15 seconds a child dies of measles in the world, and every 30 seconds a woman dies as a result of pregnancy. There are 500 million people suffering from tropical diseases. Adequate health programs including efficient universal vaccination could save 200 million lives within the last decade of the twentieth century.

It is the individual and collective responsibility of people in the industrialized world, as well as of governments in the third world and of international organizations, to provide the necessary medical help, to build the medical institutions, and to vaccinate all children of the world against infectious diseases.

It is also essential that all countries of the world that don't have universal medical insurance study and adopt the Canadian medical insurance system, which provides high quality free medical service to all people. While most industrialized countries have a universal medical insurance system which enables all citizens to have free access to quality medical services, millions of poor citizens in the United States have no access to quality medical service, and in many instances to no medical service at all. It is also important that rich countries help poor ones to make quality medical services available to all people. It must become a priority of both the developed and the developing world to have third world students study medicine at top Western medical schools, upon the condition that they return after graduation to their native countries to practice medicine as well as to help their countries to improve their medical facilities.

### 61. Understanding Responsible Mental Health and Psychotherapy

Genuine and responsible mental health is more than the absence of psychiatric symptoms of mental or emotional sickness or disturbance. It means to function relatively well, to assume life's responsibilities such as to support oneself and, if married, one's spouse and children, to develop one's potentials, to have meaningful, fulfilling work, to contribute to the wellbeing and betterment of society, to get along relatively well with people, to understand and accept oneself and others. It also implies, of course, the absence of severe and crippling psychiatric disorders like schizophrenia, paranoia, incapacitating depression, severe phobias, and disabling obsessive-compulsive disorders. Personal qualities such as sensitivity, compassion, generosity, a sense of humor, and responsible moral values also contribute to genuine, responsible mental health. Personal and moral integrity are of paramount importance as well as the ability to enjoy life and be relatively happy.

The body influences the mind and vice versa, the mind and emotions influence the physical health of people. It is not only the conscious emotions and thoughts, but also the unconscious ones that affect mental and physical health. Stress is an essential aspect of living, but too much of it, or negative stress or distress has harmful mental and physical consequences. Hard work, if it leads to positive and rewarding results, is tolerable and even health-furthering, to a certain extent. On the other hand, unemployment or humiliating work conditions can be distressful and cause mental and emotional problems.

Some psychologists, psychiatrists, and psychotherapists consider a person mentally healthy if he or she has no psychotic or neurotic symptoms. Some mental health specialists even regard the presence of guilt feelings as pathological. Guilt is regarded as dandruff which must be gotten rid of. When a person finally gets rid of all guilt (even of one which is justified), the mental disease is assumed to be cured, at the cost of having killed the moral, responsible, decent component of personality. Some feeling of guilt, especially if one has behaved legally or morally in an irresponsible manner, is appropriate, justified, and even fosters repentance, redemption, and rehabilitation. Of course, excessive guilt feelings can be crippling, as can some forms of twisted and neurotic guilt caused by a very strict and rigid parental upbringing—resulting in a person feeling guilty about satisfying even normal instinctual needs. Such neurotic guilt can have devastating and paralyzing mental health consequences. Similarly, anxiety in a moderate form stimulates improved performance, as in the case of students experiencing some anxiety before exams, who will in all likelihood perform better than their calmer colleagues. Of course, excessive anxiety is crippling and adversely affects the level of performance. It is also important to understand that in our highly competitive and often heartless society, sensitive people whose sensitivity and concern for others is not always appreciated get hurt and often develop neurotic symptoms. Similarly, shy, introverted, passive people who might have some difficulty asserting themselves might become traumatized. It is definitely better to be slightly anxious, a bit perfectionistic, moderately obsessive-compulsive with a high sense of duty and moral standards, functioning responsibly and adequately, than to be a person with no neurotic symptoms who exploits, dominates, or takes advantage of others.

Louis Bisch, M.D., Ph.D., in his book *Be Glad You Are Neurotic*, states that neurosis is a form of superiority. Neurotic people have to learn to eliminate the harmful symptoms and use their neurotic tendencies as steppingstones to success and happiness. The French writer Albert Camus expressed the opinion that people who improve the human condition are considered somewhat odd and neurotic by their contemporaries.

There is a positive and responsible evolution in the field of mental health. The discovery by physiologists that psychotics do not experience the deep dreaming sleep indicated by rapid eye movement (REM) indicates the importance of dreams for mental health. For a while in the 1960s, 1970s, and even 1980s, there was a belief among psychotherapists that the best way to deal with repressed feelings of anger and hostility is to express them openly in therapy and even in everyday life. However, this can cause strong guilt feelings and can cause a lot of problems and harm. It is often better, safer, and more responsible not to release violent outbursts of anger or hostility.

Unfortunately, a few psychiatrists have behaved in an immoral and irresponsible manner. A citizen in the former Soviet Union who criticized the despotic tyranny of the communist regime in a justifiable manner found himself or herself being referred by the authorities to psychiatrists who declared the person schizophrenic and recommended hospitalization in a psychiatric hospital where the person received drugs against schizophrenia. These often had very bad side effects on his or her general health. Dr. Cameron, chief psychiatrist at the Allan Memorial Hospital in Montreal, experimented with brainwashing techniques on psychiatric patients in the 1950s. The government compensated some of these patients.

It is also important to understand that even though Sigmud Freud made an important contribution toward helping people better understand themselves and showing that unconscious feelings and thoughts are often the cause of neurosis, his work nevertheless erred in treating morality as a form of social imposition, alien to the individual ego. Freud placed the accent on and attached too much importance to human needs as opposed to social and moral obligation, duty, and responsibility. This has led to a morally empty, irresponsible, and bankrupt view of human nature. The social and moral entities are highly important elements in an individual's self.

Responsible psychotherapy has to be based on an understanding of the factors causing mental and emotional disturbance. To some extent these factors are of an environmental nature. Contributive factors are a high level of unemployment, poverty, violent neighborhoods, a great percentage of divorce, drug addiction, racial, ethnic, sexual, age, and religious intolerance and discrimination, poor educational facilities, and a high rate of school dropouts. Some or all of the above factors can lead to violence, alcoholism, delinquency, and even suicide.

In contrast to recognizing the influence of negative environmental factors on mental and emotional problems and sicknesses, there are mental health specialists and therapists who see the individual person as an isolated unit, relatively unaffected by anything except inner or familial experiences. This is a very onesided and irresponsible view. A socially and morally responsible view is integral and based on the reality and truth that a person is influenced by his or her inherited, genetic nature, by inner experiences, including philosophy of life and world view, by family experiences as well as by the social, cultural, political, economic, and religious environment.

To a great extent, people must be held responsible for their behavior. It is important to understand and to believe that in spite of adverse circumstances people can and must triumph over adversity by improving environmental conditions, and by developing greater insight, understanding, and more respect for human differences, as well as a higher level of personal, social, and moral responsibility.

An effective and responsible psychotherapy recognizes individual differences, is eclectic, and helps a person to understand himself or herself better, become more responsible, committed, dynamic, and optimistic, and make better use of innate talents. In many instances, short-term counseling, helping a person to cope with career or marital problems, has very beneficial therapeutic effects. In other instances like depression or phobias, a longer period of help in the form of behavior or cognitive or some form of psychoanalysis might be indicated. Psychological hep could be combined with some form of medication prescribed by a psychiatrist. The important element guaranteeing psychotherapeutic success lies in the empathetic as well as sympathetic relationship between therapist and client or patient and, above all, in helping the client to become more confident, courageous, realistic, trusting, loving, and responsible.

It is also important to realize that unhappy past experiences as well as failures of all kinds can spur a person to assert his or her sense of responsibility and understand the reasons for his or her lack of success, spurring the person to improve and persevere until responsible success is achieved. Sometimes defects, failure, and traumatic experiences lead a person to try harder, overcompensate, and become exceptionally successful. The Greek orator Demosthenes (4th century B.C.) stuttered as a child.

As a result of suffering, injustice and setbacks in life, many people become bitter, cynical, and mean. A few, however, become more noble, sensitive, and compassionate, and set a beautiful and important example of fortitude, triumph over adversity, and of personal, social, and moral responsibility as well as of responsible mental health.

## 62. The Responsibility of Scientists and Doctors

Scientists must become increasingly aware of their personal, social, and moral responsibility, accept their limitations, and accept God, the creator of the universe, all living beings, and all scientific laws. Einstein, Schweitzer, and Teilhard de Chardin were brilliant scientists who had a profound faith in God. Science must work hand in hand with politics, education, and ethics to advance human progress in the direction of increased knowledge but also of greater social and moral responsibility. The same applies to technology, which must also promote economic and social wellbeing without violating humanitarian principles. The creation of ethical and moral courses by business faculties and the creation of ethical committees by medical schools and hospitals indicates that society moves in the right direction.

The Nazis misused science and technology to exterminate Jews in the gas ovens of concentration camps, where they used highly poisonous chemical substances. The production of weapons of mass destruction, whether atomic, conventional, chemical, or bacteriological—and especially their use—is another corruption and misuse of science and technology. The abuse and misuse of psychiatry by Soviet psychiatrists in the former Soviet Union, who interned people who disagreed with the system in insane asylums and treated them as schizophrenics, was also shocking. The experiments done by Nazi doctors on Jewish people in concentration camps, sterilizing and doing many other inhuman things to them, were equally cruel and despicable.

Scientists, technicians, engineers, and doctors must ask what the purpose of scientific knowledge, technical invention, or medical progress is. The answer must be to enable people to live long, healthy lives, in moderate prosperity, to produce goods without destroying the environment, to improve the quality of life in urban communities, and to promote world peace.

# CHAPTER SEVEN

# *Social Responsibilities*

### 63. Valuing Social Justice

SOCIAL JUSTICE MEANS THE CREATION AND EXISTENCE OF SOCIAL, educational, and economic conditions within a nation, state, society, or community which enable people to live above the poverty level, preferably at least in moderate comfort, having at their disposal free educational services, including college and university accessible to all students on the basis of individual potential, aptitude, and merit, adequate social security, including universal, free medicare, and adequate care and physical and social rehabilitation services for invalids and the handicapped. It further consists of the payment by the state of adequate pensions to the elderly, enabling them to continue to live decently until the end of their lives.

In view of the fact that individual talents and aptitudes differ, it is utopian to think as Marxists did (and still do) of creating a society in which everyone will be remunerated according to his or her needs. On the other hand, responsible social justice requires that people be enabled to live in moderate prosperity. However, society must also consider the quality of a person's contribution to the material, social, psychological, artistic, cultural, and spiritual wellbeing of people and the community, as well as length of training. There must be differences in earned income between people, yet the difference between the highest and lowest paid people in society must not be as large as is the case today in many countries and especially in the United States of America. Governments must regard it as their primary responsibility to implement social justice and to redistribute income through progressive taxation.

Any society based on responsible social justice must also create conditions and introduce legislation to establish equality of opportunity for all people. Every human being should and must receive as a matter of fundamental right the opportunity to fully develop his or her aptitudes and talents according to specific potential and endowment. Social justice also means that all people are materially rewarded according to the principle of equal pay for equal work and that jobs as well as promotions at all levels of society are given solely on the basis of personal merit, thus eliminating any irresponsible form of discrimination, whether on the basis of sex, race, religion, ethnic origin, or age.

Affirmative action, which means to redress the disadvantages of minorities as a group by providing them with a higher number of jobs or entries at universities or colleges, must be balanced with the principle of promoting or accepting every person on the basis of individual aptitude, talent, and merit. For instance, members of disadvantaged minorities should be enabled to enter institutions of higher learning on the basis of the group's proportion in the general population, yet admission to jobs requiring special skills, advanced knowledge, and a high degree of personal, social, and moral responsibility should only be based on skills, qualifications, and personal and moral integrity. Students, for instance, should be accepted to medical schools and allowed to practice once they have completed their medical studies only on the basis of merit, competence, and personal, social, and moral responsibility. The same must apply to all selections for jobs and promotions, where the job to be performed requires a high degree of competence and responsibility. Rosalie Abella, a Canadian judge of the Ontario Court of Appeal, has coined the phrase "employment equity" for a practice in which merit is the main basis for hiring women or members of other under-represented groups for all available jobs, when they are judged to be as qualified as other applicants. It means that in a tie game in which members of underprivileged groups compete, they should be given priority, provided they have equal competence and abilities. It is the ideal method to right the social injustice of discriminating against certain groups in hiring and promotion on the basis of sex, race, religion, nationality, or ethnic origin. It is socially and morally highly responsible, as it takes into account merit, competence, the personality of the individual, as well as redressing the wrong done to the previously discriminated group.

It is equally important that conditions are created establishing social justice in all states. It is equally vital and essential that on a global scale the disparity between rich and poor countries must be continuously diminished. The industrialized world will have to forgive a huge part of the debt owed by the developing third world. The high standards of social responsibility characteristic of some Western democracies must be introduced and become a reality in all states of the world. Universal social justice requires that people all over the world develop a strong sense of obligation and solidarity toward humankind and move toward a socio-economic-political system and superstructure consisting of the "United

States of the World," under the authority of a world government. It is only in a united world with a world government that universal social justice will have an excellent chance to flourish and become prevalent.

## 64. Fighting the Real Enemies of Humankind

Many people, including some social scientists and even some psychiatrists, believe that tribalism is a part of the inner nature of human beings, and that there is a human need for conflict and enemies. They further believe that it is also human nature to divide people into us-and-them. A good example is the destabilization in the United States following the collapse of Soviet and East European communism in the late 1980s and early 1990s. For more than four decades after the Second World War, the Soviet empire was the main enemy of the United States, which helped to focus and to channel the collective energy of the United States into containing and overcoming this foe. Many people believe that in order to find a new collective purpose, Americans must search for and find a new enemy comparable to the collapsed communist evil empire.

There is definitely strong sociological and historical evidence to support the belief that people divide themselves into us-and-them. One can see this most clearly in times of war, when a nation's and country's enemies become demonized and everything evil, vile, negative, sinister, and criminal is attributed to them. While this distortion of truth and humanity leads to a lot of devastation and tragedies, it also fosters solidarity and cooperation among the in-group.

With the globalization of commerce and communication, the transformation of the world into a global village, and the disrespect of environmental pollution on international borders, as well as the still existing, even though in a greatly diminished form, danger of a nuclear holocaust, it will become increasingly important to envisage the absolute necessity of creating a world federation in the form of the United States of the World.

The common enemies which this world government will have to fight and overcome are hunger, major sicknesses, poverty, unemployment, ignorance, prejudice, discrimination, illiteracy, wars, crime, greed, lack of integrity, personal, social and moral irresponsibility, lack of faith in God and humanity, tyranny, despotism, oppression, social injustice, disrespect for human differences, indifference to suffering and human exploitation and slavery.

Fighting against and overcoming these common enemies of humankind will create worldwide genuine human solidarity as well as global human cooperation.

## 65. The Responsibilities to the Children of the World

According to a United Nations report contained in the "State of the World's Children 1990," more than a quarter of a million small children die every week of easily preventable illnesses and malnutrition. The 1990 United Nations Children's Fund states that 8000 children die every day because they have not been immunized. This tragedy happens in spite of the fact that  80 percent of the world's children are being vaccinated against mass sicknesses. It is irresponsible and inadmissible that so many children still die unnecessarily. It is absolutely imperative that every child in the world gets vaccinated. The above mentioned report further states that spending two percent of the developed world's military expenditure would provide 2.5 billion U.S. dollars, an amount of money that could prevent the tragic death of those children.

Millions of children live on the streets of the world's cities. Many of these children become thieves, prostitutes, petty criminals, drug addicts, and drug pushers. About half of the street children live in Latin America. Asia has between twenty and thirty million street children.

It is the responsibility of governments,society, international and national institutions, parents, and teachers everywhere in the world to create conditions and implement and practice values resulting in love and respect for children and to prevent conditions that lead to poverty, crime, divorce, rejection, and abandonment of children.

Pollution of the air, water, and of food has devastating effects on the health and longevity of people. Nowhere was this more evident than in the East European countries, which, owing to outdated production methods that required the use of an excessive amount of coal and oil, and not possessing the technology to reduce pollution, were responsible for an increase in all kinds of sicknesses and in a reduction of the life span. Children especially are more vulnerable to the effects of pollution; this was obvious in Eastern European countries, not only in a considerable increase in illnesses, but also in a decreased level of their physical development, as compared with children in the Western world.

Another disaster affecting many children in some third world countries is their exploitation by unscrupulous employers, who use children, sometimes even at a very young age, as cheap labor. Not only does this irreparably harm their health, it also prevents them from getting an adequate education.

As a result of parental rejection, there are some children even in the United States who live on the streets. Many of these children become delinquents. It is also shocking that in the United States and Canada an increasing number of children are not properly fed and have difficulties concentrating and learning because of hunger.

It is also important to mention that the growing number of marriages in the Western world that end in divorce have a demoralizing and depressing effect on children. To develop properly, children need the love, respect, and attention of both parents, and it is the responsibility of parents to provide it to them by creating harmonious, lasting, and loving family ties.

Children represent the future. All the institutions of the world as well as individuals must make it a priority to ensure that children are not only wanted but also helped to develop into well-educated, competent, healthy, socially and morally, as well as personally responsible adults.

It is shocking that in many third world countries a large number of children get very little education and in many cases no education at all. It must become a top priority of governments and of society all over the world to ensure that every child receive the opportunity to get the appropriate level of education corresponding to his or her level of intelligence, aptitudes, and talents. If this is done, the child has a good chance of developing into an informed, cultivated, responsible, and competent human being.

It is especially shocking that in some countries children are still sold into slavery. This criminally irresponsible practice has to stop, and authorities should intervene to put an end to it. It is even more unbelievable that in order to eliminate their presence quite a few street children are murdered in some South American cities, by people working in cooperation with ruling elements of society. Society as a whole has to become responsible and put an end to this disgracefully criminal and irresponsible practice and do its best to help these children become educated and eventually responsible members of society.

It is also important to mention that in some parts of the world, children as young as eight fight enemies they do not know for causes they barely understand. The United Nations has estimated that 200,000 children under the age of fifteen are bearing arms around the world. Some are used in combat. In some American cities children fight gang wars which often end in tragedy.

It is important that children are not trained to kill, and not used to fight wars. The natural aggressiveness of boys must not be exploited and channeled into murder. Competitive sports are an excellent way to channel normal aggressive impulses into well-controlled, responsible, and healthy outlets. The instinct to kill is not innate. It is acquired, passed on by grownups. It is is extremely irresponsible to infect children with this criminal behavior.

In many parts of the world, parents have many children in order to help support the family, even though they are exploited at work and receive extremely low wages. This practice must stop. Women must become more emancipated, more educated, and enabled to make their contribution in many occupational fields. Their dignity and self-respect would increase and they would realize that there are other ways to be socially valuable and useful than merely giving birth to a lot of children, which they do not have the means to educate properly and responsibly. Parents should decide to have children only if they are ready to have them and can afford to support and educate them to become fully developed, responsible adults. Family planning and birth control must become an accepted universal practice and become state supported and financed. The number of children every family should have must also be influenced by the total number of people living on the planet Earth. Since there is a great danger of a population explosion, the number of children every family should have must be minimal.

A planned-for and wanted child is usually loved and has a good chance of developing into a responsible adult. The future of the human race depends on a constantly increasing number of children respected and loved by their parents as well as by society.

## 66. Understanding the Causes of Crime

Crime is caused by psychological, economic, and social factors. Some people manage to develop into decent, responsible people even in the worst slums and crime-ridden neighborhoods. Nevertheless, social and economic conditions as well as the values of society have a great influence on the incidence of crime. Democratic societies that are more egalitarian than the United States (in the sense that the difference between the very rich and the very poor is not as great and where the government has a greater sense of social and moral responsibility and responds to the needs of the less fortunate) have a far lower rate of crime. New Zealand, greatly influenced by Protestant values and strongly Anglo-Saxon, and culturally not too different from the United States, is a far less violent and crime-ridden country than the United States, due to a great extent to its greater responsiveness to the social and economic needs of people and greater sense of social justice.

There is a correlation between the rate of unemployment and crime. The higher the percentage of the unemployed, the more violent a given society will be. Insensitivity and carelessness of society about the plight of the unemployed further contribute to crime. Young unemployed people, desperate and hopeless, often express their frustration through indiscriminate, vindictive acts of violence against innocents. The vandalism of some British soccer fans, quite a few of them unemployed young people, illustrates this point well.

Other factors contributing to a high rate of crime are selfishness, excessive materialistic values, extreme individualism, lack of community spirit, an absence of cooperation and altruism, as well as the glorification of violence, illustrated by its prevalence on most television programs and movies.

Understanding the social causes of crime is only the first step in the right direction. Society must do everything it can to eliminate unemployment, to lessen the immense disparity in income and wealth between the rich and the poor, must create and implement values based on caring, moral and social responsibility, on altruism, feeling of community, generosity, and compassion for the misfortunes of others, values which must become guiding principles of every citizen. Violence should be downplayed as much as possible. Excessive competition and exaggerated accumulation of wealth should be deemphasized and devalued. As a result, people will feel less envy and greater solidarity with others.

It is also important that people lead meaningful, fulfilling, morally, socially, and personally responsible lives, which will considerably reduce, if not eliminate, the need to take drugs, further reducing the incidence of crime. Respect and appreciation for durable marital relations and greater love for and sensitivity to the needs of children are also important and responsible measures to create a society with little or no crime.

Finally, everybody must live increasingly in accordance with values like truth, decency, integrity, and responsibility.

## 67. The Duties toward the Handicapped and their Responsibilities

There are various forms of handicaps—mental, emotional, and physical. One form of mental handicap is retardation, which can vary from mild to severe. Examples of physical handicaps are blindness, hearing impairment, paraplegia, and epilepsy. Depression is an example of an emotional handicap.

By accepting all forms of disabilities and infirmities in others as well as in ourselves we become truly human, as we develop tolerance and acceptance. In their inhumanity and irresponsibility, the Nazis exterminated the mentally handicapped. So did the ancient Spartans, who killed infirm infants. Fortunately, at present there is increasing social legislation in most Western countries to make life easier and more just for the handicapped.

Terry Fox and Steve Fonyo, two young Canadian adults, each had a leg amputated as a result of cancer. In spite of this, they managed to run across half (Fox) and even the whole (Fonyo) of Canada, in order to collect money for cancer research. These men are shining examples of genuine human heroism. Likewise, the Canadian Rick Hansen, who managed to travel through large parts of the planet on a wheelchair, is another example of the transformation of a handicap into a triumph of willpower and great courage.

Handicapped children should be put in regular classes. This is already done in some countries. This helps both the normal as well as the handicapped child become more tolerant toward the other group of children. The nonhandicapped child becomes more compassionate, while the handicapped becomes socially better integrated and motivated to develop his or her potentials. By accepting other people's handicaps as well as our own we learn to accept our limitations and to use a handicap as a challenge, which motivates us to increase our effort to use all other potentials to the maximum, as well as appreciate all the blessings God has bestowed on us.

Many a handicapped person tries harder and uses his or her willpower to compensate for weaknesses and disabilities. A blind person, for example, will compensate, counterbalance, and offset the handicap by developing the senses of hearing and touch to the maximum. The ancient Greek orator Demosthenes was a stutterer, yet overcame his handicap through overcompensation, developing into an excellent orator. In some instances, an accident resulting in loss of mobility that obliges a person to use a wheelchair, can stimulate and challenge the victim to take university courses and to become a successful professional.

It is the duty of every responsible government to help the handicapped to lead normal lives. Buildings, apartments, and highways must be changed to accommodate the physically handicapped and all kinds of social services created to help people with various forms of handicaps.

It is the responsibility of society to hep the handicapped person as well as his or her duty to lead responsible lives in spite of handicaps.

## 68. The Duties toward Senior Citizens and their Responsibilities

The life span in the developed world and even in the developing countries has increased considerably within the second half of the twentieth century. In 1992, the life expectancy in industrialized countries was on average 75 years. As increasing numbers of people live until old and even advanced old age, it becomes important that they learn to age both successfully and responsibly, and continue to develop their potentials and contribute to a better society and world.

Successful and responsible aging means to remain relatively healthy, which involves eating a healthy diet, exercising regularly, and having responsible humanitarian values and an optimistic, realistically idealistic outlook. It further signifies remaining socially useful through meaningful, rewarding work (whether paid or voluntary), maintaining an interest in daily events, taking courses, engaging in enriching recreational activities, pursuing hobbies, traveling to near as well as foreign places. It also means strengthening relationships with one's spouse, family members, and friends, and continuing to develop one's personality, especially those parts that one could not develop during the years of young adulthood and middle age, when the main duties and obligations were to work, get married, and support oneself and a family. Carl Jung, the noted Swiss psychologist and psychiatrist, sees the task of old age as individuation, which means becoming whole by synthesizing various disparate conscious and unconscious personality components and integrating them into a harmonious whole. Men have a chance to develop their sensitivity, their feeling side, which society does not emphasize too strongly in young and middle-aged men, while women can and should further develop their intellectual capacities as well as their assertiveness. Psychological and moral integrity are also goals which elderly people, just as any responsible person of any age, must pursue vigorously. They should also further develop their spirituality. Research has indicated that prayer is health-furthering and prolongs life.

The increasing number of senior citizens in industrialized countries who are relatively prosperous and in relative good health owe it to the world, to society, to God, and to themselves to use their talents and life experience to continue to remain socially useful, and to work to better the world. Freed of the responsibility of making a living—with all the constraints this involves—senior citizens have a golden opportunity to improve the lives of others through altruistic activities. Retired teachers could and should counsel and teach the school dropout or learning-handicapped or socially-handicapped young person. Retired doctors should continue to use their precious talents and skills to help and cure patients who have limited access to good medical services. Counselors, specialized in various fields of helping people with problems, whether personal, vocational, legal, financial, or other difficulties, should continue to give their services, on a voluntary basis if possible. Businessmen should use their experience to advise young people how to start their own businesses.

Retired craftsmen could use their skills to help the less affluent to repair, maintain, and renovate their dwellings.

In Canada there is an organization called the "Canadian Executive Service Organization," a non-profit Montreal corporation which provides volunteer consultants to developing countries. The average age of the volunteers is 60. There are also retired executives who teach East European managers market skills on a voluntary basis. Jewish organizations send elderly Jewish volunteers to Israel for a few weeks to help make a contribution to building the country.

Senior citizens have an important role to play to the younger generation. Elderly people living responsibly motivate younger people not only to look upon getting older without fear, but also to realize that old age can and must be a period of continuing growth, of community involvement, creativity, and social usefulness.

For many people, old age is also a time when they develop a greater degree of wisdom, especially the depth of judgment and insight and also the capacity to know which values and issues are of paramount importance. And this in spite of inevitable physiological and some mental decline, especially in the area of the speed of thinking and the retrieving of information.

Responsible aging also means continuing to live in the present, planning for the future, and benefitting from past experiences. It is crucial that the concern of elderly people for the future—considering that they don't have a great many years left to live—increasingly includes society, the community, and mankind, and that each in his or her way makes a contribution to improving the world and human condition.

In February 1988, Time Magazine devoted most of one issue to the phenomenon of the graying of America—namely that Americans are living longer and are enjoying it more. In one of the articles it was mentioned that since governments have less and less money available to deal with the many social problems troubling society, a few enlightened leaders are starting to use the experience and talents of the active, youngish senior citizens to teach and guide the young. There are, however, a lot of obstacles to this highly responsible and imaginative approach. Some of these barriers are:

1) Wrong values of society, which marginalizes the elderly and casts them aside, using the hypocritical excuse and pretext that elderly people who can afford it should lead the good life of leisure, pleasure, sports, and travel, forgetting that it is highly irresponsible socially, economically, psychologically, and morally to waste the immense talents and experience of many senior citizens. To be socially useful is a basic

human need of every responsible adult of any age. It is also wrong to believe that continuing to use the skills and experience of the elderly takes away jobs from the young. There is so much human misery, family disunity, drug addiction, violence, dropouts from school, abandonment, and abuse of children that even if every senior citizen would continue to be active in helping to alleviate some of the described ills, no job would be taken away from younger workers.

2) Lack of purposeful, responsible living by many senior citizens, who sincerely but wrongly believe that after a life of hard work they deserve to live exclusively a life of leisure, pleasure, and fun, ignoring the highly responsible (and possibly repressed) needs to live purposefully and usefully.

3) Lack of psychological guidance services for senior citizens and the mistaken belief that guidance and counseling services are only for students and adults planning or changing careers. The increasing number of senior citizens studying in colleges and universities and of those who start new careers, as well as the needs of society described above, prove the importance of career counseling for senior citizens. I have helped quite a few elderly people continue to lead responsible, productive, useful social lives either as paid employees or as voluntary workers.

Some elderly people could and do continue to work on a full- or part-time basis in the same field in which they worked for the greater part of their lives. Others do or could work either in a connected field or open their own business. The important thing is that the type of work seniors do corresponds to their aptitudes, talents, interests, and experience. A retired bank manager would in all likelihood find it boring to do voluntary work delivering meals on wheels to sick or very frail elderly people. He or she might find it more fulfilling to advise young people how to obtain financial loans to start a business or how to invest in order to live in financial security in old age. A retired driving instructor could teach high school students how to drive safely.

It is also important to understand that some people are wrong to believe that voluntary work is not real work. Voluntary work—if it is socially valuable and useful, and if it also suits the psychological profile and needs of the volunteer—is in many instances more fulfilling and at least as useful as paid work. According to research, doing altruistic, voluntary work is beneficial to psychological and physical health and prolongs life.

As the birth rate declines in the Western world, and as people live longer (which results in a smaller number of working people supporting a growing number of seniors, as well as a shortage of qualified, experienced workers), many companies will be forced to ask their employees to work beyond the age of 65. A few companies have already started to do so and the trend will continue.

It is essential that governments all over the world make it possible for all elderly people to live in modest financial security, in dignity, and to receive quality medical services. It is equally important that all societies increasingly use the talents and experience of the elderly and that senior citizens develop the personal, social, and moral responsibility to use their skills and experience to improve the world.

It is also the responsibility of governments and of society to respect and value old age and to prevent any form of abuse of and disrespect for the elderly through laws and education.

## 69. Living in Moderate Prosperity

It is very important that people are materially neither too rich nor too poor. If too poor, people do not have the necessary means to eat a healthy diet, to live in adequately decent dwellings, to dress properly and appropriately, as well as to satisfy in a responsible manner their educational, cultural, and recreational needs and to keep healthy and in shape. On the other hand, if too wealthy, people might overvalue material wealth at the expense of spiritual, social, and moral values.

The widespread existence of poverty, unemployment, hunger, illiteracy, economic and social underdevelopment, the fact that energy resources are limited on a worldwide basis, and, above all, the increased desire of countries and societies in the third world for social justice and an improved standard of living, make it more and more imperative to aim to attain moderate prosperity for everyone.

In order to implement and make moderate prosperity for all a valuable and desirable objective, especially in the industrialized Western world, it will become essential that the belief in continued economic growth and in continuously increasing the level of consumption be discarded. The ancient wisdom that excess in everything is harmful and that the greatest virtue lies in moderation must also be introduced in the areas of industrial production, consumption, and ownership of wealth. Besides being socially and morally responsible, moderation is also realistic as it takes into account the fact that natural resources are not unlimited.

Accumulation of large and excessive private wealth should be increasingly discouraged, and eliminating poverty must become one of the main responsibilities of governments, society, and individuals. Moderate prosperity for all should and must become a priority for all governments.

It is neither virtuous to be too poor, nor to be too rich. While the poor cannot make ends meet and have a lot of material worries and problems, the rich provoke a lot of envy and are afflicted and plagued (even though there are many exceptions) by selfishness and by a certain degree of social and moral insensitivity and even irresponsibility. Besides, it is morally irresponsible to be too rich in a world where there is so much poverty. Former Governor Michael Dukakis of Massachusetts, presidential candidate in 1988, is an excellent example of moderate and responsible living. In 1987, he drove a five-year-old Dodge, lived in a house he bought in the early 1970s for $25,000., and bought clothes at bargain stores. Stephen Sanders, a Canadian businessman, donated the greatest part of his fortune of $110 million to charity to benefit the third world. He left for himself and his wife only an amount of $40,000 annually, which enables him and his wife to live comfortably.

Innate differences in aptitudes and talents, the difference in the degree and quality of contribution to society, and the length of time needed to complete the academic and professional studies that enable one to work in one's chosen field mean that there have to be differences in income. These differences, however, should not be too excessive.

Surviving individually and collectively in the decades and centuries to come will increasingly require an awareness of our worldwide responsibility to humankind to enable people everywhere on earth to live in moderate prosperity.

## 70. Understanding the Duties of a Responsible Society

A responsible society combines the efficiency of capitalism to produce the necessary consumer goods with the ideals of social democracy to create a moderately egalitarian society, where everybody receives free quality medical services and is insured against accidents and invalidism. Furthermore, in a responsible society there is no unemployment, and everyone receives an education in accordance with his or her level of intelligence, aptitudes, and talents. A responsible society does not allow people to live at the poverty level and endeavors to make it possible for them to live in moderate comfort or better. It also makes it possible for all elderly citizens to receive adequate pensions, enabling them to live in moderate comfort until the end of their lives.

A responsible society also ensures harmonious social relations between the various social classes and ethnic, religious, and political groups. In such a society social and community agencies cooperate with the government to find solutions to the various social ills of society such as delinquency, battered women, conjugal violence, abandoned and neglected children, excessive divorce, truancy, drug addiction and alcoholism, loneliness, homelessness, mental and emotional sickness, and other social ills.

In a responsible society there is cooperation between unions and owners of businesses and enterprises; any conflictual situation is submitted to binding arbitration in order to avoid disruptive strikes.

A responsible society is based on a strong, responsible, generous, caring, and effective government as well as on a high degree of private initiative and individual social commitment and personal, social, and moral responsibility.

A responsible society encourages people to find responsible meaning in their lives and prevents and fights all forms of prejudice such as racism, sexism, ageism, is tolerant of differences, and promotes social justice. It also fosters courage, compassion, altruism, dedication, personal, social, and moral responsibility, and humanitarianism. A responsible society helps the underprivileged and the underdog.

Finally, a responsible society protects the environment and encourages people to become world citizens in outlook. It promotes international cooperation and helps poorer countries to become industrialized and moderately prosperous in a way that does not destroy the environment. A responsible society also creates conditions leading to world peace and advances and promotes the cause of a world government ruling over the yet to be created "United States of the World."

### 71. Valuing Marriage and the Family

It is quite tragic to see increasing numbers of marriages fail and end in divorce. In previous centuries, society made it impossible for married couples who did not get along to divorce, even though some of them lived in a living hell. There is a tendency among large segments of society today, including many marriage counselors, to recommend divorce at the slightest conjugal difficulty. Spouses who should remain together are advised to separate, which is socially and morally irresponsible.

The essential important priority and main value of both marital partners must be a commitment to stay together for life. It is sad to see so many marriages today end in divorce after twenty, thirty, or forty years. While growing older can be painful, there is nevertheless tremendous meaning in living and growing old together for the rest of one's life with one's marital partner. It is also beautiful and morally full of integrity.

A successful marriage is one in which both partners love, appreciate, and respect each other and foster the expression of their unique personalities, while becoming increasingly interdependent. This interdependence has to go hand in hand with the acceptance of some degree of personal autonomy. A happy marriage is one where both partners cooperate in raising children and doing the routine household duties, as well as helping each other to develop their individual aptitudes and talents and use them in remunerative or voluntary work. And, of course, a happy marriage is one in which partners love, trust, and respect each other.

Traditionally, men valued power and competitiveness and developed their logical, analytical, and synthetic faculties almost exclusively, whereas women were encouraged to develop their feelings, sensitivity, and the quality of caring for others. To some extent this is true even today, even though as a result of the social changes of the second part of the twentieth century, including the feminist revolution, much has changed for the better. Even though feminists advocated mainly the emancipation of women in terms of better career opportunities, paradoxically their efforts could become immensely valuable to improve the quality of marriages, if both men and women become more complete. In other words, besides the intelligence of the head, men should and must also develop the intelligence of the heart, namely sensitivity, generosity, idealism and altruism, while women have to develop the intelligence of the heart and also the intelligence of the head as well as their assertiveness. Men must glorify power and competitiveness less and value cooperation, sharing, and nurturing more. This will lead to happier and more successful marriages.

A successful marriage must also deal responsibly with the bringing up of children. A mother should stay at home with a baby for at least the first two to three years, as this is absolutely essential for the healthy emotional and psychological development of the child. Society already recognizes the importance of this: In some industrialized counties a maternity leave allowance is paid for a certain period of time. In instances where the father is the sole parent of the child, or where the mother is sick, society should and must pay the father a parental leave allowance. It is very important for the balanced emotional and psychological development of the child as well as for the happiness of the marriage and of the family relations that the father take an active interest in the education of his children.

Considering the danger of a global population explosion and the burden which an excessive growth of population places on the environment and on the limited energy resources of the world, it is essential that families on a worldwide basis are not too large. China has already imposed a maximum of one child per family. Reducing the number of children per family would result in parents and society being able to appreciate and love children more, abuse them less, and ensure that they are brought up and educated in a socially and morally more responsible manner.

The important thing to understand is that to live responsibly, one should also be a responsibly successful spouse and parent. In order to succeed in both marriage and family life, one must first value them highly, understand what it takes to succeed in them, and develop the necessary psychological qualities to bring this success about. Furthermore, one must expect success, as positive expectation turns into a self-fulfilling prophecy. A lifelong commitment to one's marital partner also contributes to a responsibly successful and happy marriage.

On top of the mutual affection developed between the spouses, there must also be a duty to love the partner by principle. This strengthens the marital bond and ensures that the marriage endures and lasts in spite of difficulties. Staying married for life is not only very meaningful for both spouses, it is also very important for the emotional, spiritual, and moral wellbeing of the children. It also sets an example of social and moral responsibility and of continuity and advances the wellbeing of society as a whole.

## 72. Supporting Responsible Feminism

Responsible feminism stands for everything decent and socially just to advance the cause of equal rights for women in many areas, as well as to promote their full psychological, social, and spiritual emancipation. It fights for equal pay for equal work, for full legal rights to own property, for the right to compete on an equal basis with men to occupy every available political and managerial office and position, and equal access to all levels of education. Responsible feminism advocates the full participation of women in the so-called nontraditional professional and occupational areas traditionally dominated by men—medicine, law, engineering, architecture, the military, the police, public service, as well as the technical fields and top managerial positions. The only exception should be in the fighting, combat units of the armed forces. Since in the case of war these combat units might have to kill the enemy, this unhappy and dehumanizing task should not be done by women. It neither contributes to responsible equality between the sexes, nor does it increase human dignity.

Responsible feminism promotes the development of the whole personality. It encourages the development of the nurturing, helping, caring side of the personality as well as the full evolution of intellectual capacities and fosters assertiveness. Responsible feminism advocates the success and happiness of women in their careers as well as in their marital and family relations. It requires great responsibility, energy, maturity, self-understanding, and strength to succeed in both areas. On the one hand, some women working in such fields as medicine, engineering, and law, suffer from unconscious guilt feelings and an unconscious wish to fail, while on the other hand, some women, once they have become successful in these areas and in top management, repress their emotional need for a happy, loving marital relationship. Responsible feminism must encourage responsible human success and help women to develop the courage and wisdom to understand themselves as well as the determination to succeed in both areas—their careers and their marital and family relations.

Responsible feminism opposes discrimination against women in all areas of life, whether in the form of sexism at work or conjugal abuse and violence at home. This fight for increased dignity and respect for women must be fought globally. It must condemn and prevent the mutilation of girls' genital organs in some parts of Africa, the murder of wives by jealous husbands in some parts of the world, the abandonment of wives and making life difficult and dangerous for wives who didn't bring a sufficiently high dowry into marriage in India. Responsible feminism must fight the preference for male children in some parts of the world, of which the sex testing in India, which can spell death for unwanted female fetuses is but one horrible example. In some parts of the world, sex discrimination often means death. Worldwide research suggests the number of missing females may surpass 100 million. The tens of millions of missing include females who are aborted or killed at birth or who die because they are given less food than males, or because family members view a daughter with diarrhea as a nuisance but a son with diarrhea as a medical crisis requiring a doctor. If a boy gets sick the parents may send him to the hospital at once, but if a girl gets sick the parents may wait and see how she is the next day.

Responsible feminism fights against the rape and sexual abuse of women, condoned by some countries and governments. According to Amnesty International, soldiers and police in some states of the world regularly use rape and sexual abuse to intimidate women. Some governments turn a blind eye to these crimes, refusing to recognize rape as a serious human rights violation. The mass rape of women in Bosnia is a terrible example of criminal behavior.

Responsible feminism must also fight against polygamy, prostitution, and the selling of pornography, which is a form of human degradation and violence directed against feelings and emotions.

It is the obligation of men to responsibly help women to realize the objectives described above. The realization of the goals of responsible feminism also helps men to live happier and more responsible lives. Both men and women must develop fully the intelligence of their heads as well as of their hearts, must assert themselves responsibly, must share power responsibly, and must contribute fully and equally to create a better and more responsible world.

A beautiful example of responsible feminism, which at its best is synonymous with responsible social justice, is "employment equity." The phrase, coined by Rosalie Abella, a judge of the Ontario Court of Appeal, refers to a practice that retains merit as the main basis for hiring women or other underrepresented groups for any available job, when they are judged to be as qualified as other applicants. It means that a tie game should result in a win for the underdog, provided the underdog is as qualified as a member of a more privileged group.

It is the duty of responsible feminists to educate people all over the world to regard women's rights as human rights. Global human cooperation and friendship can be promoted if the words human brotherhood are expanded to become human brotherhood and sisterhood. In the final analysis, it is the obligation of all people of personal and moral decency and integrity in the world to support responsible feminism. The wellbeing of countless people of both sexes depends on its accomplishments and triumphs.

## 73. Being Bilingual, Preferably even Multilingual

A language is not merely a collection of words but also a vehicle and preserver of a people's culture, history, and collective world view.

Some people believe that language, even more so than politics, race, religion, or wealth, divides the human race into solitudes. As examples, they cite countries with more than one language like Belgium, India, or Canada, that are troubled by linguistic problems and quarrels .While this is to some extent true, the fact also remains that in Northern Ireland, Catholics and Protestants who speak the same language are bitter enemies.

In spite of some problems caused in some parts of the world by bilingualism or multilingualism there is nevertheless a great need for people all over the world to learn an additional language, preferably the universal language, in addition to their national language. The attempt to make Esperanto a universal language has failed, since it was an artificial linguistic construction. In our time, English has emerged as the universal language of commerce, industry, science, research, technology, and diplomacy. At the same time, however, great efforts should also be made to encourage the cultivation, preservation, and use of as many national and regional languages as possible, as this is absolutely necessary for the collective pride, dignity, continuity, integrity, and traditions of people all over the world.

It is necessary that children learn their national or regional language as well as the universal language and if possible one or more additional languages. This will help them not only to communicate with more people of different cultures than unilinguals do, but also would enable them to develop a more international, cosmopolitan outlook and to feel more like citizens of the world. Being bilingual and multilingual also helps people to develop their personality in a more complete way. For instance, a certain language that reflects an action-directed culture of a given nation, will contain more words expressing action, whereas another language might include more words concerning emotions and subtle nuances of feelings. Research has revealed that English-speaking children who started to learn French intensively from kindergarten on have improved their intelligence by the time they reached the third elementary grade. While acquiring a good working knowledge of French, they also improved their command of English and had a better mastery of the language than unilingual English children at the same level of education. Another remarkable benefit gained by bilingual children was their increased capacity to express their own ideas. They also had fewer prejudices than unilingual children, and were also more original and creative.

In the global village of today and increasingly in the future, there is and will be a growing need for as many people as possible to speak their national or regional language as well as the world's universal language and preferably an additional one or two national languages. The learning of a second, third, or fourth language should start as early as possible in life, as young children have a great facility for learning foreign languages.

### 74. Eliminating Hunger and Malnutrition

Every day 40,000 children around the world die from hunger-related causes. Every year it is estimated that millions of human beings die from the effects of malnutrition. Relatively few of these deaths are related to famine. Many occur in countries that produce plenty of food, even export it. According to the United Nations Food and Agricultural Organization (FAO), the world produces more than enough food to meet the nutritional needs of everyone on the planet, yet FAO estimates that more than 780 million people are chronically undernourished.

On December 5, 1992, ministers from 16 countries met in Rome to try to agree on a plan of action for the eradication of hunger and malnutrition in the world. The gathering was organized by FAO and by the World Health Organization (WHO). The international conference acknowledged that poverty, not lack of food, is the root cause of hunger and malnutrition. Another cause of hunger is when food sent by international aid efforts is stolen by armed bandits and as a result cannot reach those who need it. This was the case in 1992 in Somalia, and it caused the deaths of hundreds of thousands of people.

In many countries, including industrialized countries like the United States and Canada, people with little money can't afford to buy the food they need. Even when food is available, malnutrition can still be present to a wide extent. In many cases, the quality and variety of food is at issue, rather than the quantity. Quite often, the poorer people are, the more demoralized they are, and often spend more on tobacco, alcohol, sweets, and junk food, neglecting a balanced diet consisting of foods containing protein, carbohydrates, fibers, and a lot of fruits and vegetables. In some industrialized countries, especially the United States and Canada, many children of poor families, especially those where the breadwinners are either unemployed or on social welfare, go to school hungry and consequently don't have the energy to pay attention at school or to study efficiently. It is the responsibility of all levels of government to correct this scandalous situation as soon as possible. Besides, school problems, hunger and undernutrition weaken the immune system, causing all kinds of sicknesses.

Hunger can be related to a number of factors including natural disasters, war, disease, and seasonal food shortages, yet whether it is rural Bangladesh or the slum areas of New York, the underlying cause of hunger is almost universally the same—poverty.

Military spending by third world governments ($35 billion in 1988) saps treasuries of money that could be used to buy food. The resulting influx of arms fuels conflicts that hinder food production, destroy infrastructures, and make distribution of emergency food aid dangerous, and sometimes even impossible.

Ensuring that all people at all times have physical and economic access to enough food demands changes in the priority of international finance, commerce, and developmental assistance. The World Food Day Association of Canada set the goal of putting food security on the Canadian agenda. According to Gary Bellamy, communications director for the World Food Day Association, this association informs Canadians about the causes of hunger in Canada and around the world. By doing this it awakens people's personal, social, and moral responsibility to build food security.

It is crucial that governments make commitments to regard people and nutritional wellbeing as the first priority. Hunger and malnutrition must be considered unacceptable in a world that has the resources to end these human catastrophes. A global planification action must be implemented by governments and developmental agencies to provide people with sufficient supplies of adequate nutritional foods.

Rich as well as poor countries must create political, social, and economic conditions to create full employment, enabling people to live in moderate prosperity. People all over the world must be educated to develop their sense of personal responsibility to eat nutritionally adequate and healthy foods, as well as a balanced diet.

It is very encouraging that at the international meeting in Rome in December 1992, ministers from 160 Western and developing countries pledged themselves to try to reduce starvation and famine, chronic hunger, and undernutrition. It is equally encouraging and a very good omen for the future that the United Nations, under the leadership of the United States, sent military troops to Somalia at the end of 1992 to ensure that the food sent by international relief agencies was not stolen by armed bandits and reached the majority of the starving population.

## 75. Controlling the World's Population Explosion

Uncontrolled population growth is one very important factor disturbing the environmental balance of the planet. It might cause irreversible damage to the earth's capacity to sustain life. If not curbed, there could be between eleven and fourteen billion people on earth by the end of the twenty-first century. The overwhelming majority of this gigantic increase in population will be in the developing third world, which can least afford it.

The classical developmental policy which advocated the industrialization of the third world, and believed that as people became more prosperous, they would have fewer children, is not appropriate. Industrialization takes a long time and requires sacrifices. More and more people around the world want a better life now, without thinking of the future impact on the environment. In view of the population explosion,

159

many developing countries admit that their progress in education, health, and social welfare is not sufficient to improve the situation of all citizens. Family planning and birth control gain ground in third world countries and are increasingly accepted by many leaders and governments as they start to understand that they can hope to attain moderate prosperity, protection of the environment, feed their population, and keep them employed if they dramatically reduce the growth of their population.

Even though in the industrialized North the population growth has been controlled, in Africa and the Middle East the population growth doubles every twenty to twenty-five years. From 1960 to 1990 the population growth of the world declined from 2 percent to 1.7 percent, yet the absolute number of people added each year continues to rise. In 1980 the increase was 75 million, whereas in 1990 it was 90 million. The Chinese solution of only one child per family, which is drastically imposed, achieves good results in curbing the population growth. The best solution is to stabilize the number of people in a country or region of the globe at the present level. The replacement level is 2.2 children per woman. In many developing nations the fertility rate is 4.8 children per family. Many families in India have five children. Unfortunately, family planning in India is not too successful among the poor.

In some Western nations there is a decline in the birth rate per woman, below the replacement level. In view of this, some industrialized countries like France and Japan try to push the birth rate up. The desire to increase the birth rate is understandable; the decrease in the number of births and the fact that people live longer means that there would be fewer young people faced with supporting an increasing number of elderly people. However, rich countries should not increase the birth rate as it sets a bad example to the third world. The most responsible solution for rich countries is to help third world countries use family planning and to let in a greater number of immigrants from the poorer countries.

The ecologist Paul Erlich is one of the chief exponents of the viewpoint that the earth's mineral resources will deplete themselves, owing to a marked increase in population. On the other hand, Julian Simon believes that an increase in population is beneficial, as it leads to a cleaner environment, healthier humanity, and a greater supply of food and raw materials. Simon is partially right. In 1991 there were one billion more people in the world than there were in 1970, and the average person is healthier and in some countries even wealthier. Infant mortality has declined and life expectancy has increased even in many third world countries. Looking back at history one can see that as resources became scarce people found innovative substitutes. Timber shortage in sixteenth-century Britain ushered in the age of coal. Some agricultural experts believe that the third world alone could feed up to ten billion people. It is also true, however, that every 14 seconds one hectar of arable land disappears in the world. It is also important to understand that population density is not necessarily synonymous with economic misery. A good example is Hong Kong, which in spite of one of the highest population densities in the world is quite prosperous.

The responsible thing to do is to synthesize and reconcile the two opposite viewpoints mentioned above concerning the number of people which the earth can support without being destroyed by environmental pollution. We don't know the exact limits, but the death of half of Europe's forests, the deforestation in Brazil, the extremely high level of pollution of Mexico City and of other big cities indicates that the increase of population must become stabilized soon. On the other hand, it is also true that the increased number of people living today compared with 25 years ago provides the world with a greater potential of talent to solve the world's problems.

Enabling girls to complete their education and encouraging them to become technicians, professionals, and executives, and opening employment opportunities for them in these fields is a responsible way to control the population growth. Women who have careers have more self-esteem, are more fulfilled, and tend to have fewer babies than women without careers.

Among the obstacles to family planning and birth control are some fundamentalist religions that keep women in an inferior position. Half of the world's women have no access to family planning. It is not only vitally important that women all over the world have access to family planning and birth control, but also that the motivation to use them increases, and that governments in many parts of the world, including the United States, become favorably inclined toward their use. The social status of women must be improved so that they can decide as equals how many children they want. The World Bank, the International Monetary Fund, and governments from wealthy countries must give loans to third world countries on the condition that the funds are partially allocated for the education of women, for old-age pension plans, and for improved social security. Debt should be reduced if these provisions are assured.

The elderly in many third world countries must receive adequate pensions, which would make them financially less dependent on the support of their children and would contribute significantly to parents having fewer children, thereby reducing population growth.

There is evidence that the population explosion has been contained in Brazil, Mexico, and Colombia. In one generation the fertility rate of Brazil has been cut almost in half. The fertility rate of 5.7 children per woman in 1970 has declined in 1990 to 3.2. To a great extent, this spectacular success can be attributed to the increased use of contraceptives.

Other means to control the excessive growth of the population are abortion and sterilization. Abortion should be used only as a means of last resort. Decisions concerning abortions should be made by both parents as well as by the mother's physician. The factors to be taken into consideration when deciding whether an abortion should take place must be based on consideration for the mother's life as well as her physical, mental, and emotional health, on the moral responsibility to the unborn child, and on the social and moral obligation to control the population explosion. Laws concerning abortion should take into account the three factors mentioned above. Voluntary sterilization, freely accepted by one of the two parents is another means to control the population explosion.

Sex education should become compulsory in all schools, starting in elementary school, and continue until the last year of high school. Children and teenagers, depending on their level of understanding and maturity, should be taught the anatomy and physiology of the sexual organs, reproduction, prevention of venereal sicknesses, and how to avoid teenage pregnancies. Their sense of personal, social, and moral responsibility must be awakened and developed to postpone sexual relations as long as possible, preferably until their early years of adulthood. They must learn to understand their bodies, their feelings and emotions, the other sex, how to handle an intimate relationship, as well as developing empathy and sympathy for others and responsibility for their behavior.

It is important to understand that forcing pregnant women who already have one child to undergo an abortion might be an effective way to control the population explosion, but it is a solution devoid of moral responsibility. Making available means of birth control such as the pill and other contraceptives and voluntary sterilization, as well as educating people concerning their personal, social, and moral responsibility to control the excessive population growth by reducing the number of their children is more decent, respectful, and dignified.

Reducing the explosive growth of the world's population is but one problem endangering the survival of humankind, yet if this task is not accomplished, all the efforts to solve all the other threatening problems are doomed to failure.

### 76. Promoting Responsible Equality

Hand in hand with the emphasis on individual differences in the areas of personality traits, intelligence, physical and mental health, material success, and longevity, there has also been a tendency toward human equality in Western democracies and increasingly in more and more countries of the world.

Considering the differences between people outlined above, the area of equality of opportunity is one place where application of the principle of equality can even out differences and create more social justice. Any responsible society must be based on the principle of equality of opportunity for all its citizens. Every person should and must receive the opportunity to develop his or her potentials in accordance with his or her unique personal characteristics. This must be done through education. The educational system must enable every person to receive the necessary education, including university training, if indicated, to fully develop his or her aptitudes and talents. This already happens more and more in quite a few countries; it must be extended to the whole world,

Equality of opportunity also means equal access to all levels of jobs solely on the basis of merit and competence, excluding any form of discrimination because of religion, race, nationality, sex, or ethnic origin. Affirmative action in the United States has responsibly tried to correct past injustices which prevented access to jobs and entrance to higher education because of race. However, this should be done in such a manner that it not only corrects past racial or national discrimination, but simultaneously takes into account the personal merit and qualification of the individual.

Another area where progress in the interest of equality and social justice has been made is in equal pay to women for equal work. While women in many industrialized countries generally still do not earn an equal salary compared with men doing the same work, they nevertheless earn more than in the past and the gap in earning between the sexes has been reduced.

Progress has also been made in the area of equality before the courts. It is essential that all people, irrespective of sex, wealth, social position, race, religion, nationality, ethnic origin, or age are treated equally by the judicial system.

It is also very important that all countries respect the gifted, talented individual and do not prevent the creative gifts of the talented person from making a contribution to the betterment of the world. In other words, the gifted person must be encouraged and enabled to fully develop his or her superior talents, and not be prevented from doing so by jealousy, envy, or a false interpretation of democracy and equality.

## 77. The Duties of Society Toward the Young and their Responsibilities

There is a high rate of unemployment among young people in many parts of the world, including highly industrialized Western countries. There is also a high suicide rate among teenagers in some Western countries. The reasons for this tragedy are unemployment, parental divorce, drug addiction, racial prejudice, hopelessness concerning the future, and lack of motivation to complete school. In any case, the psychological unhappiness of many young people in the rich West as well as in third world countries is a big tragedy and everything must be done to bring hope to the young and create a brighter future for them.

Many young people, including university students, are less interested today in addressing some of the major critical, social, economic, and political issues, such as the global threat of the destruction of the environment, the poverty of the third world, the increasing materialism and violence in industrialized countries, and the threat of overpopulation, than they were in the 1960s and 1970s. The increasing complexity of modern technology and greater length of required studies, as well as the difficulty of finding jobs, are to some extent responsible for the lack of involvement of many young people with responsible and important social, humanitarian, economic, environmental, and political causes. There is also the feeling of powerlessness—that problems are too big and complex, and that individual efforts to improve the world don't matter. These feelings are comprehensible, but they are not justified, as every effort to better the world, no matter how small, if based on faith, hope, and a practical idealistic vision of a better world can make a difference and bring about a positive, responsible change in people's outlook and motivate them to take action, implement, and accomplish the desired change. The popular saying from the 1980s, "Think globally and act locally," has a lot of validity.

In spite of the pessimism and hopelessness of many young people described above, there are also some hopeful and positive changes as well. Graduate students in commerce at a leading American university decided in 1990 to dedicate one year of their lives to teaching the financial and marketing techniques of a free enterprise economy to executives and managers in Poland, on a voluntary basis. The new missionaries of the 1990s turn out to be commerce graduates, who only a few years ago were considered overly selfish and arch conservatives. The idealism of the Peace Corps movement, trying to help the third world, seems to become, at least partially, channeled into voluntarily helping the East Europeans become financially, economically, and industrially efficient.

It would be very responsible and efficient, in order to solve the problem of the high degree of unemployment among the young, to create a civil youth corps, which every unemployed young person would have to join for a duration of two to three years and be paid to do valuable community work like cleaning the environment, including rivers and roads, helping frail seniors, teaching illiterates to learn to read and write, preventing juvenile delinquency and drug addiction, and rehabilitating and reeducating juvenile delinquents and drug addicts. They should also be used to help the homeless. Those who did not complete their education should and must be counseled and motivated to continue their studies. The government should not only pay the young for their community work, but should also make arrangements with companies and public service institutions to provide permanent employment for them, once the two to three years of community work have been completed. Serving for a few years in a youth corps would bring about a feeling of empowerment in the young, especially when they realize that they can wield some power to improve society, and that the government helps them to do this.

Helping, motivating, and even compelling teenagers to complete high school would be a good solution to stop the disquieting phenomenon of the high percentage of North American teenagers who drop out of school. In some parts of North America the dropout rate is over 30 percent. In Quebec, it is over 40 percent. Some of the factors responsible for this tragedy are the high rate of parental divorce with its demoralizing effect on children, watching too much television, which weakens the capacity to concentrate and reduces the time left for reading good books, taking drugs, being too tired, or lacking sufficient energy to study because of working too much at a paid job, or being undernourished because of poverty. There is also the reality of many burned-out, underpaid, and overworked teachers, who lack the necessary respect, appreciation, and support from the rest of the community to be able to take up the challenge responsibly, courageously, and efficiently to help teenagers graduate successfully from high school. Overcrowded, depersonalized schools that permit little personal contact between teachers and students are also partially responsible for the lack of motivation on the part of many students to complete high school. To remedy this catastrophic situation, which will deprive the labor market of a sufficient number of workers capable of reading and writing well and having the necessary skills in mathematics to handle the increased level of sophisticated technological innovations, it is essential that parents, students, teachers, educational administrators, governments, and society as a whole cooperate to enable every intelligent student to finish at least high school. A vigorous effort must be made by parents and teachers to discourage too much television watching as well as the taking of drugs. Developing potentials through studying must become a universally respected and accepted value. Teachers must become highly respected and valued members of society.

The young must also learn to become responsible by assuming the duty of fully developing their potential. Through help and assistance from teachers and guidance counselors, they must wisely and responsibly choose a trade or profession in accordance with personal interests, talents, and personality. This choice of a trade or profession should occur only toward the end of high school or even later, when the student has acquired a certain amount of self-understanding and when he or she is to some extent familiar with the many vocational possibilities and the reality of the labor market. Employers and representatives of various trades and professions should come to the school, talk to students about the requirements and opportunities of their speciality, and students should have the possibility of visiting the various craftsmen and professionals at their places of work. Teenagers must learn to cooperate with peers, yet also to resist peer pressure, if it leads to taking drugs, committing crimes, dropping out of school, or engaging in irresponsible, premature sexual relations, which could lead to sexually transmitted diseases and to teenage pregnancies.

It is of the utmost importance that the unnecessary excessive violence dominating so much of American life come to an end. The entertainment media—movies, television programs, and popular music programs—must cease to produce films and shows where violence becomes an end itself used to cater to the lowest instincts of people in order to increase the number of viewers and make more money. Unjustified, excessive violence must be considered a poison to the mind, the human soul, and personality. Those who view or listen to unjustified, excessive violence must be warned of the detrimental effect of violence on their health and personality. Parents and teachers must inform children and adolescents that violent programs have a bad effect on their personalities and their morale.

It is also very important that educators rediscover the great value of teaching history to children and young people. Children, adolescents, and young adults must understand, value, and appreciate what happened in the past, both in their own country and all over the world. Young people must be helped to see themselves as a bridge between the past and the future, an indispensable link in the onward march of humankind to transform the world into a place of faith in God, of social justice, of personal and moral responsibility, and, above all, of universal peace and worldwide human solidarity.

It is also important to understand that the danger of a global nuclear holocaust (even though the danger is less threatening since the end of the cold war), and the devastation of the environment in many parts of the world make young people feel frightened and angry. It is understandable that they blame their elders and all authority in general for the mess the world is in. There is lack of respect and trust in authority. There is also a tendency on the part of many young people to imitate quite a few members of the older generation in their search for immediate gratification, in living only for the moment, and not planning for the future. It is essential that a new relationship of mutual respect and understanding be created between the young and the older generation, a rapport based on cooperation and the insight that the magnitude of the task to improve the world requires responsible vision and idealism, faith, experience, and efficiency. The know-how of the older generation must join hands with the idealism of the young in a relationship of partnership and solidarity to plan and find long-range solutions to the many problems confronting humankind. With God's help the endeavor will be successful.

Young people can make a contribution to a better world by writing to legislators, to cabinet ministers in their own country, and to various influential world leaders about social, economic, or political problems that bother or upset them and suggest possible solutions to deal with these problems. It is also important that young people discuss current local, national, and international events among themselves, with their parents, their teachers, and with politicians. Municipal politicians, as well as legislators and cabinet ministers, should meet periodically, more more often than they now do, with as many young people as possible to discuss current events with them, asking for their opinions as well as suggestions. By doing this, politicians would help the young to better understand the problems facing the world. The young would also feel a bit more empowered, especially when they realize that their opinions are valued. The young would also have more respect and esteem for politicians and would also develop the hope that something can be done to improve the world and the human condition. It would also help politicians to develop more idealism, integrity, and more personal, social, and moral responsibility.

## 78. Understanding that Cooperation Is Essential for Survival

We become highly motivated to perform a duty or task when we cooperate with others, since we know that they are dependent on us and we are responsible to them for the success of the common effort and endeavor. On the other hand, quite often the only interest others have in our performance in a competitive venture is to see us fail.

Cooperation means to do well, not better than others. Cooperation is enjoyable and satisfying, and contributes to personal happiness.

Harmony between conflicting groups can be achieved by a cooperative effort of finding solutions to problems and by accepting superordinate goals. As common solutions to problems are found and superordinate goals are accepted, the hostility between the groups decreases and even ceases, and friendliness increases. This has immense value to help humankind to come to grips with and to solve the many ethnic, religious, economic, and national conflicts between antagonistic groups and states, and to create harmony and peace. The superordinate goal transcending feuding and fighting should and must be the common objective to survive and to live in harmony.

A sublime example of cooperation is the relationship of parents with children, more specifically of the mother with an infant. The interaction based on love and satisfaction of needs ensures not only the baby's survival, but also that it develops into a healthy, happy child, and eventually into a successful, well-adjusted adult.

Many people have wrong values and beliefs. They believe that a non-competitive society would be mediocre and non-productive. These people fail to realize that in a highly competitive society one person's success often leads to another person's failure, which creates a lot of unhappiness, hostility, wasted human resources, and even lowered productivity. Excessive competition among scientists does not improve achievement. Competition also leads to poor performance among airline pilots. Many studies show that in the field of education, cooperation promotes higher achievement than competition. The success of many a productive effort depends on an efficient cooperative sharing of resources; this sharing does not take place when people work against each other. Cooperation also takes advantage of all the skills existing in a group and creates a spirit of positive, responsible interdependence in the group. It is comparable to a jigsaw puzzle, where every piece is indispensable to the total picture. Every person in a cooperative group is needed and is highly important. Cooperation can also bind various competitive groups together, especially when the superordinate, supreme goal is in the common interest of all groups. In this case, competition becomes integrated with cooperation and becomes subordinated to the common wellbeing of all. Cooperation can help humankind achieve a world government in the form of the United States of the World, where every nation, ethnic or religious group, and state in the world becomes indispensable to the world federation.

### 79. Understanding the Duties of the Entertainment, Advertising, and Information Media

Radio, television, the computer, and the telephone have transformed the planet into a global village in terms of communication. Television greatly influenced the successful outcome of the 1989 revolution in Rumania against the dictator Ceausescu. Awareness of the famine in Ethiopia created indignation and compassion in countless people around the world and led to material help being sent to the afflicted people. The horrors of war and of other tragedies are seen as they happen by millions of people in their homes. Television also plays an important educational role informing people of scientific and technological improvements and breakthroughs, of the deterioration of the environment in various places of the world, as well as of the geography of distant lands and the customs and cultures of their people.

Commercial publicity has a positive value by enabling the producer to inform the public about the merits of a given program. It also helps by encouraging the public to buy the product to protect and to create jobs. However, publicity must not be used to discredit the products of competitors. It should also refrain from using superlatives, like sublime, or words such as paradise to extol the merits of consumer products, as this tends to devalue the human spirit by attaching excessive importance to materialistic, pleasure-seeking pursuits. It is also socially and morally irresponsible to glamorize the sales of cigarettes through alluring advertisements, as the destructive effect of smoking on health is well known.

The excessive violence portrayed on television and in movies has a devastating effect on people's feelings of solidarity with their fellow human beings and on their concern for others and compassion for people in distress. It has a very bad effect on children, who are very suggestible. It influences not only their feelings and moods, but also their world view, and leads them to perceive the world as hostile and dangerous. Even if the behavior of a child is greatly influenced by his or her parents, watching violence on television nevertheless produces aggressive thoughts, feelings, and behavior toward others. The excessive use of violence in cartoons is equally socially and morally irresponsible.

169

Many of today's films imply that as long as the good guys triumph, the end, killing, is perfectly acceptable behavior. This means that the end justifies the means, which is morally irresponsible. Another example of irresponsible commercialism is the many horror films being produced in which there is gloating over sadistic acts. These films pander to people's most evil and psychologically sick tendencies. Films with pornographic content also do a lot of harm to viewers. They degrade women and rob intimate human relationships of warmth, tenderness, and sensitivity.

Sensationalism, widespread in newspaper reports and articles, is to some extent responsible for the fact that catastrophes or tragedies receive far more coverage than happy, positive events. This, too, is deplorable.

It is the personal, social, and moral responsibility of all people in the communication and information fields to provide news and other information which are objective, truthful, and unbiased. It is the duty of society as a whole to fight for programs free of pornography and of excessive, unnecessary violence, sadism, and killing.

The ultimate goal of film producers and of all mass media executives should and must be to make a contribution to a peaceful, moderately prosperous, responsible world and to realize that the nature and quality of their productions have an important role to play in achieving this objective.

The entertainment industry has proven that it is capable of social and moral responsibility. In the 1960s and 1970s, films like *Easy Rider* and *M\*A\*S\*H* glamorized the use of drugs, whereas in the late 1980s and 1990s the movie industry portrays the use of drugs as irresponsible, foolish, and dangerous. In a similar way, the entertainment industry should and must portray criminal, destructive violence as socially, morally, and personally irresponsible behavior, which has devastating psychological and social effects on the viewing public and on society as a whole.

## 80. Moderating the Excessive Consumption of Goods

A Worldwatch Institute study released in July 1992 concludes that the richest fifth of the world is ruining the planet by consuming too much and by producing ozone-depleting chemicals, greenhouse gases, and acid rain. The study further revealed that excessive consumption causes more environmental harm than any other cause with the exception of the excessive and rapid growth of the population.

The study by the Worldwatch Institute, a privately funded non-profit organization that studies social issues, recommends a reduction of advertising and that the richest countries give their workers and managers longer vacations rather than higher wages. Governments must stop giving subsidies to environmentally harmful industries. The study further found that the United States has more shopping centers than high schools. It states that the excessive consumer lifestyle doesn't help people feel better about their lives. Basing this conclusion on sociological research, the study found that the number of Americans claiming to be very happy has remained at the same one-third level since 1957, although personal consumption has doubled since then. Furthermore, in spite of the much greater use of many modern appliances—which were supposed to save a lot of time—many people end up saving the gained time watching television.

It is very important that society as a whole change its values and attach much less importance to the consumption of goods. People must be given much longer vacations and should be encouraged to further their education, develop their potential, and do meaningful voluntary community work on a local, national, and international level. Experts from the industrialized world in various fields of science, technology, business, and the professions should and must travel to developing countries to teach and train people in their field of competence, on a voluntary basis whenever this is possible.

It is important that the human body serve as an example. If one eats too little and not the right kind of food, one gets sick. The same happens if one eats too much. The excessive consumption of goods harms people, societies, and the global environment. It is absolutely essential for human survival that the consumption of goods become more evenly and justly spread among all people in the world, and that people learn to consume goods in a wise, moderate, and responsible manner.

## 81. Knowing When to Compromise

The ability to compromise requires openmindedness and flexibility as well as the desire for social and personal peace and harmony. Politically and socially, democracy is based on and rests on the willingness and readiness to compromise among differing opinions, synthesizing disparate viewpoints into a coherent totality or finding a middle ground among them.

However, there are occasions when it is irresponsible to compromise, when vital issues and values like human life, personal dignity and integrity, private property, peace, abolition of war, opposition to prejudice and discrimination, abolition of poverty, unemployment, and illiteracy are at stake. There are absolute moral values like integrity, decency, humanity, and human solidarity, faith in God, the creator of the universe,

171

social justice, love, altruism, compassion, truth, beauty, and philanthropy, which must be defended at all costs in a total, unadulterated, uncorrupted manner.

It requires wisdom and personal, social, and moral responsibility to know when to compromise and when not to. Even though the capacity and willingness to compromise, to understand another person's viewpoint, to give partially in to him or her in order to create a good social climate, are admirable social qualities showing emotional maturity and a conciliatory attitude and outlook, it must not prevent people from acting,when indicated, to affirm and defend responsible and absolute moral principles. It is important to build a hierarchy of values and develop the moral sensitivity and responsibility to know when to compromise and when to adhere firmly, unwaveringly, and unswervingly to responsible social and moral principles.

One cannot and must not compromise with dictators and tyrants or criminals bent on aggressive conquest and destruction. Chamberlain's attempts to appease Hitler and look for a compromise at Munich in 1938 failed miserably as he did not understand the delinquent mind, to whom appeasement and compromise are indications of weakness. One must understand human nature profoundly and know who appreciates and who responds to compromise. Above all, one must have the firmness, courage, and tenacity to stick to worthy and valuable principles.

## 82. Understanding and Valuing Responsible Tourism

Traveling to different places and countries enables us to appreciate the beauty of the world created by God as well as to enjoy and see man's artistic and architectural creations. It further helps us to discover and understand other cultures and strengthens our solidarity with mankind.

Tourism can also be irresponsible, like sex tourism in Thailand, or the case of travelers who practice nudism on the beaches of third world countries without realizing how offensive that might be in some cultures.

There is a center for responsible tourism in California that publishes a guide for tourists, recommending that travelers stay in locally owned hotels or guest houses in order to be able to appreciate the uniqueness of the host country. It further suggests the use of local transportation systems to get to know the people, to buy souvenirs from local artisans, to be sensitive and responsible when taking people's pictures, especially when they are poor.

Responsible tourists are interested in meeting third world community organizers and participating in tourist programs where they can visit the interesting sites as well as contribute to the welfare of the country they visit, possibly through voluntary activities and work. An example is a program organized by the Jewish community of Montreal and of other North American cities, where elderly tourists who visit Israel pay for their trip (including room and board) and, after taking a tour of the country, do voluntary work according to their skills and the needs of Israel.

Joanne Mills writes in the Gazette that Tensie Whelan in her book *Nature Tourism* (published by Island Press in 1991) states that ecotourism or nature-related travel is developing rapidly. Ecotourism is a highly responsible form of tourism, as it promises employment and income to local third world communities as well as needed foreign exchange to national governments, while allowing the continued existence of the natural resource base of the third world country. The organization that plans the trip must contribute to the long-term preservation of the area by returning a percentage of the profits.

Responsible tourism is not only enriching, but also makes an important contribution to a better, more cooperative, and responsible world based on human solidarity and understanding.

### 83. Understanding and Valuing Responsible Leisure

The dictionary defines leisure as freedom from the demands of work or duty, as time available for recreation or relaxation, and as spare time.

Responsible leisure means engaging in activities one enjoys in a spontaneous manner, without coercion and constraint and in which one responds to one's positive needs as well as to those of others. Responsible leisure implies that one has the obligation to use leisure as complementary to paid work to further one's wellbeing as well as that of others. Responsible leisure need not always be active in nature. A good example of this is when one engages in meditation or uses relaxation techniques to combat stress and to regenerate oneself emotionally and spiritually. This kind of leisure activity, as well as physical exercise and playing and practicing sports, is indirectly beneficial to others, since one has more psychological and physical energy to do things for others when one is in good mental, emotional, and physical shape. Playing educational games, which entertain at the same time, going to parties and socializing, visiting museums, attending lectures, pursuing a meaningful and enjoyable hobby, going to concerts, and reading good books are some examples of positive leisure. On the other hand, gambling for high amounts of money and watching films with pornographic or excessively violent content are examples of irresponsible and harmful leisure activities.

One should use one's leisure to continue to develop mentally, emotionally, spiritually, and morally in order to become a wiser and better human being. One should travel to discover and appreciate new places and to pay homage to God for the beautiful world he created as well as to the architectural and artistic genius of man. Through travel, one can become exposed to different cultures and languages and develop solidarity with humankind to become a citizen of the world. There is a form of traveling especially suited for the healthy, prosperous elderly, which makes it possible to do voluntary work in the third world. One should also become an ecotourist, which means nature-related travel, visiting tropical forests in Central or South America, for instance. This provides employment and income to local communities in the third world as well as needed foreign exchange and allows the continued existence of the country's resource base.

The Jewish community in North American cities provides senior citizens the opportunity to combine responsible leisure with voluntary work by organizing paid trips to Israel. The participants visit the country for one or two weeks and then do voluntary work for another few weeks, performing such duties as planting trees, teaching English, and looking after frail and bedridden elderly people.

# CHAPTER EIGHT

# *Psychological Responsibilities*

### 84. Valuing Differences

A LOT OF MISERY, UNHAPPINESS, AND TRAGEDIES HAVE OCCURRED in the world for countless generations because of intolerance and hostility toward people who are different, whether in appearance, behavior, customs, language, religion, nationality, race, personal beliefs, world views, political convictions, or in other ways. Differences quite often caused and continue to cause enmity, when they should have been perceived as being enriching and complementary.

God created an immense variety of living species and a great diversity of human beings. It is our responsibility to view diversity as highly useful, meaningful, and exciting. The coming together of people of diverse talents, interests, and personal traits is indispensable to the creation of a responsible community. Differences of any kind must be viewed as pieces of a giant jigsaw puzzle, where every piece becomes indispensable in relation to the total puzzle by its very difference. To look at differences as being absolutely necessary is a very responsible way of perception. This also adds value and worth to people by valuing them not only for their common humanity but also because every person is different and unique. People must be educated to regard those who are different and whose difference does not cause any harm to others as individuals who enrich society and the community. Rather than being feared and stimulating hostility and enmity, differences must be viewed as complementary.

This responsible way of looking at differences can do immense good in many areas of human activity and can being strength and harmony to marriage, family  life, and to interpersonal relationships. Accepting differences also leads to a more peaceful coexistence between people of diverse races, nationalities, religions, and political beliefs, and is conducive to genuine peace.

## 85. Asserting Oneself Responsibly

Asserting oneself responsibly is not aggressiveness, understood in its negative meaning of being inconsiderate to others, pushy, and even violent. Responsible assertion means to develop the necessary drive, motivation, will, energy, and determination to develop one's talents and aptitudes in a constructive manner, to make other people aware of these skills and talents, and to use them in a responsible manner, useful and beneficial both to others and to oneself.

This duty to assert oneself responsibly is important to everyone, but especially to women who have traditionally been taught to be docile, submissive, to value the role of mother and housewife exclusively, to develop sensitivity and altruism at the expense of their intellectual growth. Consequently, they have associated assertion with a loss of femininity.

Likewise, North American society tends to discriminate subtly against the shy, introverted person, who because of his or her passivity or introversion might have difficulty developing the necessary drive and determination to develop properly and succeed socially and vocationally. Asserting oneself has also added importance for the handicapped, the elderly, and minority groups, people who society (especially the North American one) tends to marginalize. It takes courage and willpower to overcome these social barriers. However, by understanding that one has the duty, no matter what the circumstances, to fully develop one's aptitudes and to use them in a socially useful way, one acts responsibly and contributes to the betterment of society. By doing this one also develops inner spiritual strength, fortitude, endurance, and perseverance, qualities which further lead to responsible human success.

Society too must help every person to develop his or her talents and to increasingly accept the notion that it has an additional obligation to make constructive use of fully developed human talents. Society must also encourage people to assert themselves responsibly and value this as a responsible quality.

## 86. Developing Confidence in Oneself and Others

Confidence in one's abilities is a crucial and vital personality trait of great importance in helping a person to successfully and responsibly use his or her talents. In my thirty years experience as a counseling psychologist and career counselor I have seen a large number of clients who had good intellectual potentials as well as talents, but could not use them successfully and responsibly because of a poor level of confidence in their abilities. I have helped many of my clients gain confidence in themselves;

this enabled them to make full use of their capacities and make a useful and responsible contribution to society.

It is one of the most important duties of parents as well as of teachers to help children become aware of their aptitudes and talents, to encourage and motivate them to develop these aptitudes, and to use them productively. Parents and teachers who don't encourage children, belittle them, and put them down act irresponsibly, cripple the children's personalities, and prevent them from contributing to the welfare of society and of the world.

One important confidence that people must develop is that they together with others are capable of solving responsibly the many problems confronting humankind, like eliminating wars and creating a lasting peace on earth as well as controlling the population explosion on a global scale and creating a world government. Other problems to be solved are the elimination of hunger from the world, unemployment, major sicknesses, illiteracy, and pollution of the environment.

## 87. Identifying and Satisfying Responsible Needs

A need is the fact, quality, or condition of lacking something necessary or desirable. Needs motivate people to satisfy them. There are physiological, economic, social, legal, political, psychological, artistic, spiritual, philosophical, religious, and moral needs.

Responsible needs can be divided into known needs and less well known ones. Among the responsible well known needs are the need for food, clothing, shelter, education, earning a living by doing interesting, useful, fulfilling work, the need for emotional, physical, and mental health, happiness, material, emotional, and social security, the need for friends and good interpersonal relations with others, for a good marriage and family life, and for a stable, peaceful, and moderately prosperous, pollution-free world.

Some of the less well known responsible needs are the need to develop one's potential, to find meaning in life, to understand oneself, others, and the world, to value truth, beauty, and social justice, and to contribute to society's and the world's welfare. Other less well known needs are the desire for decency, to live in accordance with practical and noble ideals, to respect one's own integrity as well as that of others, to have faith in God, to live in harmony with oneself, others, nature, and humankind. Other less well known needs are to develop a good philosophy of life, to have responsible values, and to become responsible to God, humankind, to oneself, and to other individuals. The needs to overcome prejudice, discrimination, violence, war, and to become a wiser, more mature, more compassionate, and understanding person are also less well known yet very important needs.

In contrast to the responsible needs enumerated above, there are irresponsible needs that must be recognized. These would include the need for excessive personal wealth, for oppressive power over others, for selfishness, dishonesty, unprovoked aggressiveness and war, for domination and conquest, for intolerance of differences, and for atheism. Irresponsible needs have to be recognized and overcome. The desire to satisfy irresponsible needs decreases as a person satisfies his or her responsible needs.

The responsible needs mentioned above are meaningful to everybody; however, nobody can gratify all of them. Each person has potentials as well as limitations, and the constellation of needs, values, interests, aptitudes, and aspirations differs from person to person. As a result, provided a person has become aware and has the opportunity to do so, he or she will satisfy some responsible needs, the nature of which vary from person to person. The more mature, integrated, and personally, socially, and morally responsible a person is, the more responsible needs he or she will satisfy. Satisfaction of as many responsible needs as possible leads to longevity, relatively good health, to personal happiness and fulfillment, and also contributes to the wellbeing of humankind.

## 88. Understanding and Valuing Responsible Psychological Counseling

In the past, applied psychologists as well as other mental health practitioners have viewed psychotherapy and counseling as two different approaches and procedures of dealing with personality problems, conflicts, and disorders. Psychotherapy was seen as the attempt to cure personality disorders and conflicts of a more permanent, deeper, and pathological nature and to restore the client's mental health. In contrast, counseling was seen as treating more superficial and non-pathological problems and difficulties of living. It is known today, however, that even people who have had relatively happy and secure childhoods can experience depression and other serious personality conflicts as a result of unemployment or divorce, for example.

Responsible counseling helps to restore a person's confidence in himself or herself, to regain courage and self-esteem, and to develop a greater sense of personal, social, and moral responsibility. Career counseling, for instance, enables a person to make responsible educational and vocational choices which will help him or her to work in a field and in a job compatible with his or her interests, aptitudes, talents, personality traits, values, aspirations, and acquired skills and experience.

Effective, responsible counseling helps shy people to develop the confidence, courage, and responsibility to use their talents and aptitudes in a suitable job, and to persevere in looking for this job until they find it. In this sense, responsible and effective counseling is also effective psychotherapy, because it helps a person develop the courage to be productive and useful in a rewarding and fulfilling job. This is not only highly satisfying but also induces lasting and beneficial personality changes.

Responsible and effective counseling is eclectic in nature, using the most suitable psychological techniques from various psychological schools of thought. Responsible and effective counseling must help the client to develop insight into his or her problems, to gain a better understanding of self, others, society, and the socio-economic, political system. It must also help him or her to set goals and to choose responsible social and moral values.

Responsible and effective counseling is based on listening to what the client says, but also being attuned and responsive in a highly empathetic and sympathetic manner to the client's sometimes unconscious and often unexpressed needs to find meaning in life, to develop integrity, and to devote himself or herself to a humanitarian cause.

During my thirty years of experience as a counseling psychologist and career counselor, I have helped a great many people of all ages to succeed in careers and jobs suited to the unique constellation of their talents, interests, and personality traits as well as to develop a greater sense of personal, social, and moral responsibility, and to live more meaningful, responsible, and fulfilled lives. I have received numerous written statements, describing in detail the benefits these satisfied clients have derived from the counseling sessions.

### 89. Developing Empathy

Empathy is an intellectual, imaginative, and emotional apprehension of another's condition or state of mind. It means to understand superficially as well as profoundly how others think and feel. Empathy presupposes a certain degree of personal, social, and moral responsibility.

To empathize effectively, one must first place oneself in the place of another person and to think, feel, and imagine how one would think and feel if one were in the other person's shoes. Doing this requires an awareness of one side of the coin, namely the similarity between all human beings as well as their conditions and states. The other side of the coin consists of understanding the other person's differential and unique condition and state. In order to understand the exact nature of this difference, one must ask pertinent and sensitive questions as well as listen intensively to what the person says. This requires genuine curiosity, as well a logical and intuitive understanding of what the other person says as well as what he or she implies.

Empathy also requires a profound understanding of human nature and responsible human needs.

In the final analysis, to be empathetic means to understand intellectually, emotionally, and imaginatively another's condition or state and to arrive at this understanding by using all the qualities and techniques described above.

A supreme example of empathy would be the understanding of the suffering caused by prejudice and by discrimination. One must place oneself in the place of the person unjustly persecuted by any form of prejudice. One must also think and imagine that God, who created all human beings, wants all his children to be treated in a just, compassionate, and respectful manner.

## 90. The Responsibility toward the Gifted and their Duties

Talented and gifted people exist in all fields of human endeavor, whether in science, technology, art, industry, commerce, the various professions, education, philosophy, politics, or religion. Talented people are usually highly intelligent, yet one does not have to be extremely brilliant to be creative and innovative in any of the fields mentioned above.

It is important for parents to detect special gifts in their children as early as possible in life and to foster them. It is likewise the task of responsible teachers to discover special talents in their students, and to stimulate and encourage them to develop them. The improvement and further development of culture and civilization depend to a great extent on the genius of the gifted and on our respect for their special talents.

Envy and the wrong belief that it is undemocratic to devote too much attention to the gifted are some of the obstacles which prevent gifted people from developing their talents and helping humankind to solve many of its problems.

Educational institutions must do everything possible to foster the special gifts of talented students. Gifted students should have the opportunity to receive advanced, specialized education, either individually or together with other talented students in the area of their talent.

It is the personal, social, and moral duty of talented people who have been helped by society to fully develop their talents, and to use these precious gifts in a manner beneficial to the physical, psychological, economic, social, and spiritual wellbeing of people.

## 91. Understanding and Overcoming Envy

Envy is the resentful awareness of an advantage enjoyed by another person combined with the wish to possess that advantage.

Envy is caused by a competitive socio-economic society, with little job security and fierce struggle for positions and promotions. Envy is also caused by a social climate and culture where people are constantly preoccupied with money and where greed becomes a virtue. The consumer society which promotes distorted values that everybody must have everything in abundance further strengthens envy. As a result of these wrong and false values, many people equate success with the quantity of goods they acquire and become dependent on false expectations of success. These people envy those who have managed to acquire more goods than they have, and because they have ruined their lives by adopting and following wrong values, they develop a lot of hatred against others and themselves.

Envy is an aggressive and hostile feeling. An envious person wants to have what somebody else has that he or she doesn't have, wants to take it away from the other person, and if this fails, to destroy it.

A child deprived of parental love and respect becomes an envious adult later in life. Children who were loved, respected, and disciplined in a responsible manner by their parents and consequently develop into relatively responsible and happy adults, do not harbor destructive feelings of envy.

Likewise, people who remain true to themselves, in harmony with their inner being, who develop integrity, do not tend to become irresponsibly and maliciously envious. An altruistic, cooperative, and responsible society is also less likely to generate widespread feelings of hateful envy.

Both the person who envies as well as the person who is envied suffer and are harmed. Generalized envy also destroys a culture by paralyzing solidarity and cooperation and by creating enmity and hostility. As a result of envy, creativity and the motivation to improve society become transformed into destructive hatred and sterility.

Society and individuals should and must eliminate destructive envy by creating conditions where everybody, according to his or her constellation of specific interests, aptitudes, and personality traits becomes a responsibly successful person.

## 92. Making Responsible Vocational and Employment Choices

Selecting one's vocation or career in a responsible manner and finding suitable, useful, rewarding, meaningful work are of great importance for the psychological and even physical wellbeing of a person as well as for the welfare of society.

Some people choose their vocation or career relatively early in life, as early as in the last one or two years of high school, and pursue the realization of their goal in a methodical and persevering manner. Others, who are late bloomers, make their selection later in life and often proceed by trial and error until they find the right career or occupation. Many, unfortunately, even though they might be productive, never find their work meaningful or rewarding. Some people remain faithful to one career throughout life, even though they might change companies and employers, whereas others change their careers twice or several times. The extraordinary scientific and technological developments in recent years make it necessary for many people to change careers during their working years, yet the acquisition of additional specialization should never lead a person to completely abandon an occupation or career in which one has become an expert. The change to a different occupation or career should never be a total one, but always be somewhat connected to the previous field of activity. In other words, responsible change of career or occupation means to work in a connected field, which allows one to use and integrate a great part of one's training skills and experience in the new area of work.

The important thing to know in the responsible choice of a career is that one must become aware of one's interests, aptitudes, level of intelligence, talents, personality traits, values, and expectations. To understand one's personality it is also essential that one also become aware of unconscious processes. Often, a person wishes something on a conscious level that is not in harmony with unconscious needs or desires. This creates confusion and problems. Shakespeare's dictum, "To thine own self be true," has great validity in choosing a career wisely and responsibly.

Good professional counseling by an experienced, competent career counselor is of great help. By listening empathetically, by taking a good case history, by asking pertinent questions, by administering and interpreting interest, intelligence, aptitude, and personality tests, by building up the client's confidence in himself or herself, and by giving realistic, practical information concerning the short- and long-term needs of the labor market, the career counselor guides the client to choose the career which suits him or her best.

Remaining idealistic throughout life in a practical, realistic manner is the best way to prevent burnout, which affects many professionals as well as other categories of employees.

Once a person has responsibly chosen a career and has obtained the qualifications to work in his or her chosen field through appropriate studies, it is important that he or she succeed in finding employment in the selected profession or occupation. If this is not possible, it is essential that the person try to find work in a connected field. The person might also work temporarily in his or her professional field on a full-time or part-time voluntary basis, if no paid jobs are available. Consistency and perseverance, two important characteristics of responsible behavior, quite often ensure the desired and expected success.

### 93. Understanding Oneself and Others Responsibly

A human being is born neither evil nor good. He or she has innate potentials, and if brought up by responsible, loving, sensitive, emotionally mature, and understanding parents, if educated by competent, dedicated, humanitarian, and humanistic teachers, and if social and economic conditions are propitious, the individual person will develop into a responsible, loving, competent, mature, and decent human being. On the other hand, if the development of human potentials is thwarted by insensitive, excessively authoritarian, rejecting parents, a child will develop into an evil, irresponsible person. There are exceptions—people who managed, in spite of an unfavorable upbringing to develop into decent people and who succeeded in redeeming themselves personally, socially, and morally later in life—but this does not happen too often.

In his work, Sigmund Freud treated morality as a force alien to the individual ego. Psychoanalysis has placed the accent on human needs as opposed to social obligation. This has transformed much of twentieth-century thought into a morally empty, bankrupt view of human nature. A responsible view of human nature places the emphasis on responsible human needs and on the obligation to satisfy them responsibly. Behaving in a morally responsible way is an extremely important need, and it must be absolutely satisfied.

Understanding oneself means to know that one has the need to live a full, meaningful, useful, and happy life. By understanding oneself truthfully and objectively, one also gains a better understanding of others; by understanding others one also improves the understanding of oneself. There are four parts in a person's personality: one is known by the individual but unknown by others; the second is known by others but unknown by the individual; the third is known by the person and by others; and the fourth is known neither by the person nor by others. It is a person's obligation to expand his or her knowledge of self by gaining insight and becoming aware of hitherto unknown components of personality.

Gaining a thorough and responsible understanding of oneself necessitates a knowledge of at least some aspects of one's unconscious thoughts, emotions, ambitions, and values. It also means to know that one's personality, like the one of every other person is unique and distinct, but shares many similar characteristics with the personalities of other people. Personality is also very complex, consisting of many often contradictory parts. For example, in the case of one personality component, introversion-extroversion, every person has both introvertive and extrovertive tendencies. The difference between individuals consists in the relative strength of these traits. It further means to know that there is no such thing as human perfection and also that even a very mature, responsible and decent person has some personality weaknesses and even immature and irresponsible traits.

To understand others one must develop empathy but also the ability to understand the other person's distinctiveness. Asking sensitive and pertinent questions is a good way to gain an understanding of another person by seeing him or her through his or her eyes.

Responsible understanding of oneself and others contributes to a more responsible society and world.

## 94. Developing One's Potentials and Personality Responsibly

Development of a person's potentials occurs in a responsible manner when it happens in a social context and is done to satisfy the person's needs to grow. By creating or producing something in a useful manner, by helping others, by improving the system and the world, one also helps oneself to develop competence, to find meaning, contentment, and fulfillment. Responsible human development does not occur in a vacuum, is not egoistic, but is highly social and moral.

Every person has the need to develop his or her aptitudes, talents, character traits, beliefs, and values. Aptitudes and talents must be used in a beneficial manner. If unused, they can lead a person to feel guilty, resentful, hostile, and to believe that life has no meaning.

Some psychologists believe that most people develop less than half of their innate potentials during the course of their lives. Some of the potentials to be developed are logical, analytical, and synthetic thinking, insight, memory, linguistic skills, mathematical and artistic aptitudes and talents, as well as interpersonal skills and moral qualities such as decency, integrity, fairness, responsibility, compassion, and justice. Qualities of the heart such as idealism, generosity, love, sensitivity, sympathy, and spiritual qualities such as faith, courage, endurance, and fortitude must also be developed. It is also important for good mental health to develop a good sense of humor and emotional maturity and stability. Childlike qualities like laughter, play, spontaneity, and curiosity must at all costs be preserved throughout life and should even be further developed.

It is necessary that one understand the complexity of personality and even its contradictory, paradoxical nature. While politeness, good manners, tact, and good interpersonal skills and social intelligence are very important, it is equally important to have virtuous moral inner values and beliefs. An extroverted, jovial, gregarious person can use his or her social skills to manipulate or use others in an excessively selfish manner for his or her social gain, advantage, or aggrandizement. On the other hand, a shy, reserved person can have highly positive social, and moral beliefs and values and be highly committed and altruistic.

In the past, people tended to excuse eccentric, immature, impulsive behavior in a genius like Ludwig Van Beethoven. There is no excuse for creative geniuses to have temper tantrums or behave in an emotionally immature manner. It is the duty of every human being, irrespective of his or her outstanding talents in one or more specific areas, to develop a mature, balanced, and well integrated personality.

It is important to bear in mind that only those potentials that promote other people's as well as one's own wellbeing should be realized and developed.

A person has developed a mature personality if he or she has attained a certain degree of personal and emotional independence, has relatively good relations with others, works for a living, and finds some satisfaction in work, has loyal friends, and assumes some degree of responsibility for the welfare of society and the world. The person with a mature personality must also be emotionally stable, capable of reasoning objectively, must have insight into himself or herself, and have a balanced, integrated personality. In addition, the person should also have a good, stable marital relationship and be a good and responsible parent.

It is also important that a person have some insight into his or her unconscious feelings and thoughts, and that these unconscious psychological processes become integrated to some extent into the conscious personality. Choosing a career in harmony with interests, aptitudes, talents, personality traits, values, and expectations is a characteristic of a psychologically well integrated person. Psychological integrity also reveals itself by selecting a marital partner on the basis of love, respect, sensitivity, and personality compatibility or complementarity. A person's moral integrity manifests itself through reliability and dependability and through actions and behavior that are in harmony with a person's moral principles, values, and ideals.

185

In a survey of 1517 adults conducted in Canada in 1988, the strongest expressed concern was about the honesty and integrity of politicians. Fully 82 percent said that they would be less inclined to vote for a politician who was accused of fraud in a business deal. This indicates the importance people attach to moral integrity, including politicians, and that there is hope that people will heed the warning of the Czech Republic's president, Vaclav Havel, that the future of the world depends on politicians behaving in a morally responsible manner. It is hoped they will elect politicians on the basis of personal and moral integrity as well as personal, social, and moral responsibility.

One way to explain the mystery and often contradictory, paradoxical nature of personality and behavior is to assume that a person has various selves. It is imperative for personal and collective wellbeing that the most noble, generous, responsible, sensitive, rational, and humanitarian part of a person's personality—his or her highest social and moral self—become the core of personality, and that all other selves become integrated with and subservient to the highest self. The duty to develop such a personality goes hand in hand with the obligation to foster and bring out the best and the most noble qualities in others as well.

Another major responsibility is to also aim for the development of a well balanced personality. Carl Jung describes two basic personality tendencies—introversion, which means the turning of one's interest toward one's thoughts and feelings, and extroversion, which means that one's interests are directed toward other people and outside objects and events. A well balanced person has developed both his or her introverted as well as extroverted tendencies, even though in almost all people one of the two tendencies described above is either slightly or strongly better developed than the second. A good example of a person who has developed his or her psychological qualities in a balanced manner is that of a doctor who deals empathetically and sensitively with a patient whom he or she examines and who uses simultaneously logical reason and intuition to understand the patient's problem in making a diagnosis. Similarly, a cerebral, intellectual person should and must develop qualities of the heart, such as sensitivity, courage, compassion, generosity, and idealism. Practical realism has to be balanced with socially and morally responsible idealism. Another characteristic of an emotionally and mentally mature and stable person is steadfastness of purpose.

Potentials and talents which remain undeveloped and unused can cause a person a lot of harm. Not using one's talents leads to feelings of guilt, a conscious or unconscious feeling that life has no special meaning, and can turn a person into a hostile, cynical, prejudiced, destructive, or self-destructive human being. It is also important to bear in mind that one must constantly try to develop one's interests, aptitudes, and talents. Otherwise, similar to the force of physical gravity, these interests and talents go down, decline, deteriorate, and rust. What does not go up comes down, and what is not used rusts. This applies to the body, mind, and soul. It is because of these reasons that one should and must see as one's uppermost duty to develop one's potentials and to use them in a socially and morally responsible manner.

The human growth and potential movement, inspired by humanistic psychology, is right in its belief that one should develop one's potentials. Yet it erred when it led its followers to become almost exclusively preoccupied with the self. The human potential movement looks beautiful on the surface. Unfortunately, it creates self-centered, egotistical persons, blind to the problems and needs of society, the community, and the world. Many in the personal growth movement failed because they were too concerned with themselves in a narcissistic manner. Marriages and careers were destroyed because of onesided values. Responsible personal development and growth promotes one's development and is at the same time responsive and beneficial to others. A good example is the development of one's muscular strength, endurance, and flexibility through physical exercise. By becoming stronger and more fit, one also has more energy to accomplish more, which is useful and beneficial to others as well as to oneself.

Responsible self-actualization does not occur when one thinks exclusively about oneself, but when one uses one's skills and talents to improve society and the world. God blesses people with diverse talents to be developed and used, to help, understand, beautify, and improve society and the world. People are really fortunate and blessed when they can make a contribution to creating a more beautiful as well as a socially and morally more responsible world. It results in a fulfilled, personal life, as well as wellbeing for others.

### 95. Understanding and Experiencing Meaningful Happiness

We all know how it feels to be happy. It is a feeling of wellbeing, of contentment, of being satisfied, at peace with oneself, the people around us, and with the world. Some people are ecstatically happy sometimes and not too happy at other times, whereas others neither experience extreme states of happiness, nor do they experience feelings of dejection, despair, and discouragement. In general, a stable, relatively healthy, well balanced, mature, responsible person experiences persistent feelings of contentment and wellbeing.

The determination to pursue happiness is instrumental in attaining it. Happiness also depends on the control people feel that they have over their lives as well as over events.

Love and intimacy are important factors in feeling happy. Being optimistic also contributes to happiness. Optimists, regardless of the objective circumstances of their lives, are happier than pessimists. It can also be stated that in general, altruistic, committed people who are dedicated to improving the lives of others as well as to bettering the world are content, fulfilled, happy people and know that their lives have profound meaning.

Other factors contributing to happiness are being true to oneself, having developed personal and moral integrity, and having developed one's aptitudes and talents and using them in a productive, useful way that is beneficial to others, to society, and to the world.

## 96. Believing in the Importance of the Individual

Many people feel insignificant, convinced that they are too unimportant to make a contribution to improve the system, society, the human condition, or the world. Even when they are imbued by humanitarian and humanistic ideals and work to better society, many nevertheless feel that their contribution hardly makes a difference. Others, who have been defeated by life and have become cynical, and who lack faith in God and humanity believe that the system cannot be changed.

Materialistic people, when contemplating the billions of stars existing in the universe, think of the smallness of our planet and of the insignificance of the individual in the universe. Yet when one has the faith that human beings are God's partners and coworkers whose task it is to fulfill his will to transform this planet into a earthly paradise of universal prosperity, peace, solidarity, and wellbeing, that every individual is indispensable and important in contributing to this goal, then one is not plagued by thoughts and feelings of the insignificance of people and of humanity in the vastness of the universe.

By developing one's talents, aptitudes, and personality, by developing personal and moral integrity, by becoming responsible to God, humankind, and to the individual (including oneself), by becoming a responsible spouse and parent, by being productive in a meaningful and fulfilling job, by working for peace in the world, for world government, for a clean environment, by fighting prejudice, by helping the third world, one gives importance and significance to one's life. The example set by such a person is contagious and stimulates others to likewise improve the world and the human condition.

It is also very helpful in order to develop faith in the importance of the individual to think of a jigsaw puzzle, where every piece by virtue of its distinctness becomes indispensably important to the whole puzzle. Similarly, every individual by virtue of his or her uniqueness and distinctness is indispensably important to his or her family, to the immediate community, and to humankind.

## 97. Becoming Individually and Collectively Mature

Ideally, a person who develops properly should sooner or later during adulthood reach the state of intellectual, emotional, social, and moral maturity. Many people attain some of the above-mentioned forms of maturity, but not all of them. Actually, it is rather rare today for any person to be fully mature intellectually, emotionally, socially, and morally, as society and the system do not encourage full, complete development of all dimensions of personality. Nevertheless, to assume the responsibilities and meet the various challenges confronting us today, more and more people will have to attach importance to the full development of personality in all the areas mentioned above.

Basically, a genuinely mature person is one who is personally, socially, and morally responsible, and has developed the qualities of the head as well as of the heart. He or she assumes the responsibility of making a productive contribution to society in a trade, profession, or line of business, has relatively good interpersonal relationships with friends, business associates, family members, and acquaintances, and contributes to social and community causes at a local, national, and even international level.

Maturation is a continuing, ongoing, lifelong process. It should never stop and one should constantly strive to improve oneself and become a better and more mature person.

There is a parallel between the individual maturation and the intellectual, social, emotional, and moral maturation of humankind and of society. In childhood, there is dependency on parents, whereas adolescence is characterized by ambivalence and rebellion against parental authority and other authority figures. As a person matures responsibly and turns into a well-developed, responsible, mature adult, he or she becomes capable of supporting himself or herself, of empathy, and of cooperation with parents, authority figures, and ideally also with God and humankind. Similarly, society, governments, and humankind must increasingly outgrow ethnocentrism, wars, and denial of God, and must develop human solidarity and international cooperation. Humankind must cooperate harmoniously with God to develop the wisdom, competence, maturity, and responsibility necessary to solve the many social, economic, political, educational, moral, and religious problems of the world. Mature societies and governments don't wage wars; they don't discriminate against people because they are different. They find ways to eliminate poverty, to create conditions that promote moderate economic prosperity as well as social and psychological wellbeing for all people.

## 98. Having a Balanced View Concerning the Blessings of Work

There is remunerated work and there is voluntary work. Sometimes voluntary work, which is socially useful and harmonizes with the personality traits, interests, aptitudes, talents, values, and aspirations of a person is more meaningful, rewarding, and fulfilling than paid work. Fulfilling, meaningful, socially useful work, whether paid or done for free, definitely promotes the physical health and psychological wellbeing of people.

It is also important to understand that there is increasing awareness concerning the importance of work. People have always worked to produce goods, to build cities, and to support their families as well as themselves. The increasing use of machines, including the introduction of computers, takes away a lot of the routine aspects and monotony of work, and allows manual as well as intellectual workers and professionals to attach more importance to work's psychological rewards. The psychological benefits of work consist of finding meaning in life, enabling one to use one's aptitudes and talents, allowing one to feel socially useful, and to be creative. In general, people nowadays are looking for more meaningful and satisfying jobs than in the past, jobs that are also interesting, socially useful, jobs that further personal development and offer adequate compensation. Besides remaining an economic necessity, work has also become a psychological necessity.

It is important and beneficial to work hard without, however, becoming a workaholic. Rather than finding satisfaction in hard work as hardworking people do, workaholics crave work as if it were an addictive drug, becoming depressed after working hard, rather than fulfilled and energized. Generally, workaholics don't play much, try much too hard, are perfectionistic, and have little social or love life. People who suffer from burnout have some of the neurotic tendencies of workaholics, but on top of these characteristics, they have also lost their idealism. Burnout is also induced by too much stress, too much pressure from superiors, and lack of recognition and appreciation for work well done.

## 99. Understanding and Using Positive Expectation

One's expectation of other people's behavior and performance has a profound influence on their actual behavior. The psychologist Robert Rosenthal has shown that teachers' expectations have an impact on student performance. In one study, teachers were told that all students were bright and would do unusually well in class. These students were selected at random from the general student population, yet in actual fact they all performed unusually well, even though only some of the students should have done well, and others less so, under normal conditions. In this study, the brilliant performance of all students was due to the teachers' positive expectation concerning their level of performance.

The power of expectation can also work in reverse. The poor academic achievement of many disadvantaged children from poor neighborhoods is due to some extent to their teachers' negative expectation of their performance. The teachers might visualize these students as unmotivated and dull; this negative expectation might become a reality and turn out to be a self-fulfilling prophecy. The teachers who expect brilliant performance do their best to encourage, stimulate, motivate, and praise the positive behavior; the students expected to perform brilliantly, feeling the teachers' warmth, appreciation, and encouragement, actually do their very best to excel, in order not to disappoint the teachers' positive expectation. On the other hand, students expected to function at a dull level, perceiving the teachers' low opinion of them, lose the interest and motivation to do their best, a behavior which becomes negatively reinforced by the teacher's lack of praise and encouragement.

The attitude of positive expectation could also be applied to reduce poverty, drug addiction, international conflict, unemployment, and to prevent war. To reduce and even eliminate unemployment, for example, a sufficient number of people must expect the unemployed to become productive. Industry and government must likewise expect the unemployed to become wage earners. Once this positive expectation starts to develop in people's minds, everything will be done to develop the ingenuity and resourcefulness to create new jobs as well as to share the existing jobs in a cooperative spirit of social and moral responsibility. The unemployed, in order not to disappoint the positive expectations of people and institutions, will also do their very best to work hard and, if necessary, develop new skills to improve the chance of becoming employed.

Where there is a will, there is a way. Having a vision of a peaceful, united world under the authority of a world government would induce individuals and nations not only to disarm, but also to build bridges to the hearts and minds of other people and nations, including former enemies, and to work to create a united world. This transformation to personal, social, and moral responsibility, international solidarity, and cooperation is not only desirable, but can actually be realistically achieved.

People, individually and collectively, have the potential to attain this exalted state of responsibility. The powerful tool of positive expectation must be used to tap the tremendous reservoir of human talents, which must be developed and used to create a responsible and peaceful world.

## 100. Valuing Genuine and Responsible Human Relations

Common to all forms of genuine, responsible human relations is a profound respect for the other persons involved in the relation. Responsible relations, whether interpersonal or between people of various groups, including international ones, should and must be based on mutual solidarity, cooperation, equality, awareness of interdependence, mutually shared responsibility, and a desire to promote the wellbeing of the other people as well as one's own.

Genuine and responsible human relations are based on empathy and sympathy, on an understanding of the other persons' personalities, their situation and viewpoints, on personal and moral integrity, sensitivity, and tact. It is very important to accept people as they are, yet at the same time one should also endeavor to help others to become what they could and should become. In other words, one should not only wish others well but also further and promote their development and wellbeing.

Genuine, responsible relations between parents and children should be based on love, on parents' keen interest in the physical, intellectual, social, emotional, spiritual, and psychological development of their children, and on mutual respect.

Genuine and responsible relations between spouses should and must be based on interdependence yet also on respect for each partner's unique personality. Both spouses must fully contribute to the marital relation, which has to satisfy the social, financial, emotional, and psychological needs of both marital partners.

Genuine and responsible relations at work, between management and employees, and between employees themselves should and must be based on mutual respect and solidarity. Employee participation in decision making at all levels of production, administration, and marketing is essential to the successful functioning of a business and enterprise as well as to responsible, genuine relations at work. Furthermore, some form of coownership of an enterprise by employees, in the form of owning some company stock, further increases responsible involvement and commitment to do one's best to promote the wellbeing of the company. It also contributes to better relations.

Genuine and responsible relations between elected political representatives and citizens are based on a high degree of interest for and participation by citizens in most—if not all—public and political matters of concern to the community, on a maximum participation in voting, on holding elected representatives accountable for their behavior and on the moral, social, and personal responsibility and integrity of politicians.

In general, people should and must behave in a friendly manner toward neighbors and strangers, should show a lot of compassion, and should help the less fortunate. There should and must be a great deal of acceptance of and tolerance for people of different ethnic origins, religions, nationalities, and races. Human differences should be seen as a form of enrichment. Above all, all forms of human relations should and must become increasingly based on human solidarity.

### 101. Being Idealistic in a Responsible, Practical Manner

Practical, responsible, and humanitarian idealism expresses a desire for something which is not yet accomplished, but which is desirable for the purpose either of giving meaning or beautifying life, helping individual development or happiness, or creating conditions of social justice, moderate prosperity, permanent peace, and harmonious relations between people on earth. Responsible idealism is responsive to the highest humanitarian aspirations of humankind. Responsible idealism is both realistic and visionary, considering conditions as they are as well as they could and should become. It also must be practical, which means that the ideal can be approximated and could and should become a reality. This means that one must think of possibilities which can be realized and not of situations or conditions incapable of becoming a reality. One can never help people to become perfect, but one must try to help people to develop their potentials, to constantly improve personally, socially, and morally. Practical, responsible, and humanitarian idealism is indispensably vital, as it enables us to improve the world as well as the human condition.

The great German poet Goethe said that if we only accept a person as he or she is, we cannot help him or her to become what he or she is meant to be. It is our duty to help others to become what they are meant to be, because people who do not continuously develop and improve tend to stagnate and even deteriorate and decline. To counteract the force of psychological, social, spiritual, and moral gravity pulling us downward, we must constantly strive upward by realizing our ideals to better the world and humankind.

It is very important that ideals are also based on scientific facts and not on false, criminal myths. The ideals of the Nazis to create a pure, superior, Germanic race by exterminating the Jews were irresponsible, scientifically false, and lacking in humanity. Similarly, the Marxist ideal

193

of a classless society and of the dictatorship of the proletariat leads to discrimination against and extermination of the bourgeoisie, to corruption, and to inefficient bureaucracy, in spite of its apparent egalitarianism.

Responsible idealism is the ability to see things as they should be, in a practical, humanitarian, and responsible manner. Responsible idealism differs from utopian thinking. Utopian thinking implies impracticality and incapacity to make the vision become a reality, whereas responsible idealism, based on high principles, connotes the idea of applicability and enforcement, even though the practical, responsible, and humanitarian ideal espoused can only be approximated and never completely and perfectly realized. Social justice, for instance, is a responsible ideal which can only be approximated.

On a personal level, people who do not live up to the best in themselves intellectually, socially, emotionally, spiritually, and morally tend to hate themselves and tend to feel, even if often only at the unconscious level, that the have wasted their lives. Consequently, they are not too happy.

Even though ideals cannot be fully realized, they are nevertheless extremely important for the survival of society and of humankind. People who suffer from burnout have to a great extent ceased to be idealistic, have lost their ideals, and have become cynical. In order to remain in good mental health, it is essential that people remain idealistic in a practical, responsible, and humanitarian manner throughout life.

Trusting and idealistic people, even at the risk of being a bit naive, also have better interpersonal relations with other people. The cynic, who expects negative reactions from others, usually provokes them and through self-fulfilling prophecy is often treated negatively by them. The trusting idealist, on the other hand, is quite often in a position to have his or her faith vindicated, as people tend to respond to his or her trust in a positive manner. When one sees oneself functioning at one's best or improving a situation, one increases one's motivation and often the cooperation of others as well to bring about the desired result.

Many Canadians see the objective of foreign policy as being the creation of a better world. Even though many Canadians are concerned about the effect of foreign competition on the Canadian economy, few Canadians advocate that Canada take protectionistic economic measures. This is a beautiful example of responsible, practical, humanitarian idealism.

## 102. Understanding, Valuing, and Integrating the Unconscious

Psychoanalytically, the unconscious is that part of mental life of which one is unaware. It consists of thoughts, feelings, attitudes, and values one had in childhood, which are repressed or forgotten, as well as of unrealized potentials such as aptitudes and talents. Freud was the first to understand that dreams constitute the key to the understanding of the unconscious and have great psychological importance and significance.

The personality of every person consists of four parts: the first is known to the person as well as to others; the second is known to others, but not to the person himself or herself; the third is known only by the person but not by others; and the last is known neither by the person nor by others. It is very important that people get insight into and understand as many aspects of their unconscious personality as possible. It increases their level of personal and moral responsibility by helping them to integrate unconscious contents which have been understood into their conscious personality. It makes a person more balanced, psychologically richer, more lucid, and more mature.

It is also very important that one value the unconscious. It contains all one's unrealized and unexpressed potentials. The majority of people use only a relatively small part of their potential aptitudes and realize only a part of their psychological and mental possibilities. Sometimes, extraordinary intuitive and other mental capacities slumber and lie dormant in the unconscious and help a person to find solutions to problems that preoccupy him or her. The chemist Kekule found the answer to a chemical problem in a dream. According to Swiss psychologist and psychiatrist Carl Jung, the unconscious is often in a relationship of opposition to the conscious mind. If people are extremely good and kind in their daily lives, they would often tend to repress their primitive, aggressive, and hostile impulses, which become stored in the unconscious. These emotions can burst out in the form of temper tantrums, or collectively assume the form of mass riots or mob violence. Jung calls this part of the unconscious (which he labels the collective unconscious) the shadow. The shadow is the inferior, primitive psychological component of a person. An individual has a brief awareness of this unknown aspect of his or her unconscious personality: For example, after erupting in rage, someone might say "I was not myself." The danger of repressing the shadow too drastically is that by being stored in the unconscious, it grows in strength and overwhelms the individual by erupting into the consciousness through explosive outbursts or hostile, aggressive behavior.

It is therefore vitally important that a person understand his or her unconscious thoughts, emotions, and values, and integrates them into the conscious personality. This contributes to making human beings personally, socially, and morally more responsible, and also leads to the creation of a socially and morally more responsible society.

## 103. Understanding and Valuing Dreams

The Funk and Wagnalls Standard College Dictionary defines dreams as a series of thoughts or images passing through the mind in sleep, as a fancy or vision freely entertained while awake, as a cherished or vain hope or ambition, as anything of unreal beauty or charm. To dream is further defined as spending time in idle reverie, indulging in daydreams, considering something as possible, and imagining something. Some of the meanings listed above are highly positive, realistic, and responsible. I will deal in this chapter only with the vitally important, realistic, positive, and responsible aspects and meaning of dreams.

Dreams are a psychological phenomenon. Physiologists have shown that in profound, deep periods of sleep, there is rapid eye movement (REM), associated with periods of intense deep dreaming. Psychotics don't experience periods of profound sleep and intense dreaming accompanied by REM, which indicates the importance of dreams for the preservation of mental health. Healthy, normal people dream, yet not everybody remembers his or her dreams. Understanding one's unconscious personality presupposes valuing one's dreams, making an effort and training oneself to remember them, and understanding what they mean. Dreams are the key to the unconscious, help one to be in contact with unconscious feelings and thoughts, and contribute to psychological wholeness and integrity.

For Freudian psychoanalysts dreams are a symbolic way to satisfy desires and instinctual impulses. Dreams, if properly understood, can also point to solutions of problems with which one is confronted. They are also ways to compensate for not using all one's mental and psychological potentials. They also serve to bring order into the contradictory and disparate occurrences experienced during the day and to get rid of unimportant details.

Before creating something new, whether in art, industry, business, or changing a social, economic, or political situation, or improving one's life, one must imagine and dream of new creative possibilities in the areas mentioned above. Creative imagination is a vitally important faculty which should be developed by parents and teachers in their children and students, and should be used all throughout life. After dreaming of a new imaginative, possible, and necessary improvement of an existing situation, it becomes a major responsibility to transform the dream into reality, to make it come true. Theodor Herzl, the founder of modern Zionism and the spiritual father of the state of Israel, had the vision of a Jewish state and declared at the beginning of the twentieth century that creating the Jewish state need not remain a dream if the will to create it exists. History has proven him right.

To improve the world, people must have a realistic, imaginative, responsible dream and the will to make it become a reality. Seen in this light, dreaming is a highly necessary, important, and responsible step in creating a more responsible and humane world.

## 104. Preventing Drug Addiction

The United States went though four major waves of drug use in the second part of the twentieth century: LSD in the early 1960s, marijuana in the mid to late 1960s, heroin from 1969 to 1971, and cocaine in the 1980s. Drug epidemics begin among a small elite, are then taken over by the middle class, and eventually reach the poor neighborhoods. Since 1987 there has been a decline in the consumption of cocaine among American high school and college students, yet the use of drugs by the young is still very high, especially in black neighborhoods. The main reasons for the high use of narcotic drugs are high unemployment, lack of motivation to do well in school or to attend school, lack of faith in the future, hopelessness, poverty, as well as the indifference of society to the plight of the poor. Drug addiction, however, also affects middle as well as upper class people, and one finds among its victims individuals of all ages and professions. Some other reasons why people use narcotic drugs are the negative effect which the high divorce rate has on people's lives, the competitiveness of modern life, its emphasis on materialistic values, the exaggerated emphasis on the consumption of goods, the high rate of violence and crime, the relative absence of profound moral, spiritual , and community values, and above all, society's emphasis on taking medication to remove even the slightest pain or temporary sleeplessness, which leads to a very low threshold and tolerance of pain and suffering. Finally, the blind submission of teenagers to peer pressure, which leads them to experiment irresponsibly with drugs without consideration of the terrible consequences, is another contributing factor which destroys their lives.

In spite of their different chemical compositions and dissimilar physical and psychological effects, all narcotic drugs are addictive, and their consumption leads to an irresponsible escape from reality and to the experience of irresponsibly altered states of consciousness. The pleasure and thrill people experience when using drugs lacks profound meaning, chiefly because it is chemically induced.

In addition to all the legal and police actions taken to eliminate the drug epidemic, it is essential that people learn to accept and endure a bit more of the unavoidable pain and suffering associated with living, and not try to drown the slightest pain with drugs. It is also vital that society accept the idea that full employment is an inalienable human right and create conditions that allow for more cooperation in business, industry, and in all other areas of life. Furthermore, spiritual and moral values must assume a greater role in people's lives.

It is very important that there should be no legalization of the consumption of narcotic drugs. Legalizing their use would suggest and imply government complicity and would induce many people who respect and obey the law to start consuming them.

Finally, starting as early in life as possible, people must be educated not to consume narcotic drugs and have to be made aware of the terrible consequences, in terms of destruction of their lives, which result from the use and abuse of these pernicious drugs.

## 105. Being Optimistic in a Realistic, Responsible Way

It might appear to be unusual to state that it is a duty to be optimistic, since one cannot seemingly force feelings to come into existence. Some people believe that they are either there or they are not. Psychological research on happiness, however, has shown that desiring to be happy and working toward becoming happy have the effect of inducing happiness. Likewise, thinking intentionally positive, optimistic thoughts and being determined to become optimistic lead one to become an optimistic person. It is also important to realize that being optimistic is good for the welfare of society as well as for one's own wellbeing.

To develop into an optimistic person one must also develop the confidence that difficulties and setbacks, which happen to every person as well as to every group and institution, are only temporary in nature and that through responsibility, competence, perseverance, determination, and faith, a negative situation can be transformed into a positive one.

To become optimistic one also needs a realistic, lucid, responsible understanding of history, faith in God and in humankind, as well as a responsible philosophy of life. History teaches us that in spite of innumerable setbacks, poverty, sicknesses, tragedies, and wars, people today live longer, are generally speaking more prosperous, healthier, and work fewer hours per week than in the past. They also enjoy more human rights and freedoms. This realistic and responsible awareness of progress (even though many people in the third world compared with people in rich countries are still far behind in economic and social wellbeing), leads to an optimistic vision of the future, when all people of the world will live in a peaceful world and in moderate prosperity.

Faith in God and in mankind also helps us to believe that in spite of the occurrence of countless injustices, an underlying moral order exists in the universe, as well as divine intervention to help humankind move forward toward the building of a more responsible, peaceful, and human world. The miraculous disappearance of communist tyranny in Eastern Europe in the late 1980s and in the early 1990s attests to the intervention of God in human affairs. A positive, responsible philosophy of life also helps us to understand and keep alive the conviction that in spite of all the wickedness, evil, and ugliness in the world, there is also a lot of beauty and goodness.

While being optimistic about one's own future is not always concurrent with being optimistic about the future of the world and of humankind, there is nevertheless some correlation between the two forms of optimism.

As people grow older and their faith and optimism in their own future becomes weaker, they can remain vigorous and enthusiastic and preserve hope by having a vision of a better social and moral tomorrow for the world and for humankind. According to the psychologist Martin Seligman, pessimists believe that bad events like loss of a job or a divorce are due to long-lasting permanent causes, while optimists believe that bad events are temporary. Optimists attribute success to their own efforts and abilities. Optimists tend to see the positive side in everything and are hopeful concerning the future. Optimism strengthens the immune system and prolongs life.

Seeing the bright side of things, while being realistically aware at the same time of the dark sides, and believing in a better tomorrow has a powerful impact on our physical and psychological health and wellbeing, and helps us by expecting this better future to become a reality, to actually bring about the desired better tomorrow. An optimistically envisioned and expected better future becomes a self-fulfilling prophecy. Psychological research has shown that expected success regarding people tends to lead to success. Similarly, expectation of a better future leads to the creation of a better tomorrow.

It is our responsibility to develop into responsible, optimistic persons, and to use the blessings of an optimistic outlook on life to improve the world and the human condition.

## 106. Developing Qualities of the Heart

The heart symbolizes such qualities as compassion, sensitivity, generosity, idealism, courage, being sensitive to the needs of others, as well as the affirmation of truth, beauty, and justice. It is very important for the wellbeing of society as a whole as well as for the mental health and happiness of people, that both the intellectual qualities of the head and qualities of the heart be developed and used, and that the qualities of the heart must not be considered in opposition to the qualities of the head, but must become well integrated into the total personality.

Corporate culture as well as government and industrial institutions in much of the industrialized world stimulate and reinforce attitudes essential for innovation, analytical and synthetic thinking, and cooperativeness, which are qualities of the head. On the other hand, honesty, generosity, compassion, and idealism, qualities of the heart, remain unappreciated and unused to a large extent.

The reason why qualities of the heart are neglected by business corporations is that their highest values are profit, competition, and power. Sensitivity to other people's needs becomes somewhat stifled. Corporate culture and government bureaucracies encourage the repression of feelings and emotions—without admitting it openly or even being aware of it. Intense competitiveness and lust for power lead to negative emotions of envy and hatred, which have to be repressed. In the process, the ability to be sensitive to other people's needs and feelings becomes smothered as well. While it is important that one become successful in one's work, it is also vital that one remain human by developing and using empathy and compassion. A more humane and responsible market economy, while still encouraging competition (yet not of the cutthroat type), would help managers, employees, and working people to become less detached from their hearts and emotions.

Some managers interviewed by psychologist Michael Maccoby believed that only the fittest survive and expressed little or no responsibility to the poor, nor had they thought a great deal about how to improve society or to overcome injustices. These managers have succeeded in their careers but failed to make a success of their lives. To live successfully and responsibly, one must make a success of one's marital, family, personal, and social life, as well as one's career, in a manner that preserves one's integrity and makes one both a mature, competent, and socially, morally, and personally responsible human being. The price paid for failing to develop the heart can be terrible. Some of the most creative top executives that Maccoby tested in the United States expressed self-contempt, when given Rorschach tests. They saw images of bugs, worms, and rats. When asked the reason for these perceptions, they said it was because they failed to develop their hearts and respond to the needs of others.

### 107. Preserving Some Childlike Traits throughout Life

It is very sad that many people, in growing from childhood to adulthood, while succeeding in becoming intellectually and emotionally mature, which enables them to earn a living by engaging in a useful occupation and to raise a family, nevertheless become somewhat or even very cynical, losing their ideals, becoming disillusioned and hardened. Others lose their spontaneity and the child's sense of wonder and curiosity as well as the ability to trust.

While is is absolutely essential that we become intellectually and emotionally mature, it is also important that we preserve throughout life a sense of curiosity about people, nature, and the world, and that we maintain a certain realistic degree of trust in others—without, however, being naive. Research has shown that people who trust others are less deceived by them than are cynical people who distrust others. The real winners in life are those people who are capable of seeing goodness and beauty in others and in the world, in spite of all the disappointments and setbacks they experience.

Spontaneity and creativity are also important traits that have to be preserved throughout life. Not only our wellbeing and happiness depend on retaining these precious qualities, but also our capacity to innovate, to create new things and ideas, to improve the system and the world. Playfulness and a sense of humor are equally important for being a balanced person as well as for good mental health and happiness. Preserving these childlike qualities throughout life also strengthens the immune system and helps to prolong life.

It is equally essential and vital to preserve throughout life the adolescent's idealism and the tendency to contest the existing authority and social order, especially when they are unjust, irresponsible, or oppressive. Responsible reform has its roots in adolescent idealism mixed with practical realism. Society cannot evolve and progress responsibly without this dose of responsible idealism based on the vision of how social conditions should be.

Burnout can be described psychologically as a loss of idealism. Remaining idealistic throughout life and blending it with practical realism prevents cynicism and burnout, and helps one to remain enthusiastic in the accomplishment of one's tasks and duties in life.

## 108. Listening Responsibly

The essential characteristics of listening are concentrating, paying attention, and trying to understand what others are saying . One also has to be interested in what the other person has to say. One should also be aware of the body language the other person uses and try to understand its meaning. Listening responsibly also means being sensitive to and understanding the feelings of the other person or persons.

Responsible listening goes beyond what is merely said. By using empathy and intuition one has to become aware of others' unexpressed needs to develop their aptitudes and talents, to be respected, and helped to make their contribution to society and to live fulfilled lives.

Responsible listening also means to understand that one must listen to and respond to people's needs to be spoken to in a polite manner, to be informed, educated, enlightened, and encouraged in their activities and tasks.

It is also important to know that people who live unfulfilled lives might often not be aware of the real reasons for their unhappiness. Listening to them responsibly means to empathize with them as well as to feel sympathetic, to ask questions concerning their problems in a sensitive manner, and to help them find solutions to their difficulties.

## 109. Developing a Responsible Sense of Humor

Acquiring a responsible sense of humor is a sign of good personal and social adjustment as well as of good mental health. It is important that we laugh with other people and not at others by ridiculing or making fun of them.

Humor allows us to cope with the incongruities, hardships, and trials of life. Humor helps to defuse and neutralize hostile feelings toward others and oneself. It also helps people cope with pain, to see things in perspective, and not to take life more seriously than necessary. It further enables a person to make fun of his or her weaknesses and keeps a person balanced by enabling him or her to see the lighter side of life and to laugh.

A very good example of how humor can cope with extreme adversity and great pain is found in the joke concerning the Jewish person in a Nazi concentration camp. A Nazi guard told him one day that his life might be spared if he could guess which one of the guard's eyes was an artificial one. The SS torturer pointed out that his glass eye was the best ever produced in the Third Reich, and that nobody had ever been able to guess which one it was. Terrified, the Jewish prisoner looked into the eyes of the sadist and said after a while that his left eye was the glass eye. Astonished, the Nazi said it was so, but asked the Jewish person how he had guessed. The prisoner answered that since the glass eye looked at him with such warmth, benevolence, and sympathy, it was really not difficult to have identified it.

This joke has universal relevance and appeal and indicates that humor used responsibly and courageously can sometimes help us to cope with great adversity and survive. Through laughter we can endure pain and neutralize the anguish caused by irresponsible and cruel tormentors.

# CHAPTER NINE

# *Political Responsibilities*

## 110. Preventing a Nuclear Holocaust

THE INVENTION OF NUCLEAR WEAPONS, AND THE EXISTING LARGE quantities of these arms capable of destroying all life on earth, call for a profound and radical revolution in people's thinking, feelings, perceptions, values, and their relations with God and mankind. The antidote against the threat of nuclear annihilation is more personal, social, and moral responsibility. People have to become increasingly committed to preserving life, to saving the environment, to developing a far greater degree of solidarity with their fellow men, to discovering and seeing goodness and other positive traits in others, and to seeing the will of God in human diversity.

Furthermore, governments also have to become increasingly responsible by deemphasizing national and international conflicts, by enhanced disarmament, by accepting the idea of partial or even total abdication of national sovereignty to allow the creation of the United States of the World. It is only a world government with a strong central authority, which nevertheless also accepts strong regional powers, that can effectively remove the global threat of nuclear annihilation, and can also deal efficiently with such other threats to human survival as environmental pollution and overpopulation. A world government, based on responsible worldwide human solidarity and faith in God, the creator of the universe, will also be able to enforce a more just redistribution of resources and wealth throughout the world and eliminate unemployment, hunger, illiteracy, and major sicknesses.

The main concern of governments and people everywhere should and must be the abolition of war and of all forms of killing as well as preventing further proliferation of nuclear weapons and their possession by additional states. Existing stockpiles should and must be destroyed.

The outlawing of war must go hand in hand with the creation of conditions in the world leading to genuine, universal peace. This must happen not only through legislation, but also through the creation of the necessary social, economic, psychological, political, spiritual, educational, cultural, religious, ethical, and moral conditions that will lead to generalized wellbeing, to moderate prosperity for all, to social justice, and to respect of human differences.

## 111. Creating a World Government

The numerous problems confronting humanity, such as eliminating the danger of a nuclear holocaust, protecting the global environment, controlling the population explosion, helping poor nations to develop economically without destroying the environment, eliminating poverty, hunger, and unemployment on a worldwide basis, outlawing war, and achieving global peace, will sooner or later require the creation of a worldwide political supranational structure under the authority of a world government. A plausible, appropriate, and credible name for a future politically united world might be "The United States of the World." Whether it will take a few generations, a few centuries, a millennium, or more, one must believe that humankind, in cooperation with God, will eventually succeed in creating a world government, including all the states and nations of the world.

The coming world government must have the political and judicial authority to abolish war on a global scale (the United Nations does not have this at present), must have the power to impose worldwide peace not only among nations and states but also in internal wars within states, must create global moderate prosperity, social justice, and full worldwide employment. All states and governments will have to relinquish some degree of authority and give it to the world government. National sovereignties will have to be greatly reduced and the jurisdiction of the central world government will have to be greatly increased. However, there must be a balance between the jurisdiction of the local states and the central authority of the world government. Concurrent with the world government's supreme authority, state, regional, and municipal governments would also exercise some degree of authority in many fields. The supranational government would have to possess an army capable of imposing peace and keeping it on a worldwide basis, as well as dismantling and destroying all nuclear, chemical, and bacteriological weapons. It must also have the authority over a worldwide judicial system that outlaws capital punishment globally and enforces the reeducation of criminals and delinquents to personal, social, and moral responsibility.

One of the many benefits and blessings of a world government would be the disappearance of the confrontational balance of power politics and of confrontational alliances responsible for many past wars.

It is important to understand that the United Nations was not created to be a world government, but was meant to be and is an actual fact an organization of many states. It has no authority to interfere in the internal affairs of a nation-state, even if that state persecutes and murders many of its citizens. On the other hand, some global international agencies and institutions already exist, some under the authority of the United Nations—the World Health Organization, responsible for global vaccinations among other duties, UNESCO (United Nations Educational, Scientific, and Cultural Organization)—and agencies dealing with the control of nuclear energy, environmental protection, production and distribution of food, communication satellites, and helping the children of the world.

The world government would also have to empower the World Court, which already exists at The Hague, but has very little power at present to enforce its judgments, to become the supreme global judicial authority to arbitrate and settle international conflicts.

The world government would also have to play a major part in educating young people and adults to think globally, to identify and overcome the problems confronting humankind. People would also have to be taught that God created all human beings on earth, that we are all members of the human family, and that there are as many similar characteristics as there are differences between the various individuals and ethnic, racial, religious, and national groups of the world. It is important that people be taught to tolerate and respect differences. History courses must emphasize that in spite of all the absurd and irresponsible wars and cruelties of the past, there is nevertheless a gradual, progressive movement toward more personal, social, and moral responsibility, toward more humanity, and worldwide human solidarity.

In terms of communication (and to some extent transportation), the world has already become a global village. It will become increasingly important that more and more people perceive themselves as world citizens. This perception will definitely put pressure on politicians to start dreaming about and even planning to bring about a united world and a world government in a practical way. It is also important in this respect to sympathize with people who feel more than one national loyalty, such as the Irish, Jewish, Italian, and Greek Canadians, among others, loyalties which are not in conflict with each other. These people feel loyalty to Canada, their country of birth or adoption, but are also loyal to the country their ancestors came from or to which they are linked by ethnic, national, or religious ties. People with this form of responsible double, or in some cases even multiple, loyalties are richer in a human sense, have more integrity, and are the nucleus of a future united world and world government. A good example is the former lord mayor of Dublin, Robert Briscoe, who, on his visit to the United States in the 1950s, represented the interests of Ireland, but who also as a Jew defended the interests of Israel. Jean Louis Barrault, the famous French actor, stated in 1972 in Montreal that he considered himself a world citizen.

A united world under the authority of a world government would have to work harmoniously with a multitude of national and regional governments, who have to preserve some degree of authority, especially in areas of national or local importance. Besides, it is extremely efficient and responsible to allow a lot of decentralization and local responsibility. We have all seen the inefficiency of highly centralized governments, especially the government of the former Soviet Union. National, regional, and municipal governments are also more able to respect the national and regional traditions, customs, and languages of people, an extremely important factor in producing social pride and self-respect, attitudes, and qualities which are the basis of harmony and understanding between people at the national and international level.

On the other hand, the merit of a world government would also be to do away with the irresponsible negative aspects of nationalism—excessively glorifying a province or state and belittling or insulting another one.

A world government would also demand from a central educational institutional authority that much of world history be rewritten in a more truthful, wise, humanitarian, and socially and morally responsible manner, in order that the inhumanity and moral irresponsibility of most wars in history could be exposed, and the suffering and destruction they have produced be stated and described. It is also important to remember that the ancient Greeks called foreigners barbarians. To them this connoted being primitive and uncivilized, a feeling shared by many people who lived at a later date and who were influenced by Greek civilization. The best way to see foreigners and, in fact, all human differences as potentially positive is to imagine giant jigsaw puzzles—one for states, one for religions, one for nationalities, one for races, one for cultures, and one for all the individuals of our planet, in which each constituent part, by virtue of its distinctness, difference, and uniqueness becomes absolutely indispensable to the total picture of a united world and humanity.

The tendency of European countries to unite in closer economic and political ties and the North American Free Trade Agreement point the way to the future evolution of states and nations into a united world community.

A world government would also have to enshrine the collective rights of humanity to survival, peace, to social, physical, economic, and spiritual wellbeing, to moderate prosperity, full employment, and to the preservation of the environment and a relatively pollution-free world.

The compassion which people in the rich countries showed for the starving in Africa, as well as the readiness to help by sending food, indicated the existence of profound potentials of human solidarity. These must be further developed and strengthened through socially and morally responsible education. People must learn and appreciate the customs, traditions, and values of other cultures, and ethnic and national groups. They must be helped to develop an interest in what is happening in other countries as well as being encouraged to travel extensively to various countries of the world.

It will be the duty of the world government to make one language the universal and official language of the world community, while encouraging the continuing use other existing languages. People should be motivated to learn at least a few languages. In the second part of the twentieth century, English has emerged as the universal language of diplomacy, science, commerce, and technology.

Since time immemorial, irresponsible rulers and governments persecuted their minorities and engaged in military conquest to enlarge the territory of their countries. A precedent was created at Nuremberg after the end of the Second World War, when for the first time in world history, the leaders of Nazi Germany were sentenced as war criminals for crimes against humanity, including the extermination of six million Jews, some of whom were German citizens.

A permanent World Court would have to be created to judge and sentence criminals committing crimes which fall into the category of genocide, like the atrocities in Cambodia, Bosnia and Rwanda.

Another important precedent was created in 1991, after the United Nations war against Iraq, when the United Nations—and especially the United States, England, and France—declared a large part of northern Iraq off limits to Iraqi forces in order to put the area at the disposal of the persecuted Kurdish minority. These two events are milestones in humankind's legal and moral advancement toward a world government having authority over the "United States of the World." The "'United

States of the World" could also be named "The United States of the World Human Family."

## 112. The Responsibilities of the Developed and Developing Countries

It is important that the industrialized world help the third world by providing low-interest or even interest-free capital as well as technical know-how and training in order to enable third world countries become developed and find their own solutions to the problems of creating a moderately prosperous society, as well as full employment, in an ecologically responsible manner. Achieving this is also of the utmost importance to the industrialized world. The rich countries must help the third world to improve its industry and agriculture simultaneously, as well as its educational, social, and health systems. It is also crucial that rich countries insist that the developing nations receiving aid reduce their military spending, respect human rights, and promote democracy. Together with adopting an efficient economic market system, third world countries should also wipe out corruption, redistribute income more justly, and help vast numbers of people to own land. The money lent to developing countries must help them to develop their economy and their social structure at the same time, and to protect the environment.

It is also vital that rich countries open their markets to more imports from developing nations and cancel a considerable amount of the debt owed to them by poor countries.

There is a global, ecological, economic, and political interdependence between the prosperous North and the relatively poor South. Poverty promotes deforestation and environmental degradation, which has catastrophic effects on the whole world. Poverty in the third world also creates starvation and sicknesses as well as mass population movements, which tend to destabilize the whole world. Poverty also cheapens the value of human life and leads to wars. All these factors show why it is vitally important for the rich of the world to help the poor.

One extremely responsible and ingenious way of rich creditor countries helping the developing nations (which is already being used to some extent), is to write off a financial debt partially or even totally in return for the transfer of part of the debtor's ecological treasures (rain forests, for example) to an international agency which will protect it and help the debtor country to prosper economically by using the rain forests either for tourism or for pharmaceutical purposes. This enables the developing nations to protect their environment as well as to benefit from it economically. The idea of developing economically and industrially in an environmentally friendly manner through sustainable growth should and must become a guiding principle of economic development not only in the third world but in rich countries as well.

It is also essential that Western democracies encourage third world leaders and motivate and stimulate them to introduce socially responsible structural changes in their countries in the fields of education, health, birth control, in the creation of jobs, and in social welfare.

The rich countries must also make sure that the money they lend to the developing countries does not end up in the pockets of corrupt officials, but really benefits the people it is intended for. The local population in the developing countries should be treated as partners when decisions are made concerning how the money they receive from rich countries should be best spent. Local traditions and values must be respected by investors and creditors from industrialized countries and people in third world countries should be stimulated to adapt modern technological methods to their own distinct and specific way of life.

Third world countries must make a great effort to control the population explosion by adopting responsible family planning and birth control methods. They must also learn to grow their own food efficiently and become relatively independent of outside help. The highly mechanized American way of producing food might not be totally suitable for third world countries, because it uses less and less manpower. The third world must benefit from North American agricultural know-how, but must do it in such a way as to also ensure full employment for its people. The world must also eliminate the socially irresponsible spectacle of grain surplus in some rich countries, and must find agricultural, social, moral, and political solutions to ensure that hunger disappears from the face of the earth.

It is also necessary that third world countries make it a priority to feed and house all children, run schools, and staff medical clinics even if they have incurred a large debt to the developed world. Some arrangements must be made whereby the rich creditors accept the humanitarian responsibility of the indebted in the third world to care for the young and the sick and reduce the owed debt, making it possible for the developing countries to behave in a socially and morally responsible manner toward their people.

It is encouraging to note that in spite of poverty, hunger, illiteracy, tribal rivalries, civil wars, and corrupt and incompetent leaders, there are success stories in Africa. Even after civil war, Zimbabwe has continued to feed itself and offers grain for export. There is also cooperation in Zimbabwe between blacks and whites. Generally speaking, in spite of setbacks, there are more literate children in Africa at present than was the case in the past. It is important that tribal warfare stops and that industrialized nations encourage the creation of market economies in Africa, yet African countries should also simultaneously bring into existence socially and morally responsible governments.

Another problem has to do with irresponsible tourism to third world countries. Mass tourism from the developed world is destroying many a third world country's society. Peter Davis, a member of the board of the Center for Responsible Tourism in California says that drugs, nudity, prostitution, and cultural destruction are some of the ills caused by mass tourism in third world countries. Responsible tourism tries to remedy this by encouraging tourists to have meaningful encounters with local people, understand their culture, and make a contribution to the economic development of the country.

It is also important to realize that helping the poor, homeless, and hungry of the third world is not as easy as it used to be. They don't want to be saved by Western missionaries. Furthermore, the problem of third world poverty is too massive to be fought with food packages or clinics or schools. Voluntary workers have to discover that many local people are willing and able to help themselves. There must be a better relationship and partnership between agencies in the developed world and voluntary agencies in the third world. Western values should not be imposed. Rather, cooperation with local development groups should be encouraged, as well as working together to recommend projects and priorities.

A highly responsible and successful, relatively small-scale endeavor to help people in the third world is undertaken by Accion International, an aid organization based in Cambridge, Massachusetts. It specializes in making credit available to Latin American unregistered street vendors, seamstresses, carpenters, and other craftsmen. They account for an important percentage of all the business in Latin American countries. In 1990 the organization lent out $38 million to 67,000 family businesses. The average loan was $300. The social and economic mission of Accion International succeeds in creating moderate prosperity and jobs. This example should be followed by other aid organizations and should also be introduced in other parts of the third world.

Another shining example of a remarkable twentieth-century success story is that of South Korea, which succeeded in transforming itself from a relatively undeveloped country into a highly industrialized nation within only two to three decades. While not every country can become as prosperous as South Korea has become, it is nevertheless possible for every nation to become relatively independent economically and moderately prosperous—provided people are properly educated, motivated to work hard, and have leaders who are personally, socially, and morally responsible.

Each country in the developing world must find its own way to responsible social and economic emancipation with some help from the industrialized, democratic world.

## 113. Creating a Responsible Democracy

Churchill said that democracy is the worst form of government, with the exception of all other forms. By this he meant that while democracy is far from being perfect, it is superior to all other forms of government, which are worse.

Responsible democracy means to elect leaders at all levels of government who are highly competent, well balanced psychologically, emotionally mature, wise, realistic, practically idealistic, and also responsive to the needs of the people for peace, social justice, full employment, an unpolluted environment, comprehensive social security programs, and for cities without crime and without homeless people.

Responsible democracy encourages the participation of citizens in the decision-making process, which should occur through the occasional recourse to a national referendum, where the whole population is asked to vote for or against a specific issue of great social importance. It is very important that through education citizens become knowledgeable about the issues involved and that there is no punishment for those who vote according to their conscience.

In a responsible democracy, there should be a supreme political forum composed of personally, socially, and morally highly responsible people who should make the final decision whether the result of a referendum should be accepted and used to influence government policy. The supreme political forum should only accept the verdict of the people if it is in accordance with responsible humanitarian as well as decent principles.

It is important that citizens elect highly competent, decent, mature, responsible politicians, and that citizens continue to inform the elected officials about their thoughts and feelings with respect to various political, economic, and social issues, and what they would like the politicians to do to improve society and the world.

In a responsible democracy, society and the state should have a collective purpose, like accomplishing the maximum good as well as creating a socio-economic political system based on a mixture of capitalism and social security. The system must furthermore promote peace, defend human rights and freedoms, promote political pluralism, and foster the development of everybody's potentials. Responsible democracy depends on compromise between conflicting ideas and opinions and is based on a balance between respect for the rights of individuals and those of the collectivity. It respects both the responsible values, ideals, and ideas of the majority as well as those of minorities. In a responsible democracy there is no racial, ethnic, or religious prejudice or discrimination, and there is also an absence of prejudice on account of age or sex. Responsible democracy is predicated on the conviction that no man is good or wise enough to be entrusted by his fellow men with absolute power. Responsible democracy is also based on the conviction that all people must be part of the process of making decisions that affect their lives. These decisions must be founded on the principles of truth, justice, decency, honesty, and integrity; the views of people must be disregarded if they are socially and morally irresponsible. In Bulgaria in 1989, people protested against the government's decision to give back to the Turkish minority rights taken away from them by the previous totalitarian communist government. Another example of irresponsible behavior is that of a lynch mob. They might have the power associated with large numbers but they certainly are not right. Candidates or parties advocating racial or any other form of discrimination, prejudice, or social injustice or distortion of truth must be penalized, whether they represent the majority or not.

There are other examples of irresponsible majority opinions. In 1988, 68 percent of the Canadian public favored the restoration of the death penalty, which is a cruel, vindictive form of punishment. In 1989, according to a public opinion survey, 83 percent of the Canadian public supported a bill that would limit the entry of refugees into Canada—this at a time when many third world countries are threatened by a population explosion and there are tyrannical governments in quite a few countries of the world as well as widespread hunger. Swiss voters in 1989 decided that employers have the right to fire women if they become pregnant. In a vote, 72.5 percent rejected a measure that would have given women a statutory right to retain their jobs. The Swiss federal government supported a measure allowing women to retain their jobs. In this instance the Swiss government took a position in accordance with the principle of responsible democracy, regardless of the irresponsible views of the majority of voters who were ready to support the view that women can be fired if they become pregnant.

Fortunately, however, there are also many instances when the majority of the people express highly responsible opinions. A survey conducted in 1989 across Canada revealed that a majority of Canadians are willing to pay higher taxes to have a pollution-free environment and are demanding stiff penalties for people, officials, institutions, governments, and corporations responsible for destroying the environment. Their highly responsible views must be taken into consideration and governments should raise taxes and enact laws to prevent the destruction of the environment. Laws must be enacted to severely punish polluters. Hopefully, the highly responsible views and wishes of a majority of Canadians will serve as an example to people all over the world and motivate them to express similarly responsible viewpoints and to exert strong pressure on governments to put them into action.

### 114. Creating Responsible Institutions and a Responsible World Order

The dictionary defines internationalism as the belief that mutual understanding and cooperation among nations will advance the common welfare. It is very important that people everywhere in the world learn to think globally and in terms of relations of interdependence between nations. They must also learn to feel enriched by human differences, and must also come to realize that environmental, political, demographic, and health problems, as well as the need to eliminate the threat of a nuclear holocaust, and the need to outlaw and abolish war, require more and more the creation of an authoritative world government respected by all nations and states of the world.

Eastern and Western values are different, yet highly complementary. The Western world values the individual. The Japanese have a great respect for elderly people. In India the family is more important than the individual, whereas in China the group has greater value than the individual. Japanese managers attach great importance to intuition; this to some extent explains their extraordinary economic and industrial accomplishments. North American executives, on the other hand, attach great importance to logical, analytical thinking. Better relations between the East and the West can come about if the East values the individual more and the West appreciates the group, the elderly, and intuitive thought processes more than it now does.

UNESCO (The United Nations Educational, Scientific, and Cultural Organization) is an international institution, which in spite of a lot of infighting, criticism, and the fact that the United States is no longer a member of the organization, has done a lot of good for the betterment of

213

the world. It has fought illiteracy on a global scale and has dedicated itself to preserving cultural treasures in the world. It is imperative that the Untied States again become a member of this vital institution. Two other examples of eminently important international organizations doing magnificent humanitarian work are UNICEF, the organization that promotes the welfare of children globally, and WHO, the World Health Organization, which has made a tremendous contribution to preventing and eradicating sicknesses all over the world.

The World Watch Institute in its 1988 State of the World report, supported financially by the Rockefeller Brothers Fund and the United Nations Fund for Population Activities, recommends the creation of new international institutions or expanding the authority of existing ones to promote responsible behavior. One practical possibility would be for the rich nations to create institutions dedicated to teaching and helping the developing nations produce goods without polluting the environment.

In the field of international relations, it is important that democratic governments, as well as those which are not yet democratic, behave at their best. They should and must treat other governments and people in a respectful, responsible manner conducive to international cooperation and peace.

International relations between states are increasingly based on the principle of autodetermination of people as well as on refraining from territorial conquest. This principle will have to be stressed even more in the future. Some governments are restricting and giving up some of their sovereignty, jurisdiction, and authority, subordinating themselves to a supranational structure—the European union, for example.

This tendency will have to be imitated by governments in other areas of the world as well. Supranational structures would eventually have to subordinate themselves to an as yet to be created world government, having authority over the "United States of the World."

### 115. Granting Human Rights and Freedoms

Human rights and freedoms might be viewed as the legal and political manifestation of a culture's perception of human dignity. Rights are needs that have been accepted theoretically and, in many instances, granted practically. More and more governments, institutions, and people all over the world should and must accept and grant human rights and freedoms. There has been great emphasis placed on human rights and freedoms in the second part of the twentieth century, yet humankind has not yet fully grown up to grant them to every person on earth.

Western societies have derived their belief in the dignity of human beings from the Judeo-Christian transcendental belief that human beings are made in the image of God, the creator of the universe. In the American formulation, human beings are endowed by God with inherent and inalienable rights. These beliefs are so precious, humanitarian, and responsible that they must become the universal legacy and endowment of humankind. The United Nations declaration of human rights is an important step in the right direction.

There are political, economic, social and judicial rights and freedoms—the freedom of assembly, of belief, of religious expression, of the press, of forming and joining political parties, of competing for public office, of organizing unions, of striking, of traveling, of emigration. There is the right to work, to employment, to receive adequate health services if sick, to receive an education enabling one to develop one's potentials and talents, the right to be different, the right to national and worldwide peace, to a clean environment, to live in moderate prosperity, to long-term sustainable resources, to adequate old-age pensions, and to affordable universal medical insurance and health care. Some of these rights and freedoms have already been identified, recognized, and officially granted by some societies and in some countries. Others have yet to be recognized, accepted, legally formulated, and politically granted.

In dictatorial countries, human rights and freedoms, if they exist at all, are considered a privilege rather than an inherent, inalienable right of every human being.

Some corrective measures, such as affirmative action, should and must be introduced by governments in countries and societies where discrimination exists against certain racial, religious, ethnic, and national minorities. Through affirmative action, the discriminated minority obtains some advantages and gets priority when applying for certain types of jobs or to higher education. However, these corrective measures must be integrated and harmonized with the principle of advancing and promoting people by virtue of individual talent and merit.

It is also important to be aware that there are individual and group rights and freedoms. Some rights apply more to individuals, while others more to groups. Canada, as a land of minorities, defends and grants rights to groups. The Canadian constitution has defended the rights of the English, French, Catholic, Protestant, and, since 1982, has also championed the rights of native people and of multicultural groups. Linguistic school rights as well as those of women are also in the category of group rights. Group rights apply also to individuals but only in the sense where these individuals are considered to be members of specific groups.

The responsibility to grant as many individual and group rights and freedoms as possible must become the duty of every responsible government and institution throughout the world. This is one more reason why there is an absolute need for a united world under the authority of a world government.

### 116. Understanding the Duties of Responsible Governments and of Responsible Politicians

The dictionary defines government as the authoritative administration of the affairs of a nation, state, or city. It also means the officially governing body of a nation or community. A third meaning refers to the established form of rule by which a nation or community is controlled.

Public service refers to government employment, especially in the civil department. It is synonymous with civil service, and it includes the branches of government that are not military, legislative, or judicial. It also refers to the body of persons employed in this service.

Government refers to both elected politicians and to civil servants. Public service is the administrative, non-political part of government, often referred to as the bureaucracy. In democratic countries, in contrast to dictatorships, the political branch of government consists mainly of elected officials, even though in some democratic countries some public officials can be named by the head of state or prime minister without being elected.

Civil servants very often have lifelong, permanent positions. In some countries, there is a hidden, latent conflict between politically elected officials and the bureaucratic administration, which accounts to some extent for a certain degree of lethargy and inefficiency. Politically elected officials have power and authority to effect change, but they come and go, changing every few years, while civil servants, who are there mostly for life, have to implement the decisions made by politicians, which they sometimes resist subtly and surreptitiously, or sometimes even openly.

A responsible government should and must be both efficient as well as responsive to the needs of the people. Many duties of governments are well known and are almost the same all over the world—maintaining law and order, keeping an army, providing postal service, levying taxes, maintaining relations with foreign governments, dealing with the economy and foreign trade, with education, health, social security, communication, transportation, and culture.

A responsive, socially just, and morally responsible government is characterized by introducing free universal medical insurance, similar to the one existing in Canada, by some form of redistribution of income through progressive taxation, meaning that the tax rate deducted by governments from taxpaying citizens has to increase in proportion to the increase in earned income. There should be a free education system, including university, allowing the young as well as motivated adults to develop and maximize their potentials in accordance with specific aptitudes and talents. An efficient, socially and morally responsible government will provide full employment, will prevent discrimination on the basis of sex, race, religion, ethnic background, or age, and will grant all citizens full democratic rights. It must outlaw the death sentence (in those countries where it still exists), and must reeducate criminals and delinquents to personal, social, and moral responsibility. It must not tolerate hate literature against minorities and must use some form of censorship to censor pornography and destructive, unjustified, and unnecessary violence in films, television programs, and printed material, things portrayed and mentioned only to cater to the most primitive and vilest instincts of people and to make money. Pornography is violence directed against altruistic feelings. It is also important that governments outlaw prostitution, an infamous and abject exploitation of the body as well as a form of personal, social, and moral degradation.

A responsible and responsive government must do everything possible to protect the environment by imposing severe penalties against any person or corporation who pollutes and destroys it. It must stop the population explosion and introduce some form of affirmative action to ensure social justice against discriminated groups and minorities. It must help the developing world to strengthen its economy and industries in a manner that protects the environment. It must also assist developing countries to build the necessary social, educational, and medical institutions that will enable them to attain a good quality of life. A responsible government must promote and advance the idea of the eventual creation of a world government, having authority over the "United States of the World." A responsible government must work to create cities with a high quality of life, having as little crime, poverty, and pollution as possible. It must also introduce policies to save energy and find alternate sources of energy to replace oil and coal. It must also pay for quality day care services and introduce paid maternity leave.

A socially and morally responsible government must prevent and outlaw strikes by police, firemen, teachers, doctors, nurses, and other professionals connected with health care, by public transportation workers, postal workers, and all public and municipal employees who do work that is essential for the security and the wellbeing of citizens. It must introduce forced arbitration to settle most labor conflicts, especially those where the security and wellbeing of the public is at stake. It must also assume the responsibility to educate business and industrial corporations to protect the environment and must severely punish those who pollute and destroy the environment. A socially and morally responsible government must also assume the duty of considerably narrowing the difference between the earnings of the wealthiest and the poorest segments of the population. In Japan the ratio is 17 to 1, while in the United States the difference is approximately 100 to 1. This responsible reduction of the difference in earnings and wealth can and must be done through progressive taxation.

It is essential to accept the idea that in the same way that parents have a responsibility for the wellbeing of their children, all levels of government must also assume the responsibility for the material and social wellbeing of all people. New Zealand has recognized through a series of laws the principle that the state is responsible for the health, education, and wellbeing of all its citizens, particularly the young, the old, and the distressed. In the early 1990s in Germany, banking and the economy are kept under strict government supervision, and there is a level of social protection, welfarism, that would be unimaginable in the United States. This indicates that New Zealand and Germany are examples of responsible and responsive governments. People want dynamic market economies with all their benefits, but they also want to live in a socially responsible state and community.

Another example of a socially and morally responsible government is that of Canada, where unemployment insurance, old-age pensions, and free universal medical insurance are provided to every citizen. The costs are paid through tax revenues. In the United States, on the other hand, medical insurance is private. Senior citizens are covered by government-subsidized medicare, whereas 36 million Americans, a third of them children, had no medical insurance whatsoever as recently as 1989. As a result, Canadians enjoy a longer life expectancy as well as a more equitable system. In Canada, 85 percent of the unemployed receive unemployment benefits, whereas in the United States only one in four jobless persons qualifies for unemployment insurance benefits. The Canadian system provides 60 percent of insurable earnings, while the U.S. scheme, run by individual states, provides only one-third of weekly wages.

Families with children also fare better in Canada. Family allowances (baby bonus) cover 6.6 million Canadian children. Even though a change in the system in 1992 eliminated family allowances for middle-income and rich families, the government continues to provide family allowances for poor families. Canada also has universal old-age security allowances funded out of general tax revenues, while in the United States you need to spend some time in the work force and contribute toward the old-age assistance fund to get assistance later. It should be one of the main duties of every socially and morally responsible government to provide universal medical health care, supplementary child educational funds to poor and low-income families, and universal pensions to senior citizens out of general tax revenues. Responsible governments have the duty to raise taxes to pay for these humanitarian social programs and to educate their citizens to accept them willingly and gladly.

The aim of the constitution of the United States was to oppose oppression. Struggling against a European tradition of irresponsible, authoritarian, oppressive government, the creators of the American constitution saw government as the enemy and emasculated it. Even today, republican politicians try to weaken government and emphasize too much the duty of individuals and of non-government social institutions to assume responsibilities that only governments can exercise effectively and responsibly. There has to be a balance between the responsibilities of the government and those of private institutions and individuals. Private citizens or companies cannot create universal medical insurance and quality medical services available to all citizens free of charge.

Similarly, private citizens cannot create an educational system that adequately meets the needs of all people. Only a responsible and responsive government can do these things. On the other hand, government must not become too centralized and too powerful, as was the case in the former Soviet Union, which paralyzed all private and individual initiative and responsibility and condemned the public to inadequate, scarce, and low-quality goods and services. Government must develop into an efficient, responsible, and responsive institution—and citizens must perceive it as such. A complementary and harmonious cooperation between citizens and the various levels of government has to develop all over the world.

Society must evolve to a level of development where it acts through its elected officials and civil servants as the protector and promoter of individual and collective rights and wellbeing. Laws and the police should increasingly protect individuals and groups in every country of the world from all forms of oppression, discrimination, violence, and injustice, whether committed by government agencies, business, social institutions, or by private citizens. This would require that some of the brightest, best educated, and socially and morally most responsible people select and are recruited for careers in the field of police work. Police work has to become a respected and well-paying career.

John Naisbett states that centralized structures are crumbling in the United States, where states and local governments are the most important political entities. There is an increased flowing of authority to state and local governments. Decentralized local political power can stem either from the central government delegating authority to regional municipal institutions, or from initiatives taken by neighborhoods, municipalities, provinces, or states. Central authority as it existed in the former Soviet Union, or still exists in the French educational system, is often too paralyzing, rigid, uniform, and stifling. It suppresses initiative, innovation, and progress. A lot of power and authority must be given to local political bodies and institutions. A balance has to be established between central and regional local governments. Both levels of government must be strong, and there should be no duplication of services.

Politics has traditionally been viewed as being opposed to morality. Since politics is based on the exercise of power and there is a belief that power corrupts, one can understand why politicians are disliked. Unfortunately, many politicians are guilty of corruption and of opportunism. Quite a few political leaders in some of the poorest countries of the world have become fabulously rich by robbing their impoverished subjects. Yet there are also examples of decent politicians with a high degree of integrity and social and moral responsibility. Vaclav Havel, the president of the Czech Republic, who was imprisoned by the previous communist regime for his campaign in favor of democratic freedoms and rights, nevertheless continued to remain faithful to his beliefs. In his speech to the American Congress, he said that the future of humankind depends on politicians using morality in the exercise of power. Another example is Jimmy Carter, who after having served a four-year term as American president, has dedicated his life to building houses for the poor and to promoting peace and human rights in the world. Konrad Adenauer and Willy Brandt, two post-Second World War West German chancellors, admitted the terrible crimes committed by the Nazis against the Jewish people, apologized for these crimes to the Jews, and paid billions of dollars in restitution to Israel and to survivors of the holocaust.

The survival of humankind in the future will depend increasingly on the eventual creation of a world government having authority over the "United States of the World." Only a world government can deal most effectively with the many problems threatening human survival, like the proliferation of atomic weapons, overpopulation, destruction of the environment, to name only some of the most important problems. It will become more and more imperative in coming years, decades, and centuries, that politicians who will play a very important role in solving these problems and create a world government, attach great value to developing a high degree of personal, social, and moral responsibility.

## 117. Understanding the Evil Nature of Dictatorship

Dictatorship refers to the utter subjugation of the freedom of people as well as the deprivation of most human rights by a tyrant or a despotic regime. Generally speaking, tyrants have contempt and disrespect for people. Napoleon looked upon his soldiers as cannon fodder. Hitler used German teenagers as soldiers to stop the advance of the victorious allied armies toward the end of the Second World War. Pol Pot exterminated over one million fellow Cambodians. Stalin ruthlessly exterminated political opponents and countless other Soviet citizens. All these examples point to the total moral irresponsibility of dictators.

Many members of the middle class bourgeoisie as well as of the upper class were dispossessed of their material goods and in many instances tortured and even killed by communist regimes in Cuba, China, the Soviet Union, in Eastern European countries, and elsewhere. Even the children of the bourgeoisie were prevented from attending college and university.

Political dictatorships use terror, intimidation, incitement of children to spy on their parents, or of citizens to spy on their fellow citizens, methods that are utterly evil and devoid of moral responsibility.

There are also autocratic, despotic religious dictatorships. These also forbid the responsible expression of different ideas and religious practices, and are morally irresponsible.

It is the individual and collective responsibility of people to prevent the formation of dictatorial regimes and to replace them wherever they exist with socially and morally responsible ones.

## 118. Using Power Responsibly and Wisely

Power is defined as being a force or strength, implying the ability or capacity to act, execute, or do things. Responsible power refers to its being used in a beneficial manner. Delinquents value brute strength and devalue moral goodness, kindness, and altruism as being weaknesses. Yet exactly the opposite is true. Genuine concern about the wellbeing of others, sensitivity, generosity, and a friendly smile are often more successful in overcoming opposition and hostility than the use of force. Humanitarian and altruistic help as well as genuine friendliness and authentic love are a source as well as a manifestation of real, highly responsible human power. These altruistic emotions and acts are highly motivating and stimulating,. They succeed in bringing out the best in others and also contribute to replenishing and invigorating one's own humanity. Possessing knowledge, wisdom, insight, and understanding of the world, of oneself, and of others are other examples of genuine, responsible power. Responsible power is highly moral and endeavors to respond to and satisfy other people's as well as one's own justified and life-preserving and enhancing needs.

Power and its exercise is a basic reality of life. People who don't have power, or don't want to use it condemn themselves to lives of frustration. But power should and must be used increasingly wisely and responsibly. Vaclav Havel, the president of the Czech Republic, believes that the future and even the survival of humankind depends on moral responsibility guiding politicians in the exercise of political power. Power must also be used responsibly and wisely in the military, business, industrial, educational, social, spiritual, and religious fields.

Political power, when used unwisely and irresponsibly, leads to moral corruption and bankruptcy. Power should never be used to dominate, exploit, or subjugate people. Power used to dominate and exploit is irresponsible. On the other hand, power used wisely and responsibly helps people become more competent, stimulates their maturity, and contributes to promoting human welfare, happiness, and prosperity.

People can overcome their feelings of powerlessness and improve society and the socio-economic-political system through self-motivated and self-initiated activities and through cooperation with others to protect the environment, to fight pollution, to put pressure on politicians to find solutions to the problems of unemployment, homelessness, poverty, decay of cities, violence and wars, underdevelopment of the third world, and by doing voluntary work and contributing generously to charitable causes.

People in partnership and cooperation with God and with other human beings can develop the responsible power and wisdom as well as vision to cope successfully and responsibly with all the problems threatening human survival. They must use all their psychological, spiritual, and moral qualities and energies as well as all their technical, professional, and managerial skills to accomplish this vitally important task.

This wise and responsible use of power must also create conditions in the world that will stimulate permanent peace and lead to the establishment of a world government and to the creation of moderate universal prosperity and social wellbeing.

## 119. Understanding the Value of Responsible Nationalism

The dictionary defines nationalism as a devotion to one's nation (often chauvinistic), to its political and economic interests and aspirations, and to its social and cultural traditions. Nationalism also connotes the idea of a desire or movement for national independence. The negative aspect of nationalism is chauvinism, an excessive patriotism, military overzealous glorification of one's country, and extremely exaggerated attachment to one's race or group. Nazism, with its doctrine of the racial superiority of the Aryans over the Jews and of the Germans over all other nations was an extreme example of chauvinistic, delinquent, and irresponsible nationalism.

In the increasingly economically interdependent world of today, threatened by the danger of global environmental destruction and of population explosion, irresponsible, chauvinistic nationalism constitutes a menace to the profound needs of the survival of humankind.

Responsible, positive nationalism is a necessary, historical, evolutionary step toward a better, more responsible, and socially more just world. It is an essential, transitional state toward a future world government. It also has, always had, and will always have great value, as it means to love one's country, nation, or group. It widens people's love of their fellow men, extending this love to more people than in the distant past when one identified only with one's narrower surroundings, such as one's town. At its best, nationalism is our identification with the life and aspirations of many people whom we shall never know. It is qualitatively different from the love of family or home and is related to the love of humanity and of the whole earth. Responsible nationalism with its awakening of the masses to participation in political and cultural life, prepared and continues to prepare the way for cultural contacts with all civilizations of mankind.

Responsible nationalism loves one's nation and country but also appreciates and values the love of people in different lands for their own country or nation. The responsible love of one's country also enables us to appreciate, respect, value, and love other nations and countries, and to live peacefully and in harmony with them.

On the other hand, irresponsible nationalism leads to hatred of other nationalities and often results in war. Irresponsible nationalism aims at isolation, exclusiveness, and arrogant superiority as well as domination of one's national, ethnic, cultural, religious, or linguistic group over other groups and states. Irresponsible nationalism is incompatible and inimical to the needs of humankind to survive and to live in harmony, cooperation, interdependence, and solidarity.

Responsible nationalism recognizes that nations and states have to become responsible and that the common welfare of mankind has to be placed above national interests. Responsible nationalism is also based on the understanding that nations and states will increasingly have to give up some degree of sovereignty and must eventually unite to create a world government with authority over the United States of the World. Responsible nationalism further means that each nation is unique and distinct and that this difference makes it an indispensable part of the total jigsaw puzzle of the world family of nations. Responsible nationalism does not mean "my country right or wrong," or that loyalty to my country takes precedence over everything else in the world. Responsible nationalism implies that my country is important to me, but so are other countries, and that other people love their country too. In responsible nationalism there is a progression from love of one's country to love of other countries and ideally to love of the whole world. It is important to understand that one can be in the fortunate situation where one is a citizen of two countries, like a born American who becomes a citizen of a second country through naturalization, while preserving his or her American citizenship. This double citizenship and even double loyalty constitutes an enrichment. It is a genuine and good preparation for becoming a good citizen of the world.

Paradoxically, the late twentieth-century phenomenon of the breaking up of some federal states into smaller independent states, provided it occurred in a peaceful manner, can also be seen as a step leading eventually to the creation of a world government. Through greater solidarity, people in smaller countries, united by a common culture, language, and tradition, can better solve the many economic and political problems confronting them. These smaller states also have a greater need to identify with humankind and with the whole world.

Concurrent with the breaking up of federal states like the former Soviet Union, Yugoslavia, and Czechoslovakia into smaller, more homogeneous constituent states, there is also the tendency for states to unite into a continental community, like the European union, which started as an economic association and could develop into a political union as well.

This is also an important step toward the eventual creation of the United States of the World.

## 120. Helping the World's Refugees

Wars, ethnic, religious, or national conflicts, dictatorships, oppression, discrimination, and economic hardships force millions of people all over the world to leave their countries in order to start a new and better life in a different country. Many refugees, the Vietnamese in Hong Kong, for example, live in deplorable conditions and are not wanted in their new countries. Others who make it to Canada, Germany, or a few other countries are treated far better and, if they are genuine political refugees, have a chance of remaining in their new countries.

The disintegration of the former Soviet Union and East European communist countries, and the ethnic, national hatreds leading to civil war in the former Yugoslavia, have also produced countless refugees.

It is the moral responsibility of the industrialized democracies to accept a large number of political and economic refugees, and to help them fully integrate into their societies. The industrialized democracies must also help the former communist countries as well as the third world financially, economically, and technologically to attain moderate prosperity and become democratic societies. This will make it unnecessary in the future for citizens of these countries to become refugees.

The United Nations should have a standing army at its disposal so that it can be empowered to a greater extent to prevent ethnic cleansing and genocides. Furthermore, a world court of justice must judge these crimes and have the authority to severely punish the offenders. The former communist countries, as well as third world ones must also do the utmost to make a more responsible effort, in cooperation with the West, to create democratic institutions, moderate prosperity, and some social welfare in order to keep most of their citizens in their own countries.

## 121. The Duty of Authority to Be Efficient and Morally Responsible

Throughout the ages many authority figures, such as political, military, and sometimes even political leaders, have exercised authority in a dictatorial, oppressive, domineering, and cruel manner. It is extremely important that authority be exercised in a morally, socially, and personally responsible manner, that combines efficiency with the pragmatic ability to solve problems with compassion, kindness, and responsiveness to human needs. A leader in any field can and must be both firm in his or her determination to achieve results as well as just and humane.

Research and observation indicate that many people have a wrong perception and understanding of the role of authority. Many people, because they perceive authority as harsh, cruel, and repressive, behave likewise and act with unwarranted harshness and even cruelty toward others when playing certain roles like prison guards or administering electroshocks in an experimental setting to other subjects. It is essential that people, no matter what they believe the expected demands of an authoritative role are, behave in an efficient as well as decent and responsible manner once they become authority figures themselves.

Authority has to be increasingly exercised in a way that harmonizes the head with the heart, and also is guided by a well developed social and moral conscience and responsibility. At the public service, bureaucratic level, authority must distinguish itself by excellent performance, by a high quality of service rendered to the public, by personal responsiveness to people's and society's needs, and by sensitivity.

The marriage of efficiency with social, moral, and personal responsibility should increasingly occur at all levels of authority—in politics, business, industry, science, technology, education, religion, and culture, as well as in the military and within the family and social community organizations.

## 122. The Obligations of a Socially and Morally Responsible Army

Traditionally throughout history, regional and national armies served the purpose of conquest as well as of defense. Very often they were instruments of domination and oppression. Even in our times, military leaders in some Latin American countries and elsewhere assumed dictatorial powers. Within the last forty years, since the end of the Second World War, there has been a gradual change toward a greater degree of social responsibility and internationalism. Army units of various nations, as part of a United Nations force, play an increasing role as peacekeepers and as preventers of wars in many trouble spots of the world. This tendency will continue and has to lead eventually to a situation where all armies of the world will become integrated and fused into one army structure belonging to the yet to be created "United States of the World." The mission of this global world army would be to protect and enforce peace on a worldwide basis, including regional and internal conflicts within nations. Other missions of army units should be to serve as an international police, to fight drug smuggling, to intervene and help in cases of natural disasters, and to distribute food and other items to areas of the world stricken by hunger or other calamities.

It is also important that armies become less and less ruled by a blind code of obedience of subordinates toward superiors. This must change to a responsible form of obedience, based on respect for every person, on social and morally responsible principles, where orders are explained, where a certain amount of positive, constructive criticism is allowed and encouraged.

Training of new recruits must not develop into brainwashing any more. A strong aversion and abhorrence of killing other human beings must be seen as a sign of a mature social and moral conscience and must be preserved. On the other hand killing other people should be condoned only as a measure of last resort and only in response to unjustified aggression.

Armies should not be allowed to use women for combat roles. While it is only right and normal that women should serve in the armed forces, engaging in many activities traditionally done by male soldiers, playing many roles, and exercising many nontraditional duties, it is irresponsible to train women for combat roles, as it would be an unnecessary brutalization. The egalitarian feminist demands are to a very great extent justified but training women for combat role is both a perversion of nature and socially and morally irresponsible. However, women should and must be trained to defend themselves just as their male colleagues are.

Armies should increasingly see their mission as preventing war, through intimidation of potential aggressors and dictators and by forcing them to give up their irresponsible plans of conquest and criminal aggression.

### 123. Understanding the Occasional Need for Responsible Revolutions

Revolution refers to a drastic and extensive change in a condition or idea. The industrial revolution, which drastically changed production methods in the Western world in the nineteenth century is a good example. Revolution also refers to the overthrow and replacement of a government or political system. In contrast to evolution, which implies slow, gradual progress or change, revolution occurs in a rapid, sudden manner. The sudden, speedy revolutionary overthrow of dictatorial, communist regimes in East Germany, Czechoslovakia, Romania, Poland, Hungary, and Bulgaria are good illustrations of revolutionary change.

Responsible revolutions must occur without bloodshed. The Czechs, East Germans, and Russians managed to get rid of dictatorial, oppressive communist regimes with little bloodshed, whereas the French revolution in 1789 and the Russian communist revolution in 1917 caused a lot of totally unnecessary killing. Both the French and communist

227

revolutions indicate that the revolutionaries who deposed the previous oppressive regimes behaved as cruelly and irresponsibly as the former tyrants in their mass slaughter of enemies.

All these revolutions indicate that had the overthrown oppressive regimes shown understanding and compassion for the suffering of the people, and had they introduced evolutionary, progressive change toward increased social justice, a higher level of prosperity and less corruption, they might have avoided the bloody revolutions that followed. In other words, the leaders of the tyrannical regimes were totally unresponsive and insensitive to the needs and demands of the people. The French and Russian communist revolutions also point to the foolish tendency to completely replace many of the existing and established beliefs, traditions, institutions, customs, and systems, including traditionally hallowed and consecrated ones like religion, private property, and the calendar. The French revolutionaries tried for a while to change the calendar, an attempt which failed miserably, just as the communist revolutionaries tried to eradicate religion and faith in God as well as private property—extremely important values for the dignity and spiritual, social, material, and psychological wellbeing of people. The communists failed just as the French revolutionaries did; one cannot destroy things that are highly responsible, indispensable, useful, and profoundly meaningful.

Responsible revolutions are progressive and advance social justice, democracy, responsible freedom, and human rights as well as human solidarity, peace, and moderate prosperity for all. Above all, they promote generalized wellbeing and humanitarianism.

# CHAPTER TEN

# *Economic Responsibilities*

### 124. The Responsibilities of Capitalism and Business Enterprises

THE BREAKDOWN OF STATE CONTROLLED COMMUNIST ECONOMIEs in Eastern Europe in 1989, 1990, and 1991, and their replacement by capitalistic, market-dominated economies testifies to the validity of capitalistic principles. While unchecked and unlimited greed is reprehensible and socially irresponsible, the capitalistic system is nevertheless right to advocate and encourage competition, provided it does not drive the loser into total ruin and bankruptcy. It is also right to promote initiative and risk-taking. Chinese farmers multiplied their crop output as a result of having a say in the management of their farms and not having to deliver quotas to the government. They were able to act more responsibly and to develop greater initiative, which resulted in greater production and more income. Rigid centralized planning, typical of communist dictatorship, stifles initiative, whereas decentralized planning stimulates initiative and responsibility and results in the production of a variety of goods in sufficient quantity to satisfy the needs of consumers. Private ownership, responsible competition, and responsible profit also are powerful psychological incentives to ensure a well-functioning economy.

It is very important that the capitalistic system realize that its responsibility is not only to produce sufficient consumer goods but also to ensure general moderate prosperity and economic wellbeing. Switzerland, one of the most capitalistic countries of the world, is prosperous and has an extremely low level of unemployment. Business and industry must increasingly produce goods in a way that does not destroy the environment, even though goods so produced might be more expensive. Also, greater emphasis must be given to reducing the packaging of goods and to making greater use of recycling.

A responsible business enterprise deals honestly with employees and customers, evaluates the performance of employees fairly, pays them adequate wagers, remunerates female employees equally for equal work, and ensures that promotion is based on merit. It also develops a career program for employees that encourages their vocational and professional development and institutes work-sharing programs to reduce unemployment. Furthermore, responsible business and industrial enterprises create working conditions that promote labor management cooperation by encouraging employees to participate in decision making and also by enabling them to become shareowners and coproprietors. Responsible business enterprises have competent, responsive managers and executives who see to it that employees find their work challenging and rewarding. This has a positive effect on the quality as well as the quantity of production. It must also be the responsibility of businesses to further research projects at universities, to give generously to charity, and to help in the development of the third world. Finally, all companies should pay half of the insurance premium for medical coverage of their employees and should also provide adequate retirement pensions as well as maternity leave payments.

The nature of the produced goods is also of considerable importance. Cigarette manufacturers who produce goods that destroy people's health should either fabricate cigarettes with as little nicotine as possible or should switch to the production of socially more valuable as well as healthier goods. The same can be said in the case of the manufacture of armaments. A certain number of weapons will always be needed for defense purposes as well as to impose peace and to control crime. But increasingly, arms manufacturers must switch to the production of goods that do not endanger the continuing survival of humankind.

It is also essential to understand that the profit motive is a responsible incentive to stimulate people to develop the initiative to start businesses that create employment and produce the necessary goods to satisfy people's needs. However, a part of the profits should be reinvested to keep the economy going. Accumulated wealth should be used to a great extent for philanthropic, social, and humanitarian causes. Consumer goods must be produced in sufficient numbers and varieties to satisfy people's demands and needs, yet consuming and owning goods must never become the chief value in life.

A certain amount of competition is also positive and leads to the production of cheaper products and sometimes even to the manufacture of higher quality goods, yet competition must never be cutthroat in nature.

Business, in cooperation with government, has the responsibility to create and maintain full employment. It is essential that business and capitalism develop a social conscience. In a period of economic crisis, business companies should and must introduce job-sharing procedures.

Finally, it is crucial that business executives plan on a long-term basis. Japan is an excellent example in this respect. Companies there also offer their employees lifelong job security. This ensures loyalty and devotion to the company and promotes solidarity between management and workers. Long-term planning and lifelong job security indicate a high degree of social responsibility and are also highly practical, as they result in secure, satisfied workers as well as in a successful and flourishing economy.

### 125. Eliminating Unemployment and Poverty in the World

Unemployment is one of the main causes of poverty. Apart from material deprivation, prolonged unemployment is often associated with family disruptions, conjugal violence and child abuse, drug addiction, alcoholism, depression, and sometimes even suicide.

It is the responsibility of all governments at the national, regional, and local, municipal level, business and industrial corporations, and individual citizens to create full employment. People should also be motivated and helped to create their own businesses. Full employment can be promoted by motivating business and industrial corporations to start job-sharing arrangements, as well as by shortening the average work week of white and blue collar workers and of salaried professionals. This would guarantee employment to many unemployed people and reduce the unemployment rate. As mentioned above, Switzerland, one of the most capitalistic countries in the world, has practically no unemployment. On the other hand, the unemployment rate in traditionally social democratic Scandinavian countries is also very low. The creative private initiative and social and moral responsibility of these countries should and must become an example to the whole world.

It must become one of the main priorities of the industrialized world not only to wipe out unemployment in their own countries but also to help the developing third world countries to achieve full employment. The problem of unemployment and poverty in the third world is aggravated by the fact that jobs are lost in these countries because the chemical, food, and biotechnological corporations in the Western world have produced synthetic substitutes for many raw materials, which constituted the main source of the poor nations' income. In the Philippines and Caribbean, for example, many sugar workers lost their jobs because of this. Third world countries should be helped to produce their own food as well as other consumer goods.

Ideally as well as realistically and practically every person should live above the poverty line, at least in modest comfort.

Two beautiful examples of efforts to fight unemployment and poverty can be found in the federal Canadian government's tax credit and wage subsidy programs and the efforts of the Grameen Bank in Bangladesh, which makes business loans to the poorest people in rural areas of that country. The Canadian tax credit program, which operated between 1978 and 1981, provided tax credits to employers who would create additional jobs. The wage subsidy program targeted high unemployment areas in Atlantic Canada and the Gaspe region of Quebec, and resulted in the creation of 113,000 new jobs over a three-year period among the disadvantaged. In Bangladesh, rural credit was provided to 400,000 Bangladeshis. Women represented 82 percent of the borrowers, as women are more conscious of the future of their children and want to get out of poverty as fast as possible. A typical loan consists of $60. with which a woman buys a cow and a calf. The cow's milk is sold to pay off the loan and then the woman can borrow another $60. to buy another cow. In a few years with a few cows the woman will have improved her status in the community. These beautiful examples illustrate the reality that people possess the necessary creativity and social and moral responsibility to eliminate unemployment and poverty. With the proper political will this objective can and must be accomplished globally.

## 126. Implementing Responsible Remuneration and Redistribution of Income

In Marxist theory, the ideal society is one in which people would be remunerated according to their needs. For Marxists, progress means the creation of a society which evolves from paying workers according to their abilities to compensating them according to their needs. There is some justification to this, yet it is only one aspect of the total picture. Aptitudes, talents, skills, and length of training must also be considered important factors in responsible and just remuneration. An important need which must absolutely be satisfied is to live in moderate comfort. Other important facts to be considered in just and responsible payment are the quantity and quality of output or service rendered as well as the nature and degree of the contribution made to the wellbeing of society and the community.

The difference between highest and lowest paid earners should not be as great as is the case at present, especially in rich industrialized countries. There are top executives in the United States, for instance, who earn one or more million dollars a year, while an increasing number of wage earners hardly earn more than the minimum hourly wage. This means that the richest earners make one hundred or more times what the poorest ones do. The extremely high salaries and earnings of top athletes and entertainers are also highly exaggerated.

There are very wealthy people in the world—business people, industrialists, kings or queens, members of the aristocracy, or some dictators. It should be the responsibility of every wealthy person to use his or her wealth for the material social, economic, and political wellbeing of their country, nation, society, or community, as well as of humankind as a whole.

There are examples of wealthy people, like the Rockefeller family and others, who donated and still give a large part of their fortune to philanthropic causes. .Stephen Sander, a Canadian businessman, gave almost all of his fortune of 170 million dollars to charity (after having given a share to his children), and has left himself and his wife an annual income of $40,000., enough to live decently. His considerable wealth provides for humanitarian causes all around the world, especially in third world countries.

The very low salary of a doctor in China, who earns as much or less than a specialized worker, is also irresponsible. Even though good doctors obtain a lot of fulfillment from the practice of their profession, their salary should nevertheless correspond to the immensely valuable task they perform. Similarly, it is irresponsible that elementary and high school teachers in the United States are relatively poorly paid, considering the extremely important value of their work in terms of educating the young and preparing them for their future personal, social, and moral responsibilities.

Responsible governments should see redistributing income and wealth through progressively higher taxation for higher income levels as one of their main responsibilities. Ideally and also realistically every person should and must live above the poverty level and in moderate comfort. Excessive wealth should be eliminated as well as poverty.

It is also essential that developing countries achieve economic and social conditions that will also allow their citizens to live in moderate comfort. The rich, industrialized countries must help the poorer states to increase the standard of living of their citizens in a way that does not destroy the environment. They can do this by cancelling debts incurred by third world countries, and by investing in and increasingly importing products of developing nations. The peace of the world depends greatly on doing and achieving this.

### 127. Instituting Responsible Free Trade

The European Union, the United States, and Japan put immediate short-term economic interests ahead of their own and the world's long-term needs. In 1993 the United States Commerce Department imposed 68 percent tariffs on Canadian steel and 76 and 49 percent on Mexican steel (this in spite of the creation of the North American Free Trade Area together with Canada and Mexico in 1992). These measures have ignored the purpose of a free trade agreement, which is to allow consumers of the countries involved to buy the cheapest products available. These measures are protectionistic. Similarly protectionistic are the policies of Japan, which had a trade surplus of more than 100 billion dollars in 1992, and those of the European Community, which restricted its imports from Eastern Europe and former Soviet Union countries in 1992. In order for these democracies to survive, they must be enabled to trade.

It is absolutely essential that no rich industrialized country accumulate an excessive trade surplus by exporting considerably more than it imports and that no country close its doors to imports from other countries. Furthermore, there is no future for any rich industrialized country or group of countries if they don't promote the economic development of poorer countries throughout the world.

Every country must consider the economic interests of the world as much as its own economic interests and put long-term needs ahead of short-term ones. Only such a global, highly responsible long-term economic approach can contribute to moderate global prosperity as well as to the long-term survival of humankind.

# CHAPTER ELEVEN

# *Ecological Responsibilities*

### 128. Protecting the Environment and Using Non-polluting Energy

POLLUTION OF THE ENVIRONMENT IS A GLOBAL PROBLEM. Industry, governments, and individuals are responsible for polluting the environment. The lavish lifestyle prevalent in the prosperous countries, which represent only 25 percent of the people on earth, yet are responsible for consuming 75 percent of the planet's resources, is a very large cause of the earth's pollution.

The biosphere recognizes no divisions into states or political alliances. All nations share the same climatic system. The atomic reactor disaster in Chernobyl, Ukraine had a negative effect on the environment and contaminated the air and water in countries of Europe and beyond, far removed from Chernobyl. American factories ejecting chemical pollutants into the air and water are responsible for acid rain and the destruction of the fauna and flora in nearby regions, and also in more distant areas of Canada.

The pace of environmental degradation has accelerated considerably since the advent of the industrial revolution in the nineteenth century, and especially in the second part of the twentieth.

At the Earth Summit conference held in Rio de Janeiro in 1992, world leaders asked themselves whether the earth can endure the damage done by a worldwide throwaway society. Throughout the developing world the American dream has taken hold. U.S. television, movies, and pop music dominate the world's airwaves, spreading a culture of consumption that environmentalists fear might be bad for the earth. There is also a lot of tension between the developed and developing countries concerning the speed of the third world's development. The developed countries want third world nations to slow down development for Earth's sake, while developing nations don't want to abandon their desire for prosperity, unless rich countries also reduce their standard of living. The pressure to be like the Americans is especially strong in Latin America.

Along with U.S.-style food packaging comes an American problem—city dumps bursting at the seams. The United States is the world's most recklessly extravagant country when it comes to trash. But Latin Americans are catching up. For them garbage is almost a status symbol. In Honduras, for instance, the rich throw away more than 3 kg. of trash a day, while the poor produce about 0.2 of a kg. Montrealers throw away about 1.4 kg. of garbage a day.

Experts from the World Bank and the World Watch Institute believe that the only way to control global pollution is for people to change the way they live, to rebuild cities, reduce the need for cars, redesign houses to reduce the need for energy, trade in four-wheelers for bicycles, get rid of excess packaging, and generally get by with less. That will happen, according to experts, when governments force people to pay the full environmental price for the goods they buy.

A plan to protect the earth from pollution would fail if not carried out on a global scale. How can one country keep the beaches clean if its neighbor dumps sewage into the sea? How much good can one country do by reducing carbon dioxide emissions if another nation offsets that with an increased output? Information on pollution must be gathered on a global scale. The earth must go into intensive care; its vital signs must be monitored. The public must be educated and informed. The world community must move promptly toward comprehensive treaties to protect the air, soil, and water. A framework for this global effort already exists within the United Nations. In 1972 the United Nations organized the Stockholm Conference, which set up the U.N. environmental program. In 1987, 24 countries signed the Montreal Protocol calling for a reduction in the output of ozone-destroying substances. The World bank has become environmentally responsible and has started including environmental concerns into its programs since the 1980s.

The efforts of the developing nations to catch up with the developed world are often frustrated because their efforts to industrialize rapidly poison their cities, while their attempts to boost agricultural production often result in the destruction of their forests and depletion of their soils. The impoverished third world, burdened with debt, cannot afford expensive environmental projects without outside help. Nor can the United States fund a new ecological Marshall Plan on its own. There is a need for a new North-South deal, that can pool the financial resources of the industrialized world and channel them into sustainable development plans for the poorer countries.

Maurice Strong, an influential Canadian businessman and public servant, was the president of the United Nations' first environmental conference in Stockholm in 1972 and also of the 1992 Earth Summit in Rio. He promotes the ecological imperative that mankind must change direction to survive. He states that the threat to mankind's security from environmental pollution is at least as great a danger as the traditional threat of war.

There is a great need for a worldwide agreement to protect the climate and the diversity of animal and plant life. A United Nations agency must be created through which money destined for global environmental protection can be channeled. This agency could be called "The Global Environmental Protection Agency."

### The Main Forms and Causes of Pollution and their Consequences for the Earth

1) Global Warming. Caused by fossil fuels such as coal, oil, and natural gas. The automobile is one of the main sources of this type of environmental destruction. The atmospheric accumulation of the gases produced by the fossil fuels leads to global warming, which could lead in the future to the rise of sea levels, flooding, coastal storms, and damage to marine ecosystems.

2) Erosion of the Ozone Layer. Scientists have discovered that carbon dioxide, methane, and chlorine are destroying the ozone layer, which will lead to an increase in the number of people developing skin cancer.

3) Pollution of Beaches and of the Sea Water. This is caused by the dumping of sewage into the oceans and seas.

4) Death of Forests and of Fish in Lakes. This disaster is caused by acid rain.

5) Disappearance of Rain Forests in Tropical Countries. This calamity is due to the cutting of trees in order to use the land for agriculture.

6) Erosion of Soil in the Third World.

7) Desertfication. It is the long-term biological degradation of the land's productivity through natural events and human abuses. This complex problem is caused by droughts, but also by overgrazing, overcultivating, by cutting too many trees, and by faulty irrigation projects.

8) Danger of Extinction of Some Species of Land and Sea Animals.

9) Deterioration of the Quality of Drinking Water in Many Parts of the World.

10) The Presence of Toxic Chemicals in Certain Food Products. This can lead to serious health problems.

11) Adverse Effects of Many Pesticides on Soil and Plant Life.

Terrible devastation of the environment has been caused in the former Soviet Union and the former communist countries of Eastern Europe. Their antiquated industries had absolutely no guidelines for environmental protection. Large parts of the environment have been destroyed and the quality of the air is very bad. This results in serious health problems for the general population, especially children. Many East European countries rely almost exclusively on atomic reactors for the production of electricity. Considering the rather inferior quality of their security and safeguard measures, accidents like the one in Chernobyl might recur.

There has been some progress in the fight against pollution. In 1989 the United Nations laid the groundwork for an accord between rich and poor countries to protect the environment. The river Thames in England, which was so polluted that all its fish died, has been cleaned and there is again sea life in it. Some international banks forgive debts owed by developing nations, provided that a part of the tropical forests of these countries is controlled by the bank. The forest is in trust with the bank, which uses it either to promote tourism or for sustainable development, which does not destroy the forest. Part of the revenue is given to the developed nation. The polar bear has been brought back from extinction by "The World Wide Fund." Successful efforts are being made by environmentalists to save the giant panda from extinction, as well as to reduce the terrible decimation of whales.

"The World Wide Fund" safeguards the species of a habitat by developing self-sustaining ways of using natural resources for the benefit of local communities. In 1987 the WWF purchased millions of Ecuador foreign debt to fund conservation projects like creating natural parks or preserving tropical forests.

In West Germany, which has some of Europe's toughest pollution laws, the government favors tax breaks and incentives to promote private investment in antipollution measures, as well as in a growing environmental technology industry. In 1989 the Netherlands developed a comprehensive national environmental policy plan. The program is based on the principle that the polluter must pay. In Western Europe fuel taxes are much higher than in the United States, while those in Japan are also much higher. Higher carbon taxes mean greater energy efficiency, lower growth in air pollution, smaller oil import bills, and greater security.

A test given in Canada in 1990 to 1521 adults revealed that Canadians don't fully understand the threats to the environment. They are aware of problems, but they don't know the fine points. Only slightly more than a third were able to define the greenhouse effect, responsible for global warming. Less than half the adults know that man-made chemicals are the culprit in destroying the ozone layer. Eighty percent of the people tested did know, however, that Canadians are using more energy today than ten years ago. The lack of knowledge concerning environmental issues is serious, as it might prevent people from changing their behavior or putting pressure on politicians to fight the destruction of the environment. It is imperative that people become more knowledgeable and informed concerning the dangers and threats to the world's environment.

A survey of 1500 adults conducted in Canada in 1989 revealed that Canadians are willing to pay higher prices for products that are environmentally safe. They are also willing to pay higher taxes for programs that will encourage ecological behavior and fight pollution. They want change in the way groceries are packaged and in the way garbage is disposed of. The survey further reveals that Canadians want governments to get tougher with industry. They want the leaders of industry that fail to meet environmental standards put in jail. Eighty percent want tax breaks for industries that use clean technology. Sixty-three percent would pay $1000. more for a car that pollutes less. These findings are extraordinarily important. They indicate that Canadians are highly responsible and that it is the obligation of politicians to follow, legislate, and execute the socially and morally responsible wishes and expectations of the majority of people.

To clean the world's oceans and atmosphere will require vision as well as the redistribution of wealth from the rich nations of the world to the poorer ones as well as the cooperation of the developing countries. Rich nations must change the global inequality and injustice responsible for the fact that 25 percent of the population of the world consumes 75 percent of the world's resources.

Responsible environmental management will mean a higher cost of living. Those driving big cars and owning large houses would have to pay higher taxes. Carbon taxes will have to be levied in order to raise money for mass tree planting. Oil exploitations will have to be reduced.

Rich countries must either create a zero growth economy and reduce consumption, or create a society based on moderate, responsible, sustainable economic growth. Public transportation facilities will have to be used to a much greater extent than is done at present, and people will have to rely more on bicycles and use them more. Greater use will also have to be made of electric trains and cars will eventually have to be propelled by electricity.

Politics and economics have to adapt and take economic reality into consideration. Politicians, economists, businessmen, and the public at large will have to accept the fact that environmental protection is not incompatible with a moderately prosperous economy. Governments will have to become more aggressive in fighting pollution on a local, regional, national, and global level and will have to enact legislation to reduce carbon emissions as well as chemical pesticides, to increase the tax on gasoline, to double the pace of reforestation, and to improve sewer systems, in order to prevent human waste from polluting the waterways of the globe.

People will have to be educated to become more responsible, using cars only when absolutely necessary, and only for long-distance driving. Ecological tourism has to be become more accepted and prominent. It is an effective way to preserve wildlife.

Governments must also become more socially responsible, enacting strict anti-pollution laws and enforcing severe penalties for polluting the environment. Industries must be directed by governments to act responsibly. The penalties for polluting the environment must be jail and payment of a considerable amount of money. Taxes must be raised to pay for the cleaning of rivers, for producing clean water, and for responsible forest management. Furthermore, there must be fuel efficiency guidelines and strictly enforced controls. Governments must also use tax incentives to help companies produce pollution-free products.

Industry and all people should make increased use of such alternate energy sources as solar energy, and should also conserve energy to a far greater extent.

There is also an urgent need for increaseed international action to alleviate growing climate problems. To motivate third world countries to protect the environment, rich nations will have to forgive large parts of the poor countries' debts and transfer technology and funds to the developing world. The industrialized nations must also finance developing nations' programs to protect wildlife habitats such as tropical forests.

It is extremely important that countries with very large populations, China and India, for example, develop in an environmentally responsible manner.

It is essential to realize that the amount of money spent in four days by the governments of the world on military spending is sufficient to implement a five-year plan to save some of the world's tropical forests. The world must change morally to place the protection of the environment before the production of armaments.

Governments will also have to consult more with labor and business on environmental issues and spend more money on environmental research. Soil conservation will have to be promoted to a greater extent and farmers and peasants educated to reduce agricultural pollution. Private industry must also change to plan for long-term economic goals and become aware of the terrible environmental consequences of some short-term economic gains.

A study conducted by the World Commission on the Environment and Development, the Brundtland Commission, found that countries investing in the environment did not lose in any substantial way. Some jobs were lost, but many others were created.

The Canadian Chamber of Commerce has called for global environmental coordination to ensure that every company everywhere in the world plays by similar rules. Otherwise, companies that pollute the environment have a competitive advantage over those that are ecologically responsible. It is also important that businesses view such natural resources as trees as a capital stock, and that resources of the atmosphere and oceans become included in national and international accounts of wealth.

People's values and world views have to become more responsible and they must understand that the quality of life depends as much on economic prosperity as it does on the preservation of the environment. Nature is like business. Business sense dictates that we guard our capital and live on the interest. Nature's capital is the gigantic diversity of living things. It helps us to feed and cure ourselves. Many of the unexplored species in the wild could yield cancer-fighting substances, one additional reason why we must save tropical forests.

People must promote the development of effective corporate environmental policies, such as the recycling of industrial and business waste. Every manufacturing company should pass an environmental impact checklist that addresses water, air, and noise pollution concerns. Business must become socially and morally responsible and integrate the environment into economic thinking. Companies that choose materials wisely and practice recycling do not have to deplete resources. One can make money by preserving the earth.

There must be sustainable ecological and economic development that meets the needs of the present while not compromising the ability of future generations to meet their needs.

The use of automobiles must be reduced. They must become more environmentally friendly and be driven by electrical batteries. This will cost a lot of money and will require an important change in people's lifestyle.

241

Cities must also become environmentally friendly. There must be a reduction of waste in city offices and a reduction of noise. Workplaces must become healthy places with no air pollution and as little noise as possible.

Citizens will have to become more empowered as well as neighborhood- and community-conscious and must cooperate to fight waste and pollution.

In spite of everything, there is great reason for hope. At the 1992 United Nations Conference on the Environment and Development, world leaders adopted the following essential points:

1) States must ensure that activities within their jurisdiction or control do not cause damage to the environment of other states.

2) Environmental production must be part of sustainable development.

3) States must cooperate in a spirit of global partnership to conserve, protect, and restore the health and integrity of the earth's ecosystem. In view of the different contribution to global environmental degradation, states have common but differentiated responsibilities. The developed countries acknowledge the responsibility they have to the international pursuit of sustainable development, considering the pollution their societies create to the world's environment and the technologies and financial means they have.

4) All states must enact effective environmental legislation.

After warning about environmental degradation for sixteen years, the World Watch Institute in 1990 drafted an optimistic blueprint for a sustainable global economy within 40 years. The Institute foresees a better world around 2030. There will be generalized recycling, and solar power will replace oil and natural gas. The World Watch Institute was stimulated in this optimistic thinking by the miraculous overturn of communism in Central and Eastern Europe in 1989, 1990, and 1991.

The majority of people in sixteen countries polled in 1992 by the Gallup International Institute said that they would be willing to pay higher prices so that industry would better protect the environment. In only six countries was a majority against this proposition. Among the countries willing to pay higher prices for a safer environment were Canada, Germany, Britain, the United States, and such relatively poor countries as Mexico, Brazil, and India. Countries opposed included Japan, Russia, and Turkey.

Where there is a will there is a way. In cooperation with God, humankind can and must become socially and morally responsible and create a moderately prosperous, peaceful world, in harmony with nature and the environment.

# CHAPTER TWELVE

# *Legal Responsibilities*

### 129. Enacting Responsible Laws

IT MUST NEVER BE FORGOTTEN THAT ALL THE CRIMES COMMITTED against humankind in Nazi Germany were perfectly legal. Likewise, in almost all totalitarian countries repression, torture, violation of human rights, and even extermination of people who oppose the government (even in a nonviolent manner), or who express responsible viewpoints in disagreement with official dogma, are unfortunately still widespread.

Responsible laws, which have been increasingly enacted and enforced in Western democratic countries reflect to a great extent (and should do so even more) the highest ethical and moral ideals of humankind. They are and must be based to a great extent on the ten commandments given by God to Moses.

The main emphasis in responsible laws must be the absolute sacredness of human life well stated in the biblical commandment, "Thou shall not kill." This injunction has to become increasingly universal, applicable to all people in all countries of the world, under all circumstances—except on those occasions where one has to act in responsible self-defense to save one's life or in defense to save the lives of others threatened by criminal aggression. All laws must be extended to outlaw war throughout the world, not only armed conflict between sovereign countries, but also internal violent civil conflict within existing states.

Responsible laws must also be based on the respect for other people's personalities, their integrity, their distinctness in terms of race, religion, ethnic origin, nationality, sex, and age. Disrespectful, dishonest, oppressive, discriminatory, abusive, exploitative behavior toward other people, whether in speech, writing, or in any other manner, must be outlawed.

Responsible laws must also proclaim the equality of all people before God and all laws, regardless of status, position, wealth, nationality, race, religion, ethnic origin, or sex. Responsible laws must also defend civil rights and personal freedoms of people.

Responsible laws must also defend the rights of animals and of nature and must protect the right of future generations to inherit a relatively protected and well preserved environment as well as sufficient energy resources.

Responsible laws greatly contribute to the creation of justice, including social and economic justice, and promote harmony between the peoples and nations of the world. Responsible laws also make it a crime to obey and execute irresponsible orders, even when these commands are given by superior authority, whether government or bosses. Exactly such a law was enacted in West Germany after the Second World War, according to which it is a crime for a subordinate soldier or officer to execute an irresponsible or immoral order given by a superior. Responsible laws must also prevent violence against and disrespect for truth. It is a crime in Austria and Germany to deny that the holocaust, in which six million Jews were murdered by the Nazis, took place. Finally, responsible laws must also prohibit violence against feelings, such as pornography and other forms of human degradation.

## 130. Applying Responsible Censorship

Freedom is one of the most precious values. However, it must be guided by responsibility. Otherwise, this noble ideal can degenerate into licentiousness. One responsible way to prevent excesses and abuse of freedom is through the application of responsible censorship. Responsible censorship is essential in three areas.

The first is in the area of television programs, movies, and printed material, where violence is used to cater to the vilest and most primitive instincts in order to increase profits as well as the number of viewers or readers. These films, television programs, and publications overemphasize criminal tendencies, degrade human nature by showing perverted viciousness bordering on the insane, and are very harmful to viewers, especially to children. Children identify with television and movie stars and hold them up as role models. If these role models behave in a vicious, depraved manner, this will influence the values, outlook, and even behavior of viewers in a harmful manner.

The second area where responsible censorship is necessary is pornography. Pornography, whether depicting sadomasochistic sex or the lustful, carnal aspect of sex, without love, tenderness, respect, and affection, constitutes violence against feelings, degrades both women and men, and leads in some instances to violence.

Hate literature and programs make up the third area where responsible censorship must be applied to create a humane, highly civilized, socially, and morally responsible society and world. Especially harmful are printed texts that stir up racial, ethnic, religious, and national hatred. Denial of historic truth and facts as well as the perversion and distortion of history to create prejudice, hatred, and violence against innocent people must also be prohibited.

# CHAPTER THIRTEEN

# *Responsible Cities*

### 131. The Duties of Responsible and Livable Cities

RESPONSIBLE CITIES PROMOTE THE GENERAL WELLBEING OF THEIR inhabitants. They are responsive to the needs for a relatively unpolluted environment (clean air and drinkable, pure water), proper garbage disposal, recycling of waste products, adequate control of industrial and car emissions, and a lot of parks sand green spaces. Responsible cities also have sufficient and adequate health care facilities, sufficient public transportation, and many bicycle paths and pedestrian walkways. They are created and developed in accordance with a master plan, where residential and office buildings are built to satisfy both functional and aesthetic needs. Responsible cities also provide full employment for their citizens and are well equipped with sufficient educational institutions of excellent quality at the primary, secondary, college, and university level.

Responsible cities have a low rate of crime as well as a low level of unemployment and no homeless people. They have many cultural centers, like opera houses, symphony concert halls, theaters, museums, planetariums, and aquariums. Responsible cities have a flourishing economy with many industrial factories as well as many stores to satisfy the need of consumers. They are also well provided with all kinds of counseling services to help people with psychological and social problems.

It is important that the people living in a city share a spirit of solidarity, community, and cooperation, a spirit that must be developed at all costs if it does not exist.

Population density is not necessarily an impediment to community harmony. Research has proven that under the right conditions, a high level of density can actually improve relations in a community. It is important that local neighborhoods have a lot of easily accessible social resources. A beautiful example of large, happy crowds is found at international fairs and exhibitions; it is therefore important that every city organize such cultural, scientific, business, artistic, and sport events.

By the year 2000, seventeen of the largest cities in the world will be located in developing nations. It is essential that these cities as well as all other urban communities succeed in eliminating slums and find responsible solutions to the problem of the homeless, including the countless abandoned street children.

A beautiful example of a highly responsible urban community is Curitiba, the capital of the southern state of Parana in Brazil (population 1.6 million). All factories are non-polluting, the transportation system is excellent, everybody sorts recyclable trash. The city has huge parks, well looked after, with waterfalls and lagoons. The mayor of the city, Jaime Lerner, is a prizewinning urban planner and architect, who has been a consultant to the United Nations. Unlike many other cities, which built a lot of viaducts and skyscrapers in the 1970s, Lerner created many bike lanes and pedestrian malls. He built child care centers and clinics through a united effort of business and citizens. This extraordinary example of social and moral responsibility combined with human resourcefulness, ingenuity, and creativity, should and must stand as an example to cities and people everywhere and stimulate responsible and gifted people in many other cities to do similar things for the wellbeing of all.

Governments must make it one of their priorities to give cities the necessary funds in order to enable them to function responsibly. Business and industry must also help and cooperate to create responsible cities.

# CHAPTER FOURTEEN

# *Artistic, Musical, and Creative Responsibilities*

### 132. Valuing Beauty

BEAUTY IS A MOST PRECIOUS QUALITY AND VALUE. It makes life more pleasant and enjoyable and also contributes to its meaning. Young people start out with a natural appreciation of beauty, but most have it knocked out of them in the process of growing up. This is terrible, as it explains why so many people put up with the deteriorating, ugly downtown areas in many of their cities and why they tolerate pollution.

It is important to value beauty as well as to appreciate and enjoy beautiful things and ideas. It also helps to get enthusiastic and excited and to use words like pretty and beautiful in appreciation and response to the beauty in art and nature. This helps to develop an aesthetic quality.

We owe it to God to appreciate the beautiful world he created. We see the beauty of creation in the physical traits of people of various races, in the beauty of some people's personalities, in magnificent natural scenery, in the wide variety of animals and plants.

We also owe it to our fellow human beings, those who live now and those who lived in the past, to value and appreciate their artistic, literary, musical, and architectural creations. We should educate ourselves to see beauty in many scientific and technological accomplishments as well as in lofty, exalted philosophical, religious, and moral ideas.

Last but not least, an aesthetic appreciation of and response to beauty makes us happy.

### 133. Becoming Responsibly Creative

Creativity is an extremely important quality that must be developed from early childhood. It is essential not only for artistic creation but also to innovate and produce change in business, technology, science, education, politics, and in many other areas of human activity. Imagination, originality, and spontaneity are essential ingredients of creativity.

It is important to differentiate between outstanding creative achievements associated with genius and the many creative accomplishments of ordinary people. Not everybody can be a Shakespeare, yet the majority of people, if properly encouraged and stimulated, can use their imagination to write something original and meaningful.

Creative thinking makes use of insight as well as intuition and helps in the adaptation process as well as to find meaning in life and to understand oneself, others, society, and the world. The insistence of society on conformity (or even overconformity) is a reason for the stifling of creativity. This can result in difficulty or even intolerance of accepting differences—especially divergent opinions and world views.

There is no evidence that one has to be a genius or of extremely high intelligence to be creative. A sizable proportion of people, if properly stimulated and encouraged, and provided they have the appropriate talents and interests, could write poems, do scientific research, or make some innovative contributions in many other fields.

The creative urge to add something new to the world, whether in technology, the arts, music, science, politics, business, or in personal relations, must be combined with responsible values. The Nazis, who invented gas ovens and chemical substances to exterminate people efficiently and in great numbers acted criminally and in a socially and morally irresponsible manner. Responsible, beneficial creativity means to enrich the world by producing something new or by revealing a new way of seeing reality, a way that must absolutely be impregnated with personal, social, and moral responsibility. The important thing to remember is that the creative product, work of art, or original thought satisfies the human need for usefulness, beauty, truth, decency, meaning, responsibility, peace, social justice, equality, solidarity, health, moderate prosperity, wellbeing and faith.

## 134. Valuing Responsible Art and Music

Art refers to an aesthetically pleasing and meaningful arrangement of elements as words, colors, shapes, and sounds. Literature, poetry, painting, sculpture, drawing, photography, cinematography, and music are some of the principal artistic fields. One of the main functions of art is to portray beauty and to help us to appreciate it. It also helps us to find meaning.

There has been considerable controversy as to whether art should exist for its own sake or whether it should be tendentious (having a purposed aim or intentional tendency). I believe that art should consist of a synthesis of existing for its own sake and of having purpose. The artist needs a great deal of freedom to create, and should aim to help people have an aesthetically pleasing experience, gain insight into and an understanding of social and personal reality, and also motivate them to personal, social, and moral improvement and responsibility, and to greater faith in God. Responsible art must be simultaneously realistic, educational, and uplifting.

Art must not be exploitative. Pornography is not valuable art. Neither is the portrayal of killings in literature, films, and television programs done only to excite and stimulate base, vile impulses in order to increase sales. A socially and morally responsible society must use some form of censorship to prohibit those productions and creations that cater to the vilest, most aggressive, and violent impulses of people and stimulate them to think, feel, and act in a personally, socially, and morally irresponsible manner.

Music is an art which has a considerable influence on emotions. Great music in not only beautifully melodious and entertaining, but if it is combined with an uplifting meaningful text it can also enthuse, exalt, and ennoble spiritually, intellectually, emotionally, and morally.

The Nazis misused the beautiful Viennese waltzes of Johann Strauss in the most irresponsible and criminal manner in the extermination camps, where millions of people were killed. Jews went to the gas chambers to the strains of Viennese waltzes.

Beehoven's ninth symphony is a perfect example of uplifting, great music. The beautiful melody is combined with a fiery and passionate text by Friedrich Schiller describing human solidarity and brotherhood. It would be the most fitting anthem of a united world, which will have to be created eventually, and which should assume the form of the "United States of the World."

# BIBLIOGRAPHY

## I. Books

Adler, Alfred. *The Practice and Theory of Individual Psychology*. New York: Harcourt, 1927.

Bish Louis E. *Be Glad You Are Neurotic*. New York: McGraw-Hill, 1946.

Bottome, Phyllis. *Alfred Adler*. New York: Van Rees Press, 1939.

Buber, Martin. *I and Thou*. New York: Charles Scribner's Sons, 1970.

Chalk, Frank and Kurt Jonassohn. *The History and Sociology of Genocide*. New Haven: Yale University Press, 1990.

Fordham, Frieda. *An Introduction to Jung's Psychology*. Harmondsworth, U.K.: Penguin Books, 1953.

Frankl, Viktor E. *Man's Search for Meaning*. (paperback edition) New York: Pocket Books, 1972.

Freud, Sigmund. *New Introductory Lectures on Psychoanalysis*. London: Hogarth, 1949.

Fromm, Erich. *The Anatomy of Human Destructiveness*. Greenwich, CT: Fawcett, 1975.

_____. *Escape from Freedom*. New York: Rinehart and Co., 1941.

Funk and Wagnalls. *Standard College Dictionary*. Canada, 1974.

Goodman, David. *Living from Within*. Kansas City: Hallmark Cards, Inc., 1968.

Gray, Martin. *The Book of Life*. New York: Seabury Press, 1973.

Jung, Carl. *Modern Man in Search of a Soul*. London: Routledge and Kegan Paul, 1933.

Kohn, Hans. *The Idea of Nationalism*. Toronto: Collier Mac Millan Canada Ltd., 1969.

Lorenz, Konrad. *On Aggression*. Vienna: Dr. G. Borotha Schoeber Verlag, 1963.

Maccoby, Michael. *The Gamesman*. New York: Simon and Schuster, 1977.

Middlebrook, Patricia N. *Social Psychology and Modern Life*. New York: Alfred A. Knopf, 1974.

Naisbitt, John. *Megatrends*. New York: Warren Books, Inc., 1984.

251

Peters, Thomas J. and Robert H. Watterman, Jr., *In Search of Excellence*. New York: Harper and Row, 1982.

Rosenthal, R. and L. Jacobson. *Pygmalion in the Classroom: Teacher Expectation and Pupils' Intellectual Development*. New York: Holt, Rinehart and Winston, 1968.

Schweitzer, Albert. *Reverence for Life*. Kansas City: Hallmark Cards, Inc., 1971.

Segal, J. *Winning Life's Toughest Battles: Roots of Human Resilience*. New York: McGraw-Hill, 1986.

Seligman, Martin. *Learned Optimism*. New York: Alfred A. Knopf, 1991.

Spranger, E. *Types of Men*. New York: Stechert, 1928.

Stoessinger, John G. *Why Nations Go to War*. New York: St. Martin's Press, 1978.

## II. Journal and Popular Magazine Articles

Birnbaum, Jesse. "Crybabies, Eternal Victims," *Time* (August 12, 1991), 37.

Ciabattary, Jane. "Will the 90's Be the Age of Envy," Psychology Today (December 1989), 47-50.

Fishman, Joshua. "The Security of Uncertainty," *Psychology Today* (June 1988), 28.

Goretti, Gustavo. "The Mission of Jaime Jaramillo," *Readers Digest* (January 1993), 85-90.

Hurley, Dan. Cycles of Craving," *Psychology Today* (July 1989), 54-60.

Koerbel, Kurt H. "The Indispensable and Important Contribution of Individual Psychology," *IPNL. Organ of the International Association of Individual Psychology*. vol. 34, no. 1 (April 1986), 12-13.

_____. "An Individual Psychological Approach to Help the Unemployed." *IPNL. Organ of the International Association of Individual Psychology*. vol. 34, no. 2 (November 1986), 18-19.

_____. "Helping the Young to Regain Hope and to Live Purposefully," *IPNL. Organ of the International Association of Individual Psychology*. vol. 36, no. 1 (April 1988), 12-13.

_____. "Helping the Elderly to Use Their Experience in a Purposeful, Productive, Useful and Responsible Manner," *IPNL. Organ of the International Association of Individual Psychology*, vol. 37, no. 2 (October 1989), 16-17.

_____. "Les Insucces Scolaires chez les Etudiants Brilliants (Scholastic Failures in Brilliant Students)," *College et Famille*, vol. 26, no. 2 (April 1969), 57-62.

_____. "Le Conflit des Generations aux Yeux du Psychologue (A Psychologist's View of the Generational Conflict)," *Education et Société*, vol. 1, no. 6 (October 1970), 6-7.

_____. "Considerations sur la Publicité Commerciale (Opinions on Commercial Advertising)," *Education et Société*, vol. 1, no. 8, (December 1970) 12-13.

_____. "Reflexions sur l'Orientation des Etudiants au Niveau Pre-Universitaire (Thoughts on the Guidance of Pre-University Students)," *Education et Société*, vol. 2, no. 1 (February 1971), 14-15.

_____. "La Science Contemporaine et l'Evolution du Concept de Dieu (Contemporary Science and the Evolution of the Concept of God)," *Education et Société*, vol. 2, No. 2 (March 1971), 8-9.

_____. "Le Bilinguisme comme Facteur d'Epanouissement Humain (Bilingualism as a Factor of Human Development)," *Education et Société*, vol. 2, no. 6 (September 1971), 18.

_____. "Contester pour l'Humanité entière (Contending for the Whole Human Race)," *Education et Société*, vol. 3, no. 3 (April 1972), 18-19.

_____. "The Use of Guidance Counseling to Preserve the Mental Health and to Promote the Educational and Vocational Growth of the Unemployed," *Cognica*, vol. 9, no. 6 (March 1978).

_____. "Effective Counseling Is Highly Therapeutic," *Cognica*, vol. 10, no. 8 (May 1979), 3-4.

Krauthamer, Charles. "Saving Nature, but only for Man," *Time* (June 17, 1990), 64.

Louv, Richard. "Childhood Future," *Readers Digest* (June 1991), 75-79.

Marjory, Robert. "School Yard Menace" *Psychology Today* (February 1988), 52-56.

Melson, Gail and Alan Fogel. "Learning to Care," *Psychology Today* (January 1988), 39-45.

Milgram, S. "Behavioral Study of Obedience," *Journal of Abnormal and Social Psychology*, 67 (1963), 371-378.

Nielsen, Robert. "World of Ottawa Spending," *Readers Digest* (February 1991), 115-120.

Ross, Judy. "The Healing Power of Kindness," *Homemaker Magazine* (December 1986), 22-34.

Tierney, John. "Betting on Planet Earth," *Readers Digest* (May 1991), 139-144.

### III. Newspaper articles

Broadbent, Ed. "Indivisible, Until Women's Rights Are Human Rights," Montreal, *The Gazette* (March 11, 1993).

Brogan, Patrick. "Freeing Trade, " Montreal, *The Gazette* (January 28, 1993).

Bueckart, Dennis. "Price Tag to Save Earth," Montreal, *The Gazette* (October 22, 1991).

De Bries, Christian, "Des Politiques Malades," *Le Monde Diplomatique* (October 1987).

Dyer, Gwynne. "Time to Respond to Real Arab Grievances," Montreal, *The Gazette* (March 12, 1991).

–––––––––. "As Democracy Spreads Wars Should Diminish," Montreal, *The Gazette* (August 20, 199?)

Evans, David. "Soviet Reforms Deprive U.S. of Needed Enemy," Montreal, *The Gazette* (July 4, 1988).

Fisher, Marc. "Guards Convicted in Berlin Wall Slaying," Montreal, *The Gazette* (January 1, 1992).

Ford, Tom. "Responsibilities, Communitarianism Might Save Us Much Mental Anguish in the Coming Year," Montreal, *The Gazette* (March 12, 1993).

Mathews, Jessica, "More Will Go Hungry," Montreal, *The Gazette* (January 31, 1992).

Mils, Joanne. "What People Can Do," Montreal, *The Gazette* (December 31, 1989).

–––––––. "Ecotourism," Montreal, *The Gazette* (February 9, 1992).

"Nice People Campaign Announced by Gerry Weiner," Montreal, *The Suburban* (November 13, 1991).

Richards, Bill. "Easy Come, Easy Go," Montreal, *The Gazette* (April 8, 1990).

Webster, Norman, "Timid Welcome for Dalai Lama Shames Canada," Montreal, *The Gazette* (September 22, 1990).

Wills, Terrance, "Who Calls the Tune: Harmonizing Social Progress," Montreal, *The Gazette* (July 9, 1988).

# ABOUT THE AUTHOR

Kurt Koerbel was born in Vienna, Austria. He survived the second World War in Rumania and came to Montreal, Canada in 1953. He has been a Canadian citizen since 1958.

Kurt Koerbel obtained the Master of Arts degree in psychology from the Université de Montréal in 1960 and continued his Ph.D. studies in psychology at the same university until 1961.

He worked for the Government of Québec as a counseling psychologist in the departments of Education and Manpower from 1963 to 1988. He also gave a course on the "Psychology of Personality" at Loyola College (today a part of Concordia University) in Montreal.

Kurt Koerbel has written articles on counseling, psychological, educational, spiritual, ethical, religious, philosophical and social subjects in English and French for national and international counseling, psychological and educational journals. The Individual Psychology Newsletter, organ of the International Association of Individual Psychology (Adlerian), Munich, Germany published the following articles by Kurt Koerbel:

I) - *The Indispensible and important contribution of individual psychology*; II) - *An individual psychological approach to help the unemployed*; III) - *Helping the young to regain hope*; IV) - *Helping the elderly to use their experience in a purposeful and productive manner*.

Kurt Koerbel was president of the Home and School Association of Somerled Elementary School in Montreal from 1967 to 1969. Though retired from Government since 1989, he continues to work as a couneling and career psychologist and provides free of charge psychological and career counseling to regular and continuing education university students.

In September 1993, Kurt Koerbel received an award of merit from the McGill University Association of Continuing Education Students, in recognition of his generosity, compassion and dedication.

Since September 1994, the author gives free career counseling to regular students at the École de Technologie supérieure of the Université du Québec in Montreal, and to adult education students at the École des Hautes Études Commerciales at the Univerité de Montréal.

Kurt Koerbel also gives talks to Golden Age Clubs and to various community agencies on "How to Age Responsibly, Successfully, and Gracefully."